Contemporary Issues Within Caribbean Economies

Colin Cannonier · Monica Galloway Burke
Editors

Contemporary Issues Within Caribbean Economies

palgrave
macmillan

Editors
Colin Cannonier
Jack C. Massey College of Business
Belmont University
Nashville, TN, USA

Monica Galloway Burke
Western Kentucky University
Bowling Green, KY, USA

ISBN 978-3-030-98864-7 ISBN 978-3-030-98865-4 (eBook)
https://doi.org/10.1007/978-3-030-98865-4

This Palgrave Macmillan imprint is published by the registered company Springer Nature Switzerland AG
The registered company address is: Gewerbestrasse 11, 6330 Cham, Switzerland

Foreword

The Caribbean region is at a crossroads in the quest for sustaining durable and inclusive growth for its citizens. This book is timely in casting a long arc that sketches a historical perspective of the evolution of these economies and the challenges they face at the current juncture. With the advent of slavery, these economies were locked into an extractive production relationship that exploited slave labor in the export of primary commodities to their respective colonial masters.

With independence, these economies explored various models of development, including economic integration and preferential trading arrangements with the European Union and the United States under the African, Caribbean, and Pacific Countries partnership and the Caribbean Basin Initiative respectively. However, as preferential market access was challenged and ultimately dismantled under the World Trade Organization's framework, these economies pursued continuous structural adjustment. Alternative models of development included the establishment of offshore financial centers and citizenship by investment programs.

The book deftly illustrates how tourism has emerged as the main source of foreign exchange that is complemented by remittances which act as a form of social insurance. At the same time, the lack of diversification, makes these economies vulnerable to economic and climatic shocks. Given their small size, the impact and duration of shocks are extreme. The smoothing of shocks through fiscal policy, has led to the rapid accumulation of debt which has proven to be a drag on growth. In this context, the book demonstrates the policy makers' trilemma of the limits to raising taxes, boosting spending in response to shocks, and the constraint of high debt levels. The lack of fiscal space is further compounded by the middle-income status of the majority of these economies which precludes them from concessional financing or debt relief. The book further highlights that with higher living standards, non-communicable diseases have placed stress on healthcare systems, the budget, and productivity.

The book also turns the spotlight on Haiti by illustrating the role fragility plays in undermining macroeconomic stability. The combination of weak institutions, economic instability, bouts of political unrest, and natural disasters has led to double digit inflation which is the worse tax on the poor.

Finally, the authors provide comprehensive and invaluable insights into the contemporary challenges facing Caribbean which should be of great interest to policymakers and development economists.

Oral H. Williams, Ph.D.
Advisor, African Department IMF
Technical Assistance Center
International Monetary Fund
Washington, USA

Contents

Notes on Contributors

Dr. Dillon Alleyne is the Deputy Director of the Economic Commission for Latin America and the Caribbean (ECLAC) sub regional Headquarters for the Caribbean based in Port of Spain. Before joining ECLAC, he was a Senior Lecturer in the Department of Economics at the University of the West Indies, Mona, Jamaica, where he taught Public Finance and graduate Econometrics. He has published widely and his current research interests are in public finance, including fiscal reforms, leveraging the Diaspora for Caribbean development and global financial issues affecting Caribbean SIDS.

Dudley Augustin is a Deputy Head of the Monetary Statistics Unit at the Central Bank of Haiti (BRH). He joined the Central Bank as an economist in 2007. He holds an M.A. in Quantitative Finance and Economics from the University of Rennes 1 in France and a B.A. in Applied Economics from the Centre de Techniques de Planification et d'Économie Appliquée (CTPEA) in Haiti. His areas of interest are monetary economics, finance, and econometrics.

Dr. David Mc. Arthur Baker is a Professor of Hospitality & Tourism Management in the College of Business at Tennessee State University, he has been teaching at the university level for 25 years. Dr. Baker also does consulting work in the tourism field mainly in South East Asia, the Bahamas and Islands in the Caribbean. Before assuming his current position, he worked as an Associate Professor and Assistant Professor of Hospitality Management at the University of Central Missouri, an Instructor of Hospitality Management at Eastern Illinois University and as a Resort Manager of the Frigate Bay Beach Resort Hotel in the Caribbean Nation of St. Kitts/Nevis. In the USA Dr. Baker did consulting work with the Kansas City Convention & Visitors Bureau, the Fairmont Hotel Kansas City, and the Hyatt Regency Crown Center Kansas City. He conducts international research on cruise ship tourism, Island destinations development & marketing, and teaching and learning, he has published over 30 articles in academic journals, book chapters and is a reviewer for several journals. Dr. Baker holds a Ph.D. in Workforce Education & Development (Hospitality & Tourism concentration) from Southern Illinois University-Carbondale USA, MS in Hotel & Foodservice Management from Florida International University-Miami and a B.Sc. in Hotel Management from the University of the West Indies.

Dr. Marcus Bansah is an Assistant Professor of Economics at St. Olaf College. Prior to joining St. Olaf, he was appointed as Belmont University Fellow in Economics at the Jack C. Massey College of Business. Dr. Bansah earned his Ph.D. in Economics from the University of Tennessee, Knoxville. He received his B.A. in Economics with first class honors (Summa cum laude), and M.Phil. in Economics from the University of Ghana, Legon. After receiving his master's in 2010, he spent three years working as a teaching/research assistant at the Department of Economics, and as a Principal Research Assistant at the Institute of Statistical, Social and Economic Research (ISSER), University of Ghana. While at ISSER, he was also a co-instructor at Wisconsin International University College and Ghana Institute of Management and Public Administration (GIMPA), where he taught Quantitative Methods at the M.B.A. level. Dr. Bansah also served as a Faculty Intern at Ashesi University, where he was a co-instructor of International Trade and Policy. In 2014, he joined the Department of Economics at the University of Tennessee, Knoxville, as a graduate teaching associate, where he taught six intermediate undergraduate classes in Macroeconomics, Development Economics, and Monetary Economics. He also served as graduate research assistant at Boyd Center for Business and Economic Research. His research focuses on analyzing policy-relevant development and trade issues at the macro level, particularly in small open economies. Dr. Bansah has presented his research at several conferences including the annual meetings of the Southern

Economic Association. He is a reviewer for the Journal for the Advancement of Developing Economies. Dr. Bansah is a member of Amazing Church International, where he serves as financial secretary and member of leadership team.

Dr. Madlyn Bonimy is part-time graduate faculty member in Doctoral Research at the University of Arizona Global Campus. Madlyn is a published author. She has published in several academic journals. She has also published in books and book chapters, and presented papers at various international conferences, including in the United States and Canada. Her research interests include tourism and the environment, tourism and economic development strategy, global tourism and management, citizen participation, and public policy and urban affairs. Dr. Bonimy has also served as a mentor and chair of doctoral dissertations, and supervising faculty for Master degree directed research projects. She has experience leading projects in the US, Canada, France, Africa, and the Caribbean..

Samuel Braithwaite is a lecturer in the Department of Economics, The University of the West Indies, Mona. His primary research interests are in international economics and economic development. Samuel Braithwaite is married and has a son. He is Guyanese.

Dr. Colin Cannonier received a bachelor's degree with first class honors from the University of the West Indies, Jamaica with an emphasis in Economics and Social Statistics. He also has respective master's degrees in Development Economics and Economics from Williams College and Louisiana State University, where he also obtained his Ph.D. He is currently an Associate Professor in Economics at Belmont University, a Global Labor Organization (GLO) Fellow and GLO Country Lead for St. Kitts and Nevis. He began his career working as a country economist in the Eastern Caribbean. His research focus is in applied economics with emphasis in health, labor, and education and how they intersect with public policy and economic development. He has authored several peer-reviewed articles in scholarly journals such as *Economics of Education Review*, *Journal of Labor Research*, *Review of Economics of the Household*, and *Journal of Demographic Economics*. His research has also been featured in popular outlets such as the *Harvard Business Review* and the UNESCO. In addition, he has made numerous presentations at national, regional and international forums such as the London

School of Economics, the American Economic Association, Paris School of Economics, the European Economic Association, the NBER Summer Institute and central banks. In September 2019, he delivered the feature address at the Government of St. Kitts and Nevis Annual Prime Minister's Independence Lecture Series. Dr. Cannonier has had the honor of representing his native country in two sports: cricket and soccer.

Dr. Monica Galloway Burke is a Professor in the Department of Counseling and Student Affairs at Western Kentucky University (WKU). Prior to her 24 years of experience as a faculty member and practitioner in Student Affairs and Higher Education, she worked in the field of mental health. Dr. Burke has authored numerous peer-reviewed articles in scholarly journals and contributed chapters to various books. She also served as the lead author for *Helping Skills for Working with College Students: Applying Counseling Theory to Student Affairs Practice* (Routledge, 2017) and *Helping Students in Distress: A Faculty Guide* (Routledge, 2020). She is also a co-author for *Mindful Strategies for Helping College Students Manage Stress: A Guide for Higher Education Professionals* (Routledge, 2021). Dr. Burke also served as a co-editor for *No Ways Tired: The Journey for Professionals of Color in Student Affairs*, a three-set volume (Information Publishing, 2019). Additionally, she has conducted numerous workshops and presentations at the international, national, regional, state, and local levels. Dr. Burke currently serves as the co-editor of the *Journal of the Professoriate* and has served on editorial boards of professional journals as an associate editor and reviewer. She has also supervised numerous research theses, dissertations, and research projects, some of which led to co-authored published manuscripts with students. Dr. Burke is a Global Labor Organization (GLO) Fellow and currently a Diversity, Equity, and Inclusion Fellow for the Center for Teaching and Innovation Learning as well as a Fellow for Diversity, Equity, and Inclusion in Academic Affairs for the Office of the Provost at Western Kentucky University. She is also a member of the Kentucky Council on Postsecondary Education's Faculty Advisory Network. She has been recognized for her commitment to preparing graduate students for a career in student affairs; work to promote the field of student affairs and diversity in higher education; advising and research; as well as collaboration with colleagues and students by receiving various awards from WKU, professional organizations, and her local community.

Dr. Jeetendra Khadan is a Senior Economist who holds the position of Country Economist within the Caribbean Country Department at the Inter-American Development Bank. Jeetendra has written and published books, book chapters, and articles in several peer-reviewed academic journals.

Machel Pantin is an Economic Affairs Assistant at the Economic Commission for Latin America and the Caribbean Subregional Headquarters for the Caribbean. His work focuses mainly on macroeconomic research and policy development in the Caribbean.

Dr. Amos C. Peters is a Development Economist at UCLA Institute of the Environment and Sustainability. Dr. Peters has had previous stints with the Caribbean Development Bank, the University of Cape Town, the CARICOM Secretariat and the Eastern Caribbean Central Bank. He holds a Ph.D. in Economics from the University of North Carolina, Chapel Hill. Dr. Peters is a reform-minded economist with an avid interest in designing evidence-based economic and development strategy for emerging economies. His expertise is in exchange rates, fiscal policy, and international migration policy. He possesses a high level of experience in performing complex economic analysis in academic and policy environments with vast experience working in Africa and the Caribbean.

Yves Nithder Pierre has been working at the Central Bank of Haiti (BRH) since September 2007. He is currently the Head of Macroeconomic Analysis Unit in the Money and Economic Analysis Department (the Research Department). Prior to this position, he spent one year at the International Monetary Fund (IMF) as Government-Provided Advisor (GPA) to the Executive Director for Brazil (OEDBR). He holds an M.A. in Quantitative Finance and Economics from the University of Rennes 1 in France and B.A. in Applied Economics from the Centre de Techniques de Planification et d'Économie Appliquée (CTPEA). His areas of interest are Macroeconomics, Monetary Policy, and Financial Technology (Fintech).

Carl-Henri Prophète is a Deputy Director at the Macroeconomic Analysis Department at the Central Bank of Haiti (BRH). He joined the Central Bank as an economist in 2005 and served as Advisor to the Executive Director for Brazil at the International Monetary Fund (IMF) from June 2017 to January 2018. He holds a B.A. in Economics from Université Quisqueya in Port-au-Prince, an M.Sc. in Economics from Université de Montréal and a Master of Public Policy from the University of Maryland, College Park. His main academic interests include economic growth and structural change, economic policy, and economic history.

Dr. Inder Ruprah studied at the University College London, London School of Economics, and the University of Cambridge. His last posting was Regional Economic Advisor for the Caribbean at the Inter-American Development Bank. Inder has written and published books, book chapters, and articles several in peer-reviewed academic journals.

Dr. Wendell Samuel a national of St. Vincent and the Grenadines was Deputy Division Chief in the IMF's African Department prior to assuming the position of CARTAC Program Coordinator. He also served as the IMF's Regional Resident Representative for the ECCU during 2010–2012. Mr. Samuel holds a bachelor's and master's degree in economics from the University of the West Indies, and a Ph.D. in Economics from New York University. Before joining the IMF, Mr. Samuel was Senior Director of Research and Information at the Eastern Caribbean Central Bank, and a Lecturer in the Department of Economics at the University of the West Indies.

List of Figures

List of Tables

CHAPTER 1

Introduction

Monica Galloway Burke and Colin Cannonier

The generally tropical Caribbean consists of many island nations and territories, the Caribbean Sea, and the surrounding coasts. The islands are located between North America and South America and east of Central America as well as southeast of the Gulf of Mexico and west of the Atlantic Ocean. Although the Caribbean is viewed as one region, its islands are linguistically (i.e., English, Spanish, French, Dutch, and Antillean creole), economically, politically, and socially diverse (Image 1.1) Central Intelligence Agency [CIA] (2020).

Historically, the Caribbean is rooted in colonialism in which the plantation system served as an economic driver for foreign-owned entities. Producing crops such as sugar, bananas, and coffee, primarily intended for export, was replaced with tourism as the economic driver around

M. G. Burke (✉)
Western Kentucky University, Bowling Green, KY, USA
e-mail: monica.burke@wku.edu

C. Cannonier
Jack C. Massey College of Business, Belmont University, Nashville, TN, USA
e-mail: colin.cannonier@belmont.edu

C. Cannonier and M. Galloway Burke (eds.),
Contemporary Issues Within Caribbean Economies,
https://doi.org/10.1007/978-3-030-98865-4_1

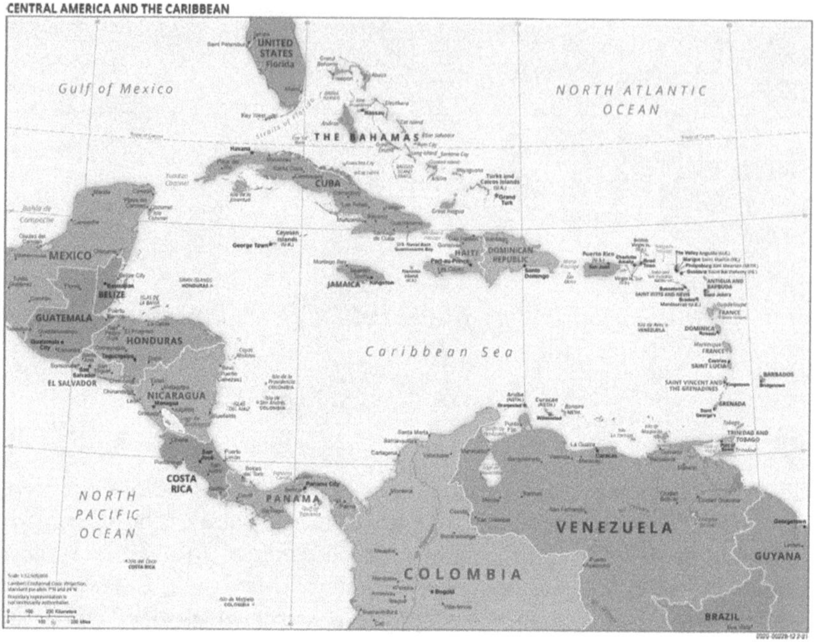

Image 1.1 Caribbean map (*Source* CIA World Factbook at https://www.cia.gov/the-world-factbook/static/025bc228cb50e875e41f1d38820ff8d8/central_america_pol.jpg)

1960s. Acemoglu, Johnson and Robinson (2002, 2005), argued that in regions like the Caribbean, Europeans were likely to set up extractive institutions that aimed to transfer as many resources from the colony as possible to the colonizer. The Caribbean was also exploited for its resources through the enslavement of Africans brought to the region to produce goods such as sugar cane and banana, solely for the profit of the slaveowners/plantation owners residing in Europe. To the extent that most of the profit was reinvested in the home country of the plantation owners, Caribbean countries became bereft of the requisite infrastructure and the level of human capital development necessary to profitably compete in a free market system. The difficult transition from plantation economies (i.e., sugar and bananas) following a downturn in agricultural manufacturing (e.g., sugar and bananas) to contemporary economies in a globalized context for economic competition and development shown vulnerabilities and created more challenges for Caribbean countries, albeit to varying degrees, such as debt, impoverishment, increased dependency on tourism and remittances, instability in the financial sector, inadequate infrastructure for growth, vulnerability to natural disasters, and reliance on foreign aid.

In addition, the limited infrastructure and slow economic development were also influenced by the restrictions imposed on the colonies and "the next century would be marked by economic, political and demographic instability throughout the Caribbean zone" (Vargas, 2012, para. 27). Caribbean economies worsened as they had to face competition for exports that were previously protected with guaranteed entry into the United Kingdom (UK) markets. Even though the Caribbean economies were negatively impacted by increased competition, the point to be made is that the history of colonialism and exploitation meant that the newly independent small island developing states are always playing catch-up.

Many will also argue that Caribbean colonies have been exploited since their incorporation into the international economy; that is why they are referred to in the literature as "colonies of exploitation" and not "colonies of settlement." Ultimately, various strategies and policies developed to address issues that remained after colonialism have not fully addressed the negative economic impact from the long-term development of colonies.

The Contemporary Issues of Caribbean Economies

Economics is an intriguing and complex concept that touches every part of our societies within our global world and has driven societies for centuries. The influence of economics can appear in something common like the prices we pay at the grocery store or at the gas station to something not as common, like a natural disaster or pandemics. Economics is also a global concept because the actions and well-being of one country can influence another, such as global market fluctuations and trade. For this book, the focus is on Caribbean economies due to the interesting combination of its assets and challenges.

The Caribbean is a diverse region, identified by its small, open economies that mostly fall into the middle-income category, and possesses uniqueness in its history, culture, music, staple dishes, and regional linguistic diversity mixed with its environmental amenities of sea, sand, and sun. Each island in the Caribbean also has its own distinct economic features but each also faces challenges. Some of these challenges include foreign debt, competition, employment, crime and violence, environmental degradation, climate change, technological innovation, energy costs, education, inflation, slowing productivity growth, remittance dependency, loss of correspondent banking relations, and domestic politics. There are also external vulnerabilities such as the export market, status of technology, and financial sector. Being a small economy with a relatively small population, land area, and gross national product (GNP), the Caribbean, like other small island economies, have characteristics like geographic isolation; narrow production bases, often with one or two primary products or industries and mainly producing for export; diseconomies of scale, translated through factor indivisibilities into higher unit costs of infrastructure, investment, and production; a restricted number of export markets and import suppliers; and high vulnerability to natural hazards and global market fluctuations (Legarda, 1984). From a global context, Caribbean, economies are developing and the importance of the services sector—especially tourism, offshore finances, and information technology—is evident and will continue to grow.

In general, there is fragility due to the small size of their individual economies in addition to their geographical location that makes the Caribbean islands more susceptible to economic and financial volatility (Zappino, 2005). The precariousness of their island ecosystems makes them among the most threatened in the world, especially because they are particularly vulnerable to natural and environmental degradation. Specifically, natural disasters can impede economic progress for islands in the Caribbean to various levels. Natural disasters (e.g., hurricanes, volcanoes, and earthquakes) are of special concern because of most of the islands' dependence on tourism. An example of a natural disaster impacting the economy is the category 5 Hurricane Dorian that occurred in the Bahamas from September 1 to 3, 2019, that not only impacted the labor market, tourism, and infrastructure of the island, but lives were lost, and many homes and property were destroyed.

Issues associated with the Caribbean cannot be simply sorted into categories because they are the result of a variety of forces. In addition to the impact of the vestiges of history, Caribbean economies are often tinged by external factors, whether they be geographical, economic, political, or environmental (or a combination thereof). As previously noted, the Caribbean islands face some obstacles to their sustained progress related to external influences as well as internal and external threats typical for small economies. These aforementioned issues could potentially pose barriers to economic development in the Caribbean region. These factors suggest a difficult road ahead, but the chapters presented in this volume aim to help to prompt discussions and a search for creative solutions to the region's problems.

The chapters in this book are authored by distinguished professionals, practitioners, researchers, and academicians who offer a comprehensive analysis of topics that impact the Caribbean economies. Notably, each chapter has a contributor who is a native of, has lived, and has worked or currently works in the Caribbean. Further, the authors have wide-ranging experiences in professional settings such as academia, government, central banks, and international organizations such as the International Monetary Fund (IMF), The United Nations Economic Commission for Latin America and the Caribbean (ECLAC), the Caribbean Development Bank (CDB), and the Inter-American Development Bank (IADB), which are integral to Caribbean economies. Thus, the perspectives these authors share are evidenced-based and informed by their extensive knowledge of contemporary issues in the Caribbean. These authors present empirical, theoretical, and contextual research focused on areas such as debt and fiscal constraints, non-communicable diseases, climate change, information and communication technologies, infrastructure, size and sustainability, migration, economic growth, investment, economic policies, tourism, employment, and remittances, to name a few.

Small states, like some in the Caribbean, face low growth, high debt, significant vulnerabilities, and limited resilience to shocks. According to the International Monetary Fund [IMF] (2013), many Caribbean economies face high and rising debt to GDP ratios that jeopardize prospects for medium-term debt sustainability and growth. In Chapter 2, Dillon Alleyne and Machel Pantin explore such challenges through an examination of the Caribbean debt burden and situation, including its particular challenges. They identify the factors that fuel high debt and the vulnerabilities which the region must address over time. Also offered are proposals related to debt reduction by the Commonwealth Secretariat, The World Bank, and the Economic Commission for Latin America and the Caribbean (ECLAC). Their analysis also addresses the requirements for fiscal sustainability, current policy prescriptions, the link between debt accumulation and the impact of particular vulnerabilities, and debt reduction proposals that have been suggested for the Caribbean and their implications.

A lack of access to digital infrastructure presents challenges for economic development in small island developing states, such as those in the Caribbean. Information and communication technologies (ICTs) can help mitigate many of these challenges. The COVID-19 pandemic truly illustrated the influence and potential of ICTs. According to Malcolm Johnson (2021) of the International Telecommunication Union, the challenge for small island developing states (SIDS) is about small domestic markets and small numbers of ICT suppliers; the lack of how to take advantage of the technologies; a lack of awareness of the advantages of connecting; a lack of relevant local content online in the local language; a much higher cost of connection in SIDS than most countries; reliance on satellite connections; and a small domestic market does not offer the industry enough return on investment. As Wendell Samuel asserts in Chapter 3, real economic growth will require an acceleration of the harnessing of technology to increase productivity that has declined in the Caribbean over the last three decades. He presents research that examines the reasons behind the slow growth and declining productivity experienced by most Caribbean countries over the last three decades related to ICT. Also included in the chapter are findings related to the ICT's impact on growth in the Caribbean and any contributing factors.

Noncommunicable diseases (NCDs), such as cardiovascular disease and type 2 diabetes, represent not only a major health problem that cannot only, according to the Pan American Health Organization (PAHO), overwhelm health services in Caribbean countries but also challenge their sustainability for economic growth and create losses in productivity while increasing economic burdens. Caribbean governments have recognized the debilitating impact of NCDs on the well-being of Caribbean people and started initiatives to address the issue and recognize that the lowering of mortality from NCDs remains a major concern. In Chapter 4, using an economic growth (macroeconomic) approach, Samuel Braithwaite estimates the economic costs of NCDs for four member countries (Barbados, Guyana, Jamaica and Trinidad & Tobago) of the Caribbean Community (CARICOM) and compared these to the costs of Cuba and the United States. Details related to these research findings are detailed, focusing on the economic burdens associated with NCDs, particularly the battle with the COVID-19 pandemic that will undoubtedly further stymie initiatives aimed at tackling NCDs.

As evidenced by expanding fiscal deficits, high debt levels, and slowing productivity growth, the Caribbean development model, primarily based on tourism and financial services for some countries and commodities for others, is no longer delivering. Consequently, Caribbean countries have earned the moniker of "high debt, low growth." Debt can adversely impact economic growth and large increases in the debt-to-GDP ratio could lead to much higher taxes, lower future incomes, and intergenerational inequity; thus, have negative or significant (or both) effects on the growth rate of an economy (de Rugy & Salmon, 2020). Unfortunately, fiscal deficits will rise due to increased COVID-19-related expenditure and revenue fall due to the combined effects of discretionary tax measures that reduce tax liabilities and fall in economic activity. In Chapter 5, Jeetendra Khadan and Inder Ruprah examine several channels and feedback loops that contribute to Caribbean countries' low economic growth-high debt status. They review the region's main fiscal problems, focusing on the tax system and how tax reforms can improve the countries' fiscal positions and considering how the region's tax system is undermined by a large shadow economy, perverse effects of tax expenditures and weak tax administration, among other issues. The authors present four critical objectives that should be pursued by Caribbean countries as it relates to tax reforms.

Migration flows between Caribbean islands for a variety of reasons are not unusual but influenced by economic conditions and legislative restrictions. People may migrate to improve their livelihood, and if applicable their families; seek refuge from a country's conflicts; fulfill family reunification; or search for better employment opportunities. In particular, Connell and Aldrich (2020) noted that economic fluctuations, employment opportunities, hazard events, and pursuit for healthcare and higher education have influenced migration and that immigration has played a major role in the expanding tourism and financial center, particularly in the Turks and Caicos Islands. In Chapter 6, Amos Peters examines the impact of Belonger status and country of birth on labor market outcomes in the Turks and Caicos Islands. The economics of how immigrants affect native wages and employment can impact labor market performance. Although immigrants possess a variety of skills and useful attributes that contribute to the diversity of the host country, they are often stigmatized, discriminated against, and blamed for many of the problems in the host country. The author presents research findings and a discussion that attempt to address this gap in the literature by analyzing the labor market outcomes of immigrants and natives in a developing small island state and seeks to identify and explore earnings and employment disparities by immigrant status, and among immigrants by country of birth.

Haiti, the Caribbean's second-largest nation by population, is the poorest country in the Caribbean region and among the poorest countries in the world with more than half of its population living below the World Bank's poverty line and ranking 170 out of 189 countries in 2020 on the UN's Human Development Index (World Bank, 2020). Haiti has had its share of challenges that has thwarted its economic development such as foreign interventions, debt, lingering political instability, corruption, criminality and violence, intergenerational poverty, illiteracy, lack of access to clean water and basic sanitation, and natural disasters (i.e., earthquakes, tornadoes, tropical storms, and drought) that have displaced Haitians and destroyed housing and land. Two chapters focus on Haiti's economic challenges related to its exchange rate and inflation dynamics and the effectiveness of monetary policy as well as migrant workers' remittances and the country's real exchange rate. In Chapter 7, Yves Pierre examines inflation in Haiti which is recurrent and relatively strong in country. The author explores the inflation process that is fed by a permanent monetary expansion and the monetary effect. Pierre further investigates these monetary effects and their strength on the dynamics of inflation in Haiti with some conventional econometric methods using quarterly data from different sources. The strength and the stability of these dynamics are also analyzed. Chapter 8 focuses on remittances, which have become a major segment of Haiti's economy as it has been increasingly reliant on migrants' transfers over the past 30 years increasing almost tenfold between 1998 and 2018. Carl-Henri Prophète and Dudley Augustin examine the relationship between the increasing flow of remittances and the country's real exchange rate in Haiti using annual data while controlling for other macroeconomic factors that might affect the country's external competitiveness.

Like Haiti, remittances represent a significant source of inflows to most Caribbean countries, following tourism and foreign direct investment. In terms of contribution to economic output, remittances are more important to the Caribbean than any other region around the world and account for approximately 4 % of the region's GDP (World Bank, 2019). The impact of remittances on Caribbean economies is also important because of the region's close proximity to the United States, which represents the largest source of remittances and where more than half the migrants emigrate. Against this backdrop, Colin Cannonier and Marcus

Bansah, the authors of Chapter 9, use panel data across several Caribbean countries over four decades to explore the influence of workers' remittances on financial development. Their approach is based on a variety of empirical methodologies to identify the causal impact of remittances on various measures of financial development. Overall, their findings offer some clear policy implications. If a goal is to increase the level of financial inclusion of households receiving remittances, then policymakers should consider pursuing policies that improve the mechanisms that offer easier channels for remittances to enter the domestic banking system.

The tourism sector plays a vital role in economic growth in many Caribbean communities, which are mostly dependent on tourism and exceeds that in other regions of the world. Tourism in the Caribbean, which relies heavily on the financial sector and contributes to the gross domestic product (GDP), has significant and positive impact across two main categories: depth and efficiency (Cannonier & Burke, 2017). In addition, tourism provides volume to the smallness of Caribbean countries to overcome insufficient market demand; increases competition by encouraging new entrants in the marketplace; and raises the standard of living and thus, the quality of life of those in the Caribbean (Croes, 2006). Tourism expenditure in Caribbean countries also represents the single largest inflow of foreign exchange and is associated with a significant amount of international capital flows, increased employment, increased local business revenues, access to foreign direct investment and increased tax revenues, to name a few. In the end, tourism has a positive effect on growth and tourism's contribution to economic output and to the extent that tourism accounts for a sizable proportion of GDP in the Caribbean in particular, policymakers can play a role (Cannonier & Burke, 2019). Chapters 10 and 11 focus on different aspects of tourism in the Caribbean. David Baker discusses sustainable tourism in Chapter 10, especially as it relates to health threats due to COVID-19. No other event, natural or human-caused, has disrupted the travel and tourism sector as much as COVID-19 and the related reductions in tourism have devastated communities. Per the author, public health threats of tourism on local communities will only increase post-COVID-19 pandemic. This chapter also highlights the need for more dialogue between industry executives and community officials in the Caribbean region regarding island governance and potential strategies involving public, private, and mixed partnerships to develop a tourism strategy that supports its development and sustainability. In Chapter 11, Madlyn Bonimy provides a summarization of historical aspects of tourism in the Bahamas and deliberates on the role of the Bahamas' government in tourism. The author examines three components related to the role that the Bahamas government plays in tourism and can enhance in tourism, which are government legislation in tourism development, government policy in tourism development, and government programs in tourism development.

The Caribbean is beautiful and yet complex, as well as strong and yet fragile in many ways. Of course, as with most small state islands, there are obstacles that need to be moved to boost economic growth in the region but there are opportunities for growth too. Analyzing and understanding salient and current economic issues as well as exploring strategies to address these issues in the Caribbean are needed and as such, this book takes a closer look at pertinent contemporary issues. This book contributes to scholarly discussions and provides research-based insights into the current economic landscape of the Caribbean, which can broaden the scope for future policymaking and future economic growth.

References

Acemoglu, D., Johnson, S., & Robinson, J. A. (2002). Reversal of fortune: Geography and institutions in the making of the modern world income distribution. *The Quarterly Journal of Economics, 117*(4), 1231–1294. https://doi.org/10.1162/003355302320935025

Acemoglu, D., Johnson, S., & Robinson, J. A. (2005). The rise of Europe: Atlantic trade, institutional change, and economic growth. *The American Economic Review, 95*(3), 546–579. https://doi.org/10.1257/0002828054201305

Cannonier, C., & Burke, M. G. (2017). Tourism and financial development in small states—Evidence from Caribbean countries. *Tourism Economics, 23*(6), 1369–1377. https://doi.org/10.1177/1354816617689870

Cannonier, C., & Burke, M. G. (2019). The economic growth impact of tourism in small island developing states: Evidence from the Caribbean. *Tourism Economics, 25*(1), 85–108. https://doi.org/10.1177/1354816618792792

Central Intelligence Agency [CIA]. (2020). *World and regional maps: Central America and the Caribbean*. Map. https://www.cia.gov/the-worldfactbook/static/c0e0198c123b78e404c04b3b742113e1/central_america_phy.pdf

Connell J., & Aldrich, R. (2020). Migration: Holding on to home? In J. Connell & R. Aldrich (Eds.), *The ends of empire: The last colonies revisited* (pp. 291–320). Palgrave Macmillan. https://doi.org/10.1007/978-981-15-5905-1_6

Croes, R. (2006). A paradigm shift to a new strategy for small island economies: Embracing demand side economics for value enhancement and long term

economic stability. *Tourism Management*, *27*(3), 453–465. https://doi.org/10.1016/j.tourman.2004.12.003
de Rugy, V., & Salmon, J. (2020). *Debt and growth: A decade of studies* [Policy Brief]. Mercatus Center, George Mason University. https://www.mercatus.org/system/files/de_rugy_and_salmon_-_policy_brief_-_debt_and_growth_a_decade_of_studies_-_v1.pdf
International Monetary Fund [IMF]. (2013). *Caribbean small states: Challenges of high debt and low growth—Executive summary*. https://www.imf.org/external/np/pp/eng/2013/022013b.pdf
Johnson, M. (2021, September 17). *Connecting the world means connecting small islands too.* https://www.itu.int/en/myitu/News/2021/09/17/08/33/Connecting-small-islands-SIDS-digital-transformation-Malcolm-Johnson
Legarda, B. (1984, June). Small island economies. *Finance & Development*, *21*(2), 42–43. https://www.elibrary.imf.org/downloadpdf/journals/022/0021/002/article-A012-en.pdf
Vargas, H. (2012). *Sugar and slavery in the 17th century*. https://enciclopediapr.org/en/encyclopedia/sugar-and-slavery-in-the-17th-century/
World Bank. (2019). *World Development Indicators (WDI)*. http://data.worldbank.org/data-catalog/world-development-indicators
World Bank. (2020). *The World Bank of Haiti*. Retrieved November 1, 2021, from https://www.worldbank.org/en/country/haiti/overview#1
World Tourism Organization [UNWTO]. (n.d.). *Small developing states*. Retrieved November 1, 2021, from https://www.unwto.org/sustainable-development/small-islands-developing-states
Zappino, V. (2005). *Caribbean tourism and development: An overview*. (ECDPM Discussion Paper No. 65). https://ecdpm.org/wp-content/uploads/2013/11/DP-65-Caribbean-Tourism-Industry-Development-2005.pdf

CHAPTER 2

Debt Burden in Small Island Caribbean States and Prospects for Debt Relief

Dillon Alleyne and Machel Pantin

Introduction

This chapter is divided into three sections. The first describes the evolution of the Caribbean debt burden, its structure and composition, and the particular challenges which have resulted from the debt overhang. The analysis also addresses the requirements for fiscal sustainability. The

The views expressed in this chapter are those of the authors and do not necessarily reflect the views of the organization they are affiliated with.

D. Alleyne (✉) · M. Pantin
Economic Commission for Latin America and the Caribbean (ECLAC), Port of Spain, Trinidad and Tobago
e-mail: dillon.alleyne@un.org

M. Pantin
e-mail: machel.pantin@un.org

C. Cannonier and M. Galloway Burke (eds.), *Contemporary Issues Within Caribbean Economies*,
https://doi.org/10.1007/978-3-030-98865-4_2

second section explains the factors that gave rise to the debt accumulation since such an explanation is critical to an appropriate policy response. The discussion addresses the fact that the current policy prescriptions assume that the debt arises largely from fiscal discretion and in the extreme case fiscal excess. It is suggested that debt accumulation also arises from falling export capacity that shows up as persistent deficits on the current account. The chapter also examines the link between debt accumulation and the impact of such vulnerabilities—i.e., extreme events and climate change. The third section reviews debt reduction proposals that have been suggested, namely those put forward by the Commonwealth Secretariat, the World Bank and the Economic Commission for Latin America and the Caribbean (ECLAC), as well as the implications of each to address the underlying challenges posed by the overhang. The chapter then concludes.

The Evolution of Caribbean Debt

The Caribbean region has had a long-standing problem with public debt accumulation beginning in the 1970s with the debt crisis among developing countries and then in the 1980s before the intensification of World Bank/IMF structural adjustment programs. This section examines in detail the evolution of public debt for the period 2000 to 2020 and compares it with the debt burden of other developing countries. In 2001, the average gross general government debt was 69.7% of GDP for Caribbean[1] countries which was just below the average for developing countries of 71.9%. Subsequently these two debt trajectories began to diverge with the Caribbean sustaining higher levels of debt throughout the period. The debt burden of the Caribbean peaked at 78.6% in 2004 while it was 66.1% for developing countries. The Caribbean debt began to fall just before the global financial crisis of 2008–2009 and was 66.1% in 2007. This was due to, among other factors, an expansion in growth consequent of the buoyant tourism sector and the primary commodity boom which benefited commodity exporters in the region.

In the case of developing countries, the debt to GDP ratio declined steadily to 42.6% in 2007. Following the global financial crisis, the debt

[1] For this section, the Caribbean refers to Antigua and Barbuda, The Bahamas, Barbados, Belize, Dominica, Grenada, Guyana, Jamaica, Saint Kitts and Nevis, Saint Lucia, Saint Vincent and the Grenadines, Suriname and Trinidad and Tobago.

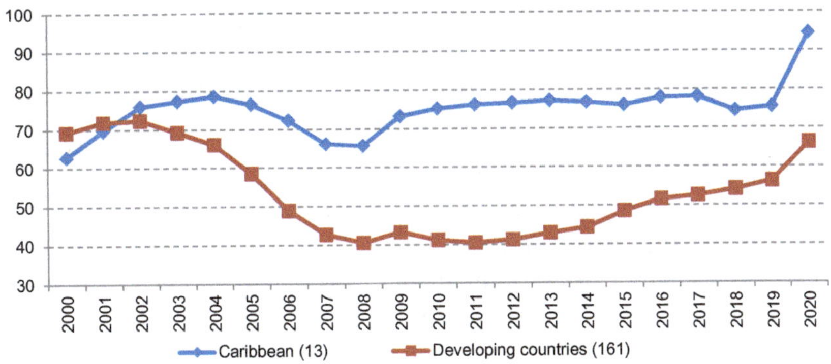

Fig. 2.1 Gross general government debt (Percent of GDP) (*Source* International Monetary Fund, World Economic Outlook Database, April 2021)

burden of both sets of countries rose but again the trajectories were very different. For the Caribbean between 2009 and 2019, the debt to GDP ratio never fell below 70% and was 75.5% of GDP in 2019. For developing countries, the average rose from 43.1% in 2009 to 56.2% in 2019. The COVID-19 pandemic has affected all countries and both the developing countries' average debt and that of the Caribbean increased sharply in 2020. The latter is due to the collapse of the tourism sector, the decline in primary commodity prices, border closures, and the spillover effects at the domestic level. As is observed in Fig. 2.1, the average has increased for both groups, but substantially more in the Caribbean due to the limited fiscal space and lack of concessional finance. Clearly the debt challenge is not peculiar to the Caribbean, but they represent outliers in the debt accumulation process.

Decomposing the Caribbean Debt

It is of interest to decompose the change in debt to determine what impulses led to its increase or decrease over most of the periods, 2001–2005, 2006–2008, and 2009–2015. A standard decomposition technique is used to separate the change in central government debt over the periods into the following effects:

- The real exchange rate effect: a devaluation increases the debt ratio and vice versa.
- The growth effect: If growth is positive this effect decreases debt and vice versa.
- The interest rate effect: Increases the debt ratio if nominal interest rates increase and/or economic growth decreases, and vice versa.
- The primary balance effect: A primary balance surplus decreases the debt ratio and vice versa.
- The residual: Effects from all other sources, including the government taking on contingent liabilities (Fig. 2.2).

In 2001–2005, the real interest rate effect and a large residual effect (due mainly to unanticipated shocks in a number of countries) pushed debt up. In this period economic growth and primary balance effects were not large enough to reduce the debt.

In the second period, the Caribbean managed to achieve a decrease in average central government debt due to strong economic growth and reduced real interest rates. A major contributor to the decline in this period was the decline in Guyana's debt ratio, which fell from 188.3%

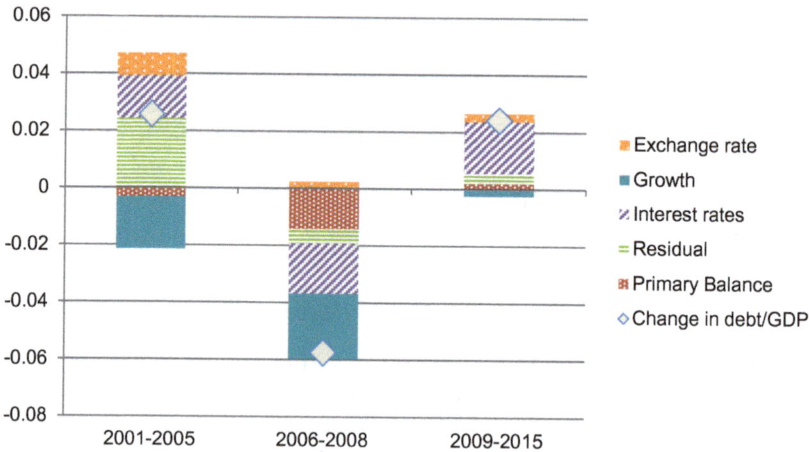

Fig. 2.2 Average contribution to debt accumulation in the Caribbean, 2001–2015 (Percent of GDP) (*Source* Authors calculations, based on official sources and World Bank data)

of GDP in 2005 to 97.0% of GDP in 2006. Guyana was a beneficiary of the Highly Indebted Poor Countries (HIPC) debt relief initiative, later followed by the MDRI initiative. Trinidad and Tobago, which was in the midst of an oil boom, saw its debt to GDP ratio fall from 37.6% in 2002 to 10.9% in 2008. In this period, the global financial crisis also took place but its effect was generally felt from 2009.

In the post-crisis period, the debt to GDP ratio increased again as a result of reduced growth. Despite falling interest rates, the real interest rate effect was still positive as growth had been absent. Service producing economies fared particularly poor in the wake of the global financial crisis. In more recent years, the commodity producing economies[2] like Suriname and Trinidad and Tobago saw their previous strong growth disappear in the face of falling commodity prices.

The Heterogeneity of Caribbean Debt

While the average Caribbean debt to GDP ratio is in excess of the arbitrary limits suggested by the IMF of 60% for debt sustainability, a closer look reveals a very diverse situation. In 2020, total public sector debt varied from 156.9% of GDP in Suriname to 24.8% in Guyana. Twelve of the fourteen Caribbean countries had higher public debt to GDP ratios than the average for developing countries (48.5%), and all except Guyana have debt ratios of over 60% of GDP.

Countries also had different debt profiles in terms of the composition of creditors. Six of the Caribbean countries had a higher share of domestic debt in the total debt, while the rest had a greater share owed to external creditors. The highest domestic debt to GDP ratio in 2020 was observed in Barbados (96.9%), and the highest external debt ratio belonged to Suriname (106.0%) which faces severe foreign exchange risks (Fig. 2.3).

The available data allow for a further examination of external debt for seven Caribbean countries. The overall results for the seven countries show that in 2010 49.3% of the debt was owed to the private sector, 14.8% to bilateral creditors, and the rest (36.0%) was owed to multilateral creditors. For 2019 the ratios were 50.5%, 12.8%, and 36.8% respectively.

[2] The commodity (or goods) producing economies of the Caribbean are defined as Belize, Guyana, Suriname and Trinidad and Tobago. The remaining Caribbean economies constitute the service producers.

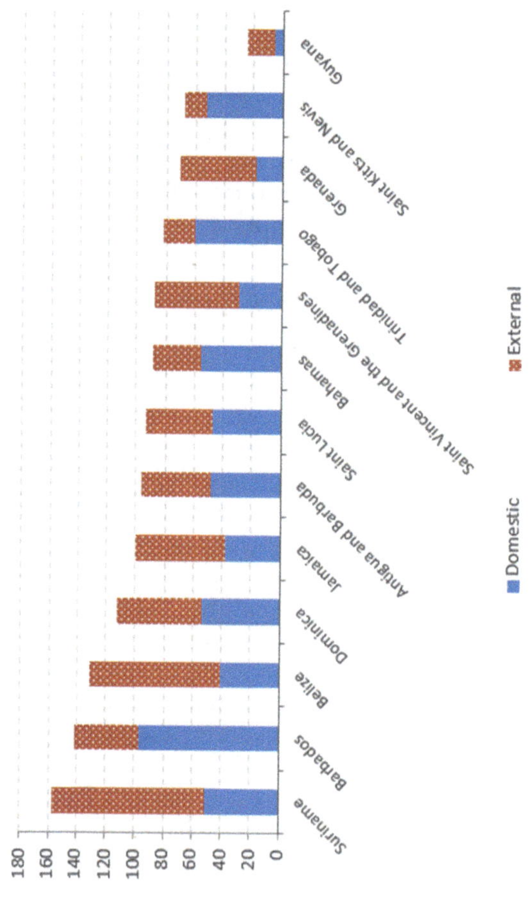

Fig. 2.3 Caribbean domestic and external public sector debt, 2020 (Percent of GDP) (*Source* Economic Commission for Latin America and the Caribbean, on the basis of official figures)

The high share of private debt reflects the lack of concessional finance and the need to go to the private market. In some cases, domestic debt is denominated in foreign currency and these could bear foreign exchange risks.

The external debt structure also displayed a high level of heterogeneity between countries (see Fig. 2.4). In 2010 three of the seven countries, (Belize, Grenada, and Jamaica) had debt to private creditors in excess of 40% of total external debt. In 2019 as well, three of the seven countries (Belize, Jamaica, and Saint Lucia) had the share of debt to private creditors greater than 40%; of these three, only in Jamaica was the share greater than 55%. Debt from multilateral sources was clearly more dominant, particularly in Guyana and Saint Vincent and the Grenadines, where it accounted for 65.2% and 80.9% respectively.

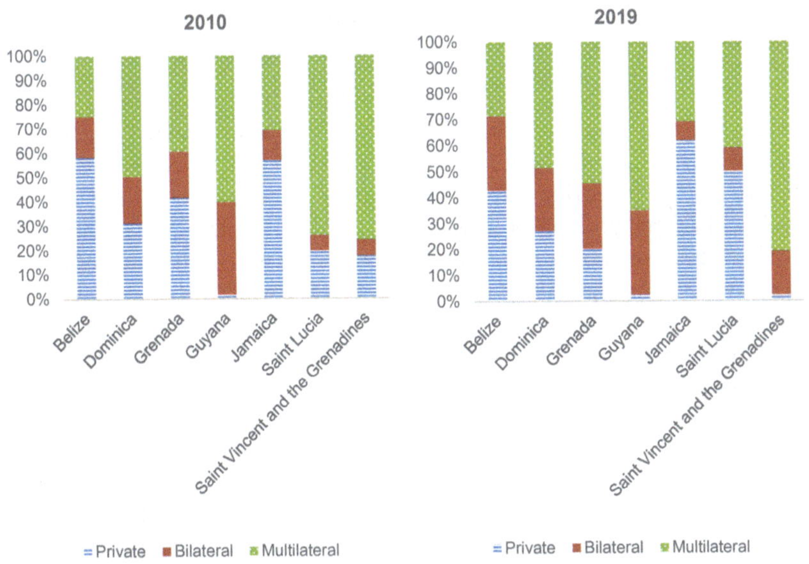

Fig. 2.4 Composition of public and publicly guaranteed external debt, 2010 and 2019 (Percentage) (*Source* World Bank International Debt Statistics database)

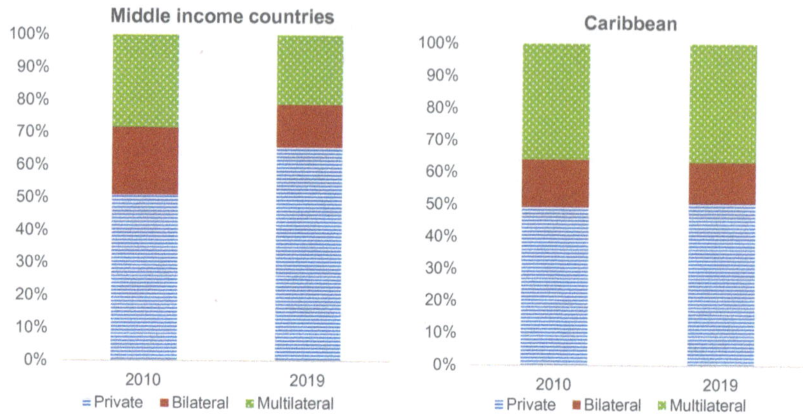

Fig. 2.5 Average composition of public and publicly guaranteed external debt, 2010 and 2019 (Percentage) (*Source* World Bank World Development Indicators Database)

The figure below compares the composition of external debt for the Caribbean to that of middle-income countries.[3] Whereas almost half of the Caribbean countries' external debt is from private sources, 49.3% in 2010 and 50.5% in 2019, for middle-income countries it was 50.9% and 65.5% respectively. Meanwhile multilateral debt was 36.0% and 36.8% in 2010 and 2019 respectively for the Caribbean, while for middle-income countries it was 28.4% and 21.3%, demonstrating that the Caribbean relies more heavily on multilateral sources than most other middle-income countries (Fig. 2.5).

The Debt Repayment Burden

The burden of high debt is not only demonstrated in the debt to GDP ratio, but in the debt service costs. Every dollar spent repaying debt is a dollar not spent on health, education, or any other form of economic development.[4] The chart below plots the external debt service payments

[3] Middle-income economies are defined by the World Bank and this chapter as those in which 2015 GNI per capita was between $1,026 and $12,475.

[4] This assumes that past debt accumulation was to support consumption rather than investment and capital accumulation either human or physical.

Fig. 2.6 Debt service payment ratios for the Caribbean, 2015–2019 average (*Source* Economic Commission for Latin America and the Caribbean, on the basis of official figures)

as a percent of exports of goods and services against total debt service payments as a percent of government revenue. On average, external debt service payments amounted to 7.5% of exports of goods and services and absorbed 29.9% of government revenue. The highest external debt service ratios were seen in Jamaica, Dominica, and Saint Vincent and the Grenadines, while the highest total debt service ratios were seen in the Antigua and Barbuda, The Bahamas, Barbados, and Jamaica, where they absorbed over 50% of government revenue (Fig. 2.6).

Unpleasant Fiscal Arithmetic

A debt sustainability analysis was conducted to determine just how difficult it is to stabilize the debt and what primary surpluses are required (ECLAC, 2016).[5] Using the standard approach outlined in the work of Buiter (1985) and Blanchard (1990), the primary surpluses, in percent of GDP, required to stabilize debt at its 2013 levels for Belize, Dominica, Grenada, Guyana, Jamaica, Saint Lucia, and Saint Vincent and the

[5] The results are based on ECLAC's debt strategy paper (ECLAC, 2016).

Grenadines were computed. The results were that the debt stabilizing surpluses ranged from 0.56% of GDP in Dominica to 3.82% in Jamaica.

More importantly, the exercise also calculated the fiscal adjustment, in percent of GDP, required to achieve the debt stabilizing primary surplus. It is calculated by subtracting the current primary surplus from the debt stabilizing primary surplus. It gives an idea of how difficult it would be for governments to contain debt at its current levels. The calculated adjustments to achieve debt stabilizing primary surpluses ranged from 0.00% of GDP in Jamaica[6] to 5.41% in Grenada.

As part of the debt sustainability analysis, the primary surpluses required to reduce debt to 60% of GDP over 10 years (ECLAC, 2016)[7] and their corresponding fiscal adjustments were computed. The results were mixed, given the varying levels of government debt. Belize, Dominica, Saint Lucia, and Saint Vincent and the Grenadines had government debt to GDP ratios of 75.8%, 75.1%, 79.6%, and 74.0%, respectively, in 2013 (IMF, 2014). To reduce their debts to 60% of GDP, they would have required fiscal adjustments of 1.54%, 2.93%, 5.02%, and 4.49% of GDP, respectively. Grenada and Jamaica had much higher government debt levels of 109.8% and 141.6% of GDP, respectively. While Grenada[8] would have required a massive 10.04% of GDP adjustment to reduce its debt to 60% of GDP, Jamaica only required an adjustment of 3.4% of GDP since its primary surplus was already so high in 2013. The results from this analysis provide some evidence of the difficulty that Caribbean governments face in stabilizing their debt ratios, much less reducing them.

[6] Jamaica's primary surplus in 2013 was already above the debt stabilizing value. Jamaica has since achieved success in reducing its debt to GDP ratio. It is important to note that the primary surplus posted by Jamaica of around 7% of GDP is not congruent with their historical experience and may itself be stifling growth.

[7] The required primary surplus would have to be maintained over the period.

[8] The debt burden of Grenada has fallen since due to Paris Club restructuring.

Structural Factors Contributing to Debt Accumulation Over Time

The Major Structural Factors

In light of the heavy debt burden facing Caribbean countries, an important question is: what are the factors contributing to debt accumulation? Does the problem stem from fiscal mismanagement, structural constraints, or a combination of both?[9] There is empirical evidence that fiscal policy in the Caribbean tends to be pro-cyclical, which means that fiscal buffers cannot be easily built. In addition, the fiscal multipliers are relatively weak (Alleyne & Pantin, 2013; Guy & Belgrave, 2012) which implies that expanding public spending results in pressures on foreign exchange through the important intensity of consumption and intermediate imports.[10] More generally, however, it is not obvious that debt accumulation is simply a fiscal challenge because in open Caribbean economies there are multiple sources of such accumulation including fiscal sources, the current account sources, and impulses coming from the monetary policy focus of the central bank.

The policy diagnosis has tended to suggest that the immediate fiscal challenge characterized by high debt and repayment costs are the result of fiscal excesses. As a result, much of the emphasis of adjustment has been on fiscal reforms designed to squeeze expenditure and raise taxes.[11] Implicit in this view is that cutting government spending inspires confidence in the private sector to expand consumption and investment.[12] In addition, some governments have been persuaded to implement fiscal rules to guarantee fiscal discipline—for example, in the case of Grenada and Jamaica. The adjustment exercises, whether home grown, as in Barbados, or under the IMF/World Bank group, assume that correcting

[9] None of the major debt initiatives maintain that the debt was accumulated solely due to vulnerabilities and the ECLAC proposal maintains that fiscal management and structural reforms are both important.

[10] When the economy is buoyant various social groups try to improve their position lost during the downturn. Often this is because there is not enough social dialogue to address costs and benefits of adjustment.

[11] A recent IMF paper argues for improving tax administration. See Stephane Schlotterbeck (2017).

[12] Ironically fiscal compression is taking place at a time of reduced external and domestic demand.

the fiscal imbalances will place these countries on the path to renewed growth. This approach runs counter to the functional finance position expounded by Sawyer (2009) that is based on Keynesian lines along which it is argued that fiscal policy has a positive impact on growth.[13] However, in an open economy context, this latter position may be too optimistic given that fiscal multipliers are weak. From a small states perspective, the critical issue is not the presence of a current account deficit but the persistence of such deficits and their sustainability.

In order to clarify these issues, the relationship between the current account deficit and fiscal deficits, the so-called twin deficit hypothesis, was examined using a vector autoregressive moving average (VARMA) framework developed to determine the percentage of the variation attributable to both the fiscal and current account deficits resulting from shocks arising from either of the two variables. The results suggest that for several Caribbean countries, the current account deficit Granger causes the fiscal deficit and in others, the relationship was bidirectional (Alleyne et al., 2011). Ramirez and Wright (2017) also echoed this conclusion using a framework of macroeconomic fundamental and fiscal policy variables to derive the fiscal limits of 18 Central American and Caribbean countries. They pointed out that trade volatility in these small open economies significantly impacted their ability to service their sovereign debt. According to Haque et al. (2016), the major driver of increased debt accumulation for small states was the size of the current account deficit (11.5% of GDP for lower middle-income small states, 10.4% of GDP for upper middle-income small states, and 5.6% of GDP for larger states). They also point out that slower growth in smaller states also exacerbated negative external debt dynamics. Birchwood and Matthias (2007) examined the factors that drive positive or negative fiscal balances in developing countries and concluded that persistent fiscal deficits were the result of both fiscal indiscipline and structural factors.

The chart below shows the current account balance and the overall fiscal balance for Caribbean countries distinguished by goods and service producers. Since the global crisis, the goods producers have experienced deterioration in their current account balance aggravated by the steep decline in commodity prices while for the service producers there has been an improvement aided by reduction in import prices and

[13] This is the perspective of functional finance.

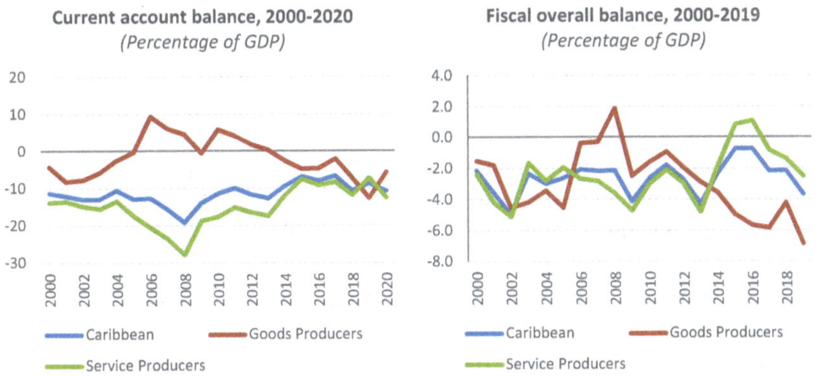

Fig. 2.7 Balances: Current account and fiscal (Percent of GDP) (*Source* Economic Commission for Latin America and the Caribbean, on the basis of official figures)

improved tourism receipts. The overall fiscal balances have also moved correspondingly between the two groups of countries (Fig. 2.7).

The current account balance is linked to reduced competitiveness and falling productivity (Alleyne et al., 2011; Ruprah et al., 2014). McLean (2017) has shown that the capacity of Caribbean economies to service their trade agreements is very low and there has been increased concentration on a few services and commodities in the export basket. The implication is that reducing the fiscal balance to stabilize the public debt offers a partial response to factors underlying debt accumulation.[14] The solution lies in solving the problems in the external sector through investment in those sectors and activities that improve the current account as against those that create an unsustainable balance. One area for careful support would be sectors that use domestic capital to raise the level of innovation and the share of new and existing products and services in dynamically growing markets.

[14] A number of goods exporting economies have been facing balance of payment difficulties in light of the significant reduction in foreign exchange inflows and this has led to implicit foreign exchange rationing.

The Impact of Disasters and Climate Change

Countries have also accumulated debt as a consequence of increased expenditures to address the impact of extreme events and climate change attendant difficulties.[15] Most Caribbean countries are located in the hurricane belt and are prone to earthquakes and other hazards. Indeed, a disaster resulting in damage and losses in excess of 5% of GDP can be expected to hit any Caribbean country every few years. Moreover, over the period 2000–2014, it is estimated that the economic cost of natural disasters (CRED)[16] in Caribbean countries was in excess of US$30.7 billion. In addition to the exposure to natural disasters, climate change represents the most serious challenge to the sustainable development of the Caribbean (ECLAC, 2011). The figure below shows the level of vulnerability of Caribbean states based on UNEP's vulnerability index (Fig. 2.8).

With respect to climate change, the region produces less than 1% of emissions of greenhouse gases (GHGs) in the world, while the impact of climate change in the subregion is disproportionately greater (UNEP, 2008). The Intergovernmental Panel on Climate Change has observed in the Caribbean an increase in sea level of about 1.8 mm per year. The consequences of this increase in sea level, associated with increased ocean temperatures, are visible in the subregion. It is estimated that 70% of the beaches are affected by loss of shoreline at a rate of between 0.25 and 9 mm per year. This loss causes damage to private and public infrastructure (roads, airports, power generators, etc.), which is particularly critical because it is estimated that 70% of the population lives in coastal areas. Similarly, the loss of coast negatively affects the quality of coastal and marine resources, which has two main effects. First, a reduction in protection against storms and hurricanes, accelerating erosion, and damage caused to infrastructure. Second, apart from the environmental degradation that it causes, it also affects the tourism sector, which represents approximately 15.5% of employment and contributes 13% to GDP. The disproportion between greenhouse gas emissions and the effects

[15] The recent passage of Hurricane Irma, a category 5 storm, through the Caribbean makes this point vividly.

[16] EM-DAT database is compiled by the Centre for Research on the Epidemiology of Disasters (CRED).

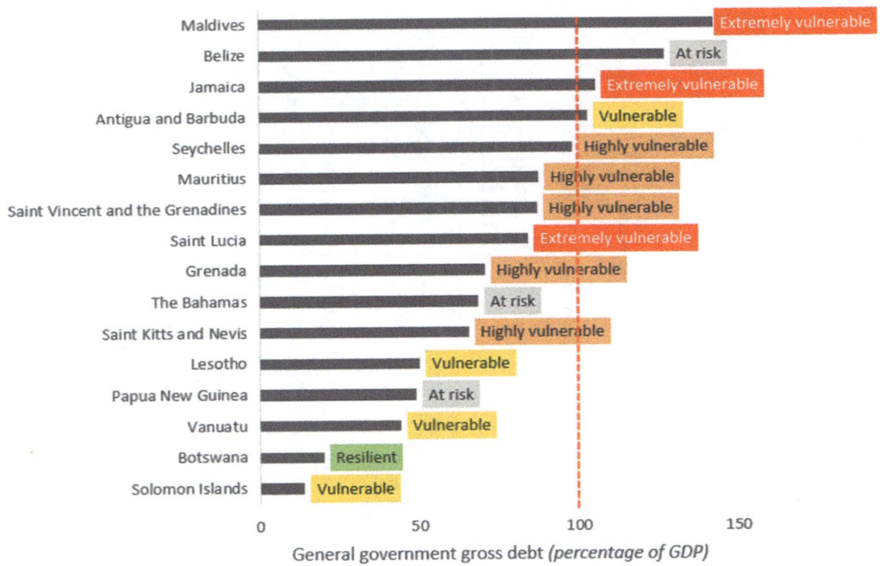

Fig. 2.8 Indebtedness and environmental vulnerability of Commonwealth Small States, 2020 (*Source* IMF World Economic Outlook April 2021 database, UNEP Environmental Vulnerability Index 2000)

generated by climate change in the Caribbean is one of the fundamental problems facing the subregion as it pursues sustainable development.

Despite these obvious threats, governments have had to focus their spending on addressing the debt burden. In addition, severe adjustment has been taking place on the capital side since this is easier to reduce in the short run. This modification has two consequences—the first of which is that countries have to forego funding much needed mitigation and adaptation programs, which will yield returns over the medium term. Second, by forgoing public capital investment, those aspects of infrastructural investment that are a complement to private investment will cause the private sector to underinvest, which harms growth. The next section examines three proposals for Caribbean debt reduction.

Proposals for Debt Reduction

Proposal by the Commonwealth Secretariat

A variety of proposals have been offered to address the severe debt challenge of Caribbean countries. Among these are three approaches that are worth considering given their differences in perspectives and degree of coverage of the debt. The first of these to be discussed is an initiative by the Commonwealth Secretariat (Commonwealth Secretariat, 2013a, b; Mitchell, 2016).

The proposal makes a number of initial assumptions, including that donors would wish to increase the sum of their climate finance disbursements in order to close the climate financing gap, and that climate finance providers do not have funds earmarked for particular recipient countries, especially when such funds are delivered through the Green Climate Fund (GCF). The proposal further assumes that debtor governments have identified a set of environments projects through an environmental plan. They also assume a trust fund is already set up either nationally or via a regional entity through, for example, the Caribbean Biodiversity Fund. The fund can then invest received resources into risk free securities to add to investments in climate adaptation projects. Finally, there is a legal agreement that provides for the write down of the debtor government's liabilities held by multilateral creditors and that the debt service previously owed will be paid to the trust fund to deliver climate adaptation projects.

Under this scheme, climate finance providers will contribute some proportion of their pledges to debt reduction based on the liabilities to the multilateral institutions. The debtor governments' equivalent transfer to the trust fund is made in local currency. Assuming that relief is to be granted, then debt could be purchased at a discount (haircut) or repayment can be made at a lower interest rate or the repayment period could be extended to ease the liquidity burden. The Commonwealth Secretariat specified a number of scenarios that reflect a combination of all three of these conditions, or some combination of them, as a path to relief. The optimum condition is the scenario in which the climate provider gets the most development finance with the least up-front financing. The Commonwealth Secretariat point to the benefit of fast-tracking disbursements and improving the economic viability of indebted countries through the conversion of foreign debt to domestic debt. The proposal recognizes that due to the heterogeneity of the debt, some countries will benefit more than others. The proposal also argues that this same mechanism can also tackle commercial and bilateral debt; however, the argument along these lines is not developed. The main challenge with this approach is that it does not offer any succor for the most indebted and speaks just to multilateral debt for which only a few countries will benefit. The multilateral debt in 2013 for seven Caribbean countries was US$4.7 billion, of which less than half was concessional. As shown in the previous section, "The Evolution of Caribbean Debt," for some countries multilateral concessional debt is quite substantial relative to their external debt. The Commonwealth Secretariat proposal is a minimalist approach developed to first determine how the markets will react and then push for further debt relief and hangs heavily on negotiating with multilateral creditors.

Proposal by the World Bank

The World Bank has also offered an approach that it hopes can begin first as a pilot with at least one member state (Haque et al., 2016). In this approach, two perspectives are offered. The first refers to a debt for nature and resilience swap and the second is a guarantee instrument that will leverage private financing in international financial markets. The World Bank argues that for countries facing high debt, the persistence of low growth will make it difficult for them to address the debt overhang. They recognize that the debt can be so large that it is difficult to refinance the current debt while financing future growth-enhancing projects. They argue that these countries face solvency and liquidity issues while needing to address debt and address climate change effects plus exposure to extreme events issues. The debt swap initiative is designed to retire high-cost commercial or bilateral debt while strengthening the policy and institutional framework for environmental sustainability and climate resilience.

Their debt swap strategy would be optional for countries in a World Bank program and where there is a track record of reform implementation. It would work through two important steps. First, the country in question would have to implement policy changes to strengthen its environmental management and its policies on climate resilience. Second, expensive debt could be bought at a discount or replaced by cheaper debt with longer maturity under World Bank terms. The savings would be absorbed by the budget, thus increasing the fiscal space to finance capital spending. It is not clear who would purchase this debt at a discount, but it could be speculated that the World Bank might persuade the creditors (bilateral donors) to participate. Of course, it is not clear whether such donors have the appetite to assist so-called "middle-income" and "high-income" Small Island Developing States (SIDS) at this time.

The other suggested option is to help countries to leverage funds in the international capital market and to obtain additional liquidity to deal with their debt situation through a guarantee instrument, or a so-called Policy-Based Guarantee. They argue that those eligible would be governments with a strong macroeconomic management objective and have shown progress toward their development goals. Specifically, those offered must have a strong track record of performance; a sustainable external financing plan; and a coherent borrowing strategy to establish borrowing in the country's own name without a guarantee over the medium term.

From this third plank, the countries can benefit from the World Bank's support and improved market access terms and possibly, good relations with the private sector. While the World Bank's plan is more comprehensive than the Commonwealth Secretariat's approach, it reflects a menu based on a case-by-case basis. While countries will continue to face new borrowing requirements, contracting more debt—especially among highly indebted countries—would be a hard sell. Given the challenges faced by the most highly indebted countries, it is not clear how the first two of three criteria under the second strategy will be fairly operationalized.

Proposal by the Economic Commission for Latin America and the Caribbean (ECLAC)

The ECLAC proposal is more comprehensive that the other two since it takes the view that the high debt levels in the Caribbean area are a regional issue and that a comprehensive regional resolution is optimal. However, in light of the heterogeneous nature of the debt structure in the various countries a menu approach which recognizes country differences is advocated. ECLAC observes that a number of factors explain debt accumulation and among these are four that can be highlighted:

- Firstly, the Caribbean is one of the most vulnerable regions with respect to exposure to extreme events. A significant proportion of debt was accumulated due to expenditure required to address such events and despite the presence of the Caribbean Catastrophic Insurance Fund (CCRIF), reconstruction expenditures are never enough to address the effects of such events.
- Secondly, the Caribbean lacks fiscal buffers which make it difficult to employ countercyclical measures in response to negative shocks. It is also the case that in post recessions, the Caribbean economies respond more slowly than other regions to increasing investment (ECLAC, 2012; Alleyne et al., 2011; Guy & Belgrave, 2012; Pentecost & Turner, 2010).
- Thirdly, there is no doubt that weak fiscal management has been an important factor in debt accumulation; however, the lack of good fiscal management is not the only factor driving debt.
- Fourthly as was suggested in section two the debt accumulation is the result of declining competitiveness and pressures coming from the expanding current account deficit. Recent work by Ramirez and Wright (2017) corroborate this finding when they concluded that, "... the open economy model with terms-of-trade and flexible exchange rate shocks produced lower distribution fiscal limits than the model without terms of trade. This shows that trade volatility in these small, open developing economies significantly impacted their ability to service sovereign debt."

The proposal also recognizes that the primary balances required for stabilizing the debt are also the cause of low growth and in addition the high debt service limits the ability of Caribbean countries to address the agenda for sustainable development.

The ECLAC debt for climate adaptation swap initiative is anchored by a central proposal to establish a Caribbean Resilience Fund (CRF). It will be designed as a Pan-Caribbean Segregated Portfolio Resilience Trust Fund. This approach will allow for the segregation of its risks and portfolios, enabling investment in a range of areas including debt reprofiling and debt swaps, and accommodating the receipt of resources from all donors, investors or enterprises deemed eligible. This is essentially a special purpose financing vehicle intended to leverage long-term low-cost development financing for the Caribbean, while at the same time ensuring the availability of resources for investment in adaptation and mitigation initiatives, in the development of green industries, thereby promoting both resilience building and the structural transformation of Caribbean economies.

The structure of the CRF comprises three distinct windows. The first window, called the resilience building window, is intended to attract finance for the development of blue and green industries and for wider investment in mitigation and adaptation as indicated above. Importantly, this window, with its in-built mechanism for the design of projects that respond to climate vulnerability in the Caribbean, will serve as a mechanism to leverage concessional financing from the Green Climate Fund to finance climate-related projects and other investment in resilience building.

The second window, called the growth and competitive window, will be dedicated to attracting funds from multiple sources for investment in projects that promote growth and economic recovery, and that enhance the competitiveness of the subregion. This window would seek to harness innovative instruments, appropriately calibrated to address individual country risks.

The third window, addressing liquidity and debt reduction, will be devoted to debt reprofiling, including the operationalization of ECLAC's debt swap initiative, with the requisite resource mobilization. The approach to debt relief proposed by ECLAC is that for countries with high debt from private creditors, a debt buyback scheme, as well as debt for equity swaps will be utilized. The debt repayment (in local currency) will be placed in a Caribbean Resilience Fund to finance green growth aimed strictly at mitigation and adaptation projects as agreed by the parties. In the case of multilateral and bilateral debt negotiations with the Paris Club and with the international financial institutions would be necessary; their participation would be important to guarantee success in such a scheme.

ECLAC proposes a pilot phase to launch the debt swap initiative, involving Antigua and Barbuda, Saint Lucia, and Saint Vincent and the Grenadines as the three pilot countries. It is hoped that this initiative can be expanded to include other indebted Caribbean countries.

The ECLAC proposal has several advantages over other schemes. It is focused on sustainable debt reduction which has so far not been the case in debt reduction schemes in the Caribbean. This proposal should also be attractive to all creditors. It proposes an initiative which guarantees reduced repayment risks, strengthens the resilience of Caribbean countries, and helps to build up a Fund that over time may be augmented by investments that have positive rates of return. It also is an opportunity for member states, to secure the fiscal space to generate much needed investment while pursuing adaptation and mitigation strategies. Finally, the proposal can inspire region-wide approach to improved fiscal management, designed to help to address future debt build up.

Conclusion

This chapter has examined the evolution of the Caribbean debt focusing on its structure and composition. It argues that the explanations which treat the debt accumulation as a fiscal problem is a partial explanation since Caribbean economies are affected by a variety of vulnerabilities which threaten their fiscal resilience. It is shown that at least for some countries, structural factors are important to the debt build up and this is manifest in the persistent current account imbalance in the Caribbean. The chapter suggests that in light of large primary surpluses required to stabilize or reduce the debt, the Caribbean needs some relief in order to properly address the sustainable development goals. The chapter also evaluates proposals for debt reduction presented by the Commonwealth Secretariat, the World Bank and by ECLAC respectively. It argues that the ECLAC initiative is more comprehensive and has the potential for supporting sustainable development.

References

Alleyne, D., Lugay, B., & Dookie, M. (2011). *The relationship between fiscal and current account balances in the Caribbean* (LC/CAR/L.345). Economic Commission for Latin America and the Caribbean (ECLAC). Subregional headquarters for the Caribbean. http://repositorio.cepal.org/bitstream/handle/11362/4084/1/S2011925_en.pdf

Alleyne, D., & Pantin, M. (2013, March 10–11). *The relationship between fiscal policy and growth in the Caribbean* [Conference Presentation]. The XXVII Regional Seminar on Fiscal Policy, United Nations Economic Commission for Latin America and the Caribbean (ECLAC).

Birchwood, A., & Matthias, R. (2007). Structural factors associated with primary fiscal balances in developing countries. *Applied Economics, 39*, 1235–1243. https://doi.org/10.1080/00036840500447716

Blanchard, O. J. (1990). *Suggestions for a new set of fiscal indicators* (Working Paper 79). OECD Economic Department. https://www.oecd-ilibrary.org/economics/suggestions-for-a-new-set-of-fiscal-indicators_435618162862

Buiter, W. H. (1985). A guide to public sector debt and deficits. *Economic Policy, 1*(1), 13–79. https://doi.org/10.2307/1344612

Centre for Research on the Epidemiology of Disasters (CRED). *Guha-Sapir, D. EM-DAT: The Emergency Events Database—Universite catholique de Louvain (UCL).* Brussels, Belgium. https://www.emdat.be

Commonwealth Secretariat. (2013a). *Multilateral debt relief for climate change adaptation and mitigation.* Commonwealth Secretariat Proposal [Unpublished]. The Commonwealth.

Commonwealth Secretariat. (2013b). *A time to act: Addressing Commonwealth small states' financing and debt challenges* [Background Paper]. High-Level Advocacy Mission.

Economic Commission for Latin America and the Caribbean [ECLAC]. (2011). *The economics of climate change in the Caribbean—Summary report* (LC/CAR/L.299). Port of Spain, Trinidad and Tobago. https://www.cepal.org/en/publications/38620-economics-climate-change-caribbean

Economic Commission for Latin America and the Caribbean [ECLAC]. (2012, August 27–31). *Structural change for equality* (Conference Presentation). An Integrated Approach to Development, Thirty-fourth Session of ECLAC.

Economic Commission for Latin America and the Caribbean [ECLAC]. (2016, April 21). *Proposal on debt for climate adaptation swaps: A strategy for growth and economic transformation of Caribbean economies* (LC/CAR/L.492). Fourth meeting of the Caribbean Development Roundtable. https://repositorio.cepal.org/handle/11362/40253

Guy, K., & Belgrave, A. (2012). Fiscal multiplier in microstates: Evidence from the Caribbean. *International Advances in Economic Research, 18*(1), 74–86. https://doi.org/10.1007/s11294-011-9338-8

Haque, T., Partow, Z., Varma, S., & Oliveira, L. E. (2016). *Addressing debt vulnerabilities in small states: The potential role of new financing instruments* (Discussion Paper No. 10). MFM Global Practice. World Bank Group. http://hdl.handle.net/10986/24009

International Monetary Fund. *The multilateral debt relief initiative factsheet*. https://www.imf.org/external/np/exr/facts/mdri.htm

International Monetary Fund. (2014, October). *World economic outlook database*. https://www.imf.org/en/Publications/WEO/weo-database/2014/October

Mclean, S., Singh, R., & Charles, D. (2017). *The Caribbean conundrum of improving its export competitiveness while enhancing intra-regional trade: A selective examination of Caribbean economies*. Studies and Perspectives (Unpublished).

Mitchell, T. (2016). *Commonwealth multilateral debt swap for climate change adaptation and mitigation proposal: An exposition of the operational features* (Discussion Paper No. 21). Commonwealth Secretariat. https://doi.org/10.14217/5jlwqtt2tj0t-en.

Pentecost, E., & Turner, P. (2010). Demand and supply shocks in the Caribbean economies: Implications for monetary union. *The World Economy, 33*(10), 1326–1336. https://doi.org/10.1111/j.1467-9701.2010.01275.x

Ramirez, F. A.& Wright, A. (2017, May) *What are the fiscal limits for the developing economies of Central America and the Caribbean?* (Working Paper No. IDB-WP-813). Country Department Caribbean Group, Inter-American Development Bank- IDB. https://publications.iadb.org/publications/english/document/What-are-the-Fiscal-Limits-for-the-Developing-Economies-of-Central-America-and-the-Caribbean.pdf

Ruprah, I., Melgarejo, K. & Sierra, R. (2014). *Is there a Caribbean sclerosis? Stagnating economic growth in the Caribbean*. Inter-American Development Bank. https://publications.iadb.org/en/publication/12057/there-caribbean-sclerosis-stagnating-economic-growth-caribbean

Sawyer, M. (2009). *Budget deficits, public debt and the level of public investment*. Department of Economics, University of Milan, Italy. Departmental Working Papers.

Schlotterbeck, S. (2017). *Tax administration reforms in the Caribbean challenges, achievements, and next steps* (IMF Working Paper WP/17/88). International Monetary Fund. https://www.elibrary.imf.org/view/journals/001/2017/088/001.2017.issue-088-en.xml

United Nations Environment Programme. (2008). *Climate change in the Caribbean and the challenge of adaptation* (No. DEW/1088/PA). Regional Office for Latin America and the Caribbean. http://www.pnuma.org/deat1/pdf/Climate_Change_in_the_Caribbean_Final_LOW20oct.pdf

CHAPTER 3

Technology, Growth and Productivity in the Caribbean

Wendell Samuel

Introduction

Real economic growth in most of the Caribbean has been disappointing over the last three decades.[1] The growth rate in the Caribbean has lagged similarly placed small states, which in turn have underperformed other groups of countries internationally (Leigh et al., 2018). Among Caribbean countries, the countries of the Eastern Caribbean Currency Union (ECCU) have exhibited secular decline since the late 1980s with average growth rates declining from around 6% to less than 2%. Barbados

[1] The Caribbean is defined as the independent countries in the Caribbean Community (CARICOM) except Haiti for which the data provides an even more significant challenge. The thirteen countries are Antigua and Barbuda, the Bahamas, Barbados, Belize, Dominica, Grenada, Guyana, Jamaica, St. Kitts and Nevis, St. Lucia, St. Vincent and the Grenadines, Suriname, and Trinidad and Tobago.

W. Samuel (✉)
Jewell Services LLC, Herndon, VA, USA
e-mail: wendell.samuel@gmail.com

C. Cannonier and M. Galloway Burke (eds.),
Contemporary Issues Within Caribbean Economies,
https://doi.org/10.1007/978-3-030-98865-4_3

and Jamaica have experienced chronically low growth rates averaging around one percent over the last three decades. Meanwhile, growth has been more volatile in the Caribbean commodity producers reflecting the boom and bust in commodity prices. The slow growth of real GDP is reflected in the evolution of social indicators. While relatively high for developing countries, progress on social indicators has slowed arresting the convergence to developed countries and allowing other developing countries to catch up. If the current low growth scenario persists, by the middle of the century, the Caribbean would fall behind most groups of countries internationally.

Recovery from recessions has been slow, creating a downward ratchet effect on real economic growth. The slow rate of recovery after recessions, as noted in World Bank (1990), appears to have slowed even further since then. The Caribbean countries were the slowest to recover from the great recession and were on the verge of recovery when they were hit by the global pandemic in 2020. The slow recovery from recessions leaves them ill prepared to deal with the next recession when it inevitably comes along. This slow recovery reflects inflexibility in resource flows between sectors. Low educational outcomes have been a contributing factor to the inflexibility of resource flows. One exception is St. Kitts and Nevis which had the financing to complete the switch from agriculture to tourism during the last 10–15 years, making it one of the faster growing economies in the region.

Declining productivity growth has been a key contributor to the declining real growth in the Caribbean. Total factor productivity (TFP) has been declining in tandem with growth. The contribution of labor to growth, albeit imperfectly measured, has been stable while the growth of the capital stock has made the most significant contribution. Investment has been relatively high for most Caribbean countries averaging about 20% of GDP (Table 3.1). The region has attracted significant amounts of foreign direct investment (FDI), largely in tourism and commodity production which has helped to keep investment high. However, FDI has been generally procyclical—increasing when the economies are expanding and leading the contraction when the economies fall into recession. The size and indivisibilities of FDI projects tend to exaggerate growth cycles. At the same time, domestic investment, which does not receive the same level of incentives, is too small to offset the large movements in FDI.

High investment and low productivity create a pair of paradoxes for Caribbean economies. The literature on embodied technical progress

Table 3.1 Caribbean Countries, Selected Social and Economic Indicators

	GDP $US billions	*Population (Millions)*	*GDP per capita*	*HDI Rank of 189*	*GDP growth 2019*	*GDP growth 20-year*	*FDI/GDP 20-year*	*Invest/GDP 20-year*
Bahamas	15.06	0.39	39,557.40	58	1.22	1.13	4.66	27.69
Barbados	4.68	0.29	16,291.66	56	−0.10	0.68	8.13	17.79
Belize	2.91	0.39	7,124.40	103	1.79	3.48	6.69	19.17
Guyana	10.67	0.78	13,604.23	122	5.35	2.83	8.09	12.80
Jamaica	30.01	2.95	10,99,054	101	0.97	0.74	5.15	23.74
Suriname	10.01	0.58	16,767.77	105	0.27	2.88	−1.46	n/a
Trinidad and Tobago	3755	1.39	26,920.09	67	−1.25	2.87	3.08	n/a
Eastern Caribbean Currency Union	*10.92*	*0.61*	*17,938.93*	*n/a*	*2.96*	*2.17*	*10.8 e*	*22.9 e*
Antigua and Barbuda	2.18	0.09	22,567.84	78	3.35	2.53	11.65	18.78
Dominica	0.92	0.07	12,216.20	94	7.57	1.41	5.8	25.50
Grenada	1.99	0.11	17,720.83	75	1.91	2.73	11.38	20.22
St. Kitts and Nevis	1.46	0.05	25,749.43	74	2.84	2.52	14.96	28.12
St. Lucia	2.94	0.18	16,367.92	86	1.73	1.74	7.62	19.99
St. Vincent/Grenadines	1.43	0.11	13,011.36	91	0.34	2.10	13.91	25.12
Memorandum items								
Latin America and the Caribbean	42,353.65	n/a	16,203.90	n/a	0.18	2.54	0.64	20.48
Emerging and Developing Asia	10,212.08	n/a	11,61,458	n/a	5.28	7.57	1.29	3755
Sub Saharan Africa	4,146.89	n/a	4,063.50	n/a	3.18	4.84	0.95	21.27

Source International Monetary Fund, WEO Database; World Bank World Development Indicators; author's calculations

(Banerjee, 2012; Boucekkine et al., 2003; Solow, 1960) point to increased productivity from investment in capital. Similarly, the literature on FDI suggests that one of the benefits of FDI is the technology that comes embodied in the new investment. For many Caribbean countries, the high level of investment has had little impact in the way of higher productivity. The contribution of capital appears to come from an increase in the physical volume. The second paradox is the virtual non-existence of the expected productivity increases associated with the expansion of information and communications technology (ICT). In most countries the use of broadband internet is associated with an acceleration in real growth and productivity increases as broadband facilitates production, employment and exports (Hjort & Poulsen, 2019; World Bank, 2016). Most Caribbean countries have yet to reap this digital dividend.

This chapter tries to uncover the factors behind this secular decline in growth and productivity and examines the role that ICT can play in reversing this trend. The chapter also outlines the growth accounting framework and estimates productivity growth as a residual after accounting for growth in labor and capital inputs. The robustness of the estimates is checked by making several adjustments to the standard growth accounting framework including for the impact of natural disasters reflecting the effects of climate change. This chapter focuses on factors behind the secular decline in productivity and some of the idiosyncratic reasons for the variability across countries and discusses the role of ICT in growth and productivity. The estimation of the effects of ICT on growth in the Caribbean is also discussed along with the results. Discussed next is a role for ICT in reversing productivity decreases in the region, as well as some of the challenges to achieving this. The contributions of this chapter are (i) to explain the diverse movement in TFP in terms of the structural shift shifts in the Caribbean economies; and (ii) to articulate a role for ICT in enhancing productivity growth which is necessary to accelerate growth and employment in the Caribbean region. To the knowledge of the author, these issues have not been analyzed in the context of the Caribbean. The analysis also explicitly accounts for the effects of climate change and natural disaster in the growth accounting framework in the Caribbean.

Growth and Productivity

The paucity of data on the Caribbean countries limits the type of analysis that can be undertaken. Consistent labor market information exists only for Barbados, Jamaica, and Trinidad and Tobago. For the other countries there are ad hoc data from the 10-year census and occasional special studies. This precludes the calculation of series for human capital, employment, labor compensation as a share of GDP and other labor market aggregates. Enterprise-level data is even more sparse. There have been only two enterprise-level surveys conducted for Caribbean countries. The Latin America and the Caribbean Enterprise Survey (LACES) conducted in 2010 along the lines of the World Bank Enterprise Survey (WBES) for Africa includes 14 Caribbean countries. A second survey conducted by Compete Caribbean in 2014, the Productivity, Technology, and Innovation (PROTEqIN) survey, was conducted on the same basis and includes 13 of the countries covered in the LACES survey. These surveys contain a wealth of micro level information on a sample of Caribbean enterprises, but they are snapshots over a very short period and would not shed much light on the longer-run issues on which this chapter focuses. This chapter, therefore, analyzes growth and productivity in a growth accounting framework and uses the micro level data as corroborative information.

The growth/development accounting framework dates to the middle of the last century with the Solow (1957) decomposition of growth into the contributions from capital, labor and technology. Numerous refinements through the years have sought to improve the measurement of capital and labor, adjust for factor quality and embed the analysis in more complex production functions (Denison, 1962; Denison et al., 1972; Jorgenson & Griliches, 1967). In recent times, Feenstra et al. (2015) and Hsiek and Klenow (2007) have improved the estimate of capital by disaggregating the capital stock into buildings and machinery that have different rates of depreciation. The asset composition of capital generates differences in capital goods prices across countries and through time. For example, buildings are cheaper to construct in lower-income countries while imported machinery is more costly relative to more developed countries.

Recent enhancements to the measurement of labor have sought to address labor quality by improving the measurement of human capital while allowing for variations in output elasticity. Enhancement of estimates of human capital was a big part of improving the measurement of the labor input (Barro & Lee, 1994, 2013; Lee, 2005). Loayza et al. (2004) also extended the analysis to multiple countries. The standard assumption of a constant labor share of income across countries has been questioned by Bernanke and Gürkaynak (2002) and Gollin (2002) who find significant cross-country differences. Meanwhile, Karabarbounis and Neiman (2014) show that labor's share of income has been declining over time. Applying the insights of recent studies to the Penn World Tables data for as many countries as possible, Feenstra et al. (2015) concluded that the share of labor averaged 0.52, significantly lower than the average of 0.7 used in earlier studies. They also found that there was no systematic relationship between labor share of income and the level of development of the economies, and that the labor share declined over time for 89 of the 127 countries studied.

Applications of the growth accounting framework to the Caribbean have been few (Ruprah et al., 2014; Thacker et al., 2012; Vasilyev, 2019). They found that the slowing real growth was associated with declining TFP and slower accumulation of capital. Analyses of the firm-level data from the PROTEqIN surveys show that only 26% of Caribbean firms showed a tendency to innovate (Dohnert et al., 2017). This finding held broadly for foreign owned and domestic firms, with foreign-owned firms slightly less likely to innovate. Foreign firms tend to use the region as distribution centers and hence, used technology from their headquarters with little innovation in the Caribbean. Domestic firms, on the other hand, have little incentive to innovate in protected markets. Accordingly, with little innovation productivity suffers.

The growth accounting framework derives TFP from an aggregate production function. This can be illustrated with a Cobb-Douglass production function:

$$Y = AK^{\alpha}L^{1-\alpha}$$

Where Y is real output; K is the capital stock, L is labor and α is the output elasticity of capital. A is a measure of aggregate/total productivity and represents a residual unexplained by changes in capital and labor input. Changes in productivity reflect the effects of improvements in technology. Since productivity is measured over a period of time, we can calculate it by differencing the production function.

$$\frac{\Delta Y}{Y} = \frac{\Delta A}{A} + \alpha \frac{\Delta K}{K} + (1 - \alpha)\frac{\Delta L}{L}$$

Rearranging this equation yields:

$$\frac{\Delta A}{A} = \frac{\Delta Y}{Y} - \alpha \frac{\Delta K}{K} - (1 - \alpha)\frac{\Delta L}{L}$$

This shows that the growth rate of productivity is a residual that equals the growth rate of output minus the weighted growth rates of capital and labor, where the weights are the respective output elasticities.

The Data

The main source of data for the calculation of TFP is the Penn World Tables Version 10.0 (PWT 10) launched in January 2021. Apart from the overall enhancements in data quality, the PWT10 has several innovations that enhance the calculation of TFP. In this version, both the capital stock and the capital services are provided. As mentioned earlier, the capital stock is based on the unique composition of capital assets for each country and for each country over time. This decomposition of the capital stock implies that depreciation rates not only vary across countries but also with time. PWT10 also provides measures of human capital based on the average years of schooling that are consistent with Barro and Lee (2013). However, estimates of human capital are only available for Barbados, Jamaica and Trinidad and Tobago.

While the enhanced estimates of the capital stock are welcomed additions to the PWT tables, they do not adequately address the effects of climate change and natural disasters on the capital stock. The Caribbean is one of the regions of the world most prone to natural disasters. The Emergency Disaster Database (EM-DAT) shows that of the over 500 natural disasters that hit small states during 1950–2018, about 350 were in the Caribbean.[2] Over the same period, the average yearly damage caused by hurricanes in the Caribbean was about 2.5 of GDP, six times

[2] The EM-DAT database records information on natural disasters since 1900 and contains information including the type of disaster, number of people affected, and in some cases, estimates of the damage.

higher than the average for all countries. Accordingly, ensuring that the effects of natural disasters are accurately reflected in the measures of capital formation and the capital stock has been an area of concern. This concern was underscored by the passage of devastating hurricanes in recent years.[3]

The PWT series for the capital stock for Dominica is an interesting example. The series shows a growth in the capital stock in 2017 despite hurricane damage of over 200% of GDP. While much of the damage was related to the housing stock and government infrastructure, there was significant damage to hotels and manufacturing that reflects a decline in the capital stock. In this case, the standard depreciation factor would vastly understate the loss of the capital stock. Much of the spending on investment in 2017 and 2018 would be replacement not captured by a standard depreciation factor. A similar situation occurred for Grenada which also had hurricane damage of over 200% of GDP in 2005. Over time, the PWT estimate would consistently over-estimate the capital stock and would be reflected in lower TFP. While this might be inconsequential for many countries, it could be quite significant for disaster-prone small countries.

The PWT calculates the capital stock as the accumulated depreciated capital stock.

$$K_{t+1} = (1 - \delta_t)K_t + I_t$$

.

Where K_t is the capital stock at time t; I_t represents investment; and δ_t is the rate of depreciation of the capital stock.

To account for the damage caused by hurricanes the equation is adjusted for the estimated damage when they occur.

$$K_{t+1} = (1 - \delta_t)(K_t - D_t) + I_t$$

Data on hurricane damage are from the EM-DAT which contains estimates of the damage caused by natural disasters in current US dollars. Since all PWT variables are indexed with base year 2017, the current value of hurricane damage is deflated by the GDP deflator with the same base

[3] Hurricane Maria caused damage of over 200% of GDP in Dominica in 2017, while hurricane Ivan caused about the same level of damage to Grenada in 2005. Storms of greater severity and intensity are expected in the future.

year. The estimate of hurricane damage includes loss of income along with damage to housing and infrastructure. For purposes of the analysis, an estimate of 30 of the total damage is used to measure damage to capital the capital stock.[4]

Given the absence of labor market information in most Caribbean countries, the PWT does not have a measure of employment or the labor force for all countries. Following Lee (2005) and Thacker et al. (2012), the population age 15–64 from the World Bank World Development Indicators WDI is used to measure the labor force in countries with no employment data.

Results

To facilitate this analysis, the Caribbean countries are divided into three broad groups. The ECCU countries constitute one group because of their size and similarity of characteristics. It is also useful to look at these countries together since they are further along the road to a single economy with a common currency. The second group are non-ECCU tourist-dependent economies which constitutes Barbados, the Bahamas and Jamaica. The third group of countries are the commodity exporters, Belize, Guyana, Suriname and Trinidad and Tobago.

The ECCU countries show a secular decline in growth since the late 1980s (Fig. 3.1). The lowest growth rates were recorded during the great recession 2007–2009 followed by a slow recovery. During the period 1971–2019, the contribution of labor to growth in the Caribbean has been remarkably stable, averaging about 1.3%. The largest contributor to growth was capital, but it has been a significant source of growth variability. The growth in the capital stock largely reflects movement in FDI. TPF declined in tandem with the decline in the growth rate and turned negative during the 5-year period of 2010–2014 as the economies struggled to recover from the recession. The variability of TFP has been the largest source of growth instability for the ECCU countries.

The tourism dependent economies, especially Barbados and Jamaica, have experienced low growth almost for the entire period. Accordingly, TFP has been low throughout the period except for short periods of

[4] This estimate is derived from post assessment damage report for the 2017 hurricane in Dominica which provides a breakdown of the total damage. Estimates of 40 and 50% yield broadly the same trend.

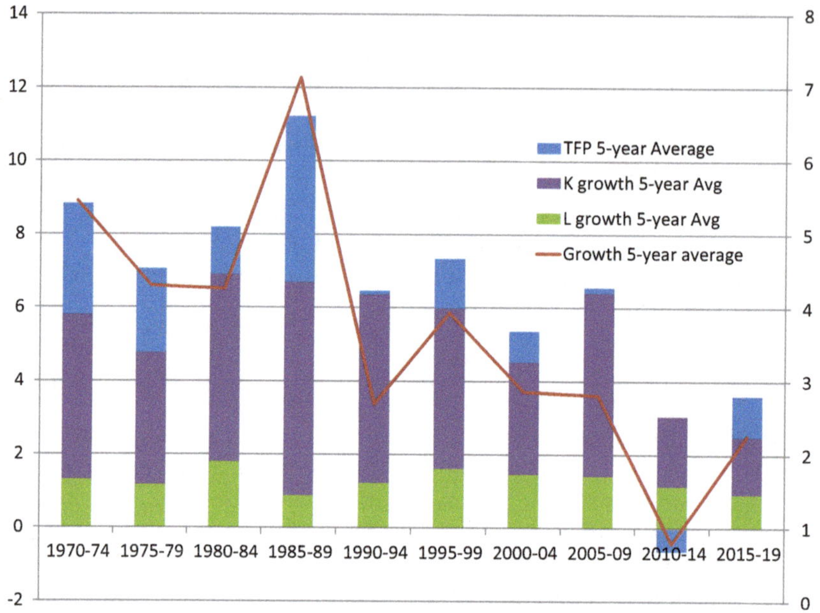

Fig. 3.1 Total factor productivity in the ECCU countries, 1970–2019

above average economic activity. The contribution of labor input has been roughly stable over the five decades (Fig. 3.2). On the other hand, the contribution of capital has been less stable, reflecting the ebb and flow of investment partly related to movement in FDI inflows. Much like the pattern in the ECCU, growth peaked in the Bahamas in the late 1970s reflecting a surge of investment in the tourism sector in the post-independence period. In the ensuing years, there has been in secular decline with growth, averaging about 1.5% since 1990. In line with these developments, TFP for the Bahamas has been on a declining trend over the period.

The commodity producers have experienced alternating periods of boom and bust, reflecting the swings in commodity prices (Fig. 3.3). Among the commodity exporters, the story is more idiosyncratic depending on the commodities that the country exports. Despite the classic boom and bust cycles, growth in Belize has been higher than most other Caribbean countries averaging about 4.5% between 1971 and 2010.

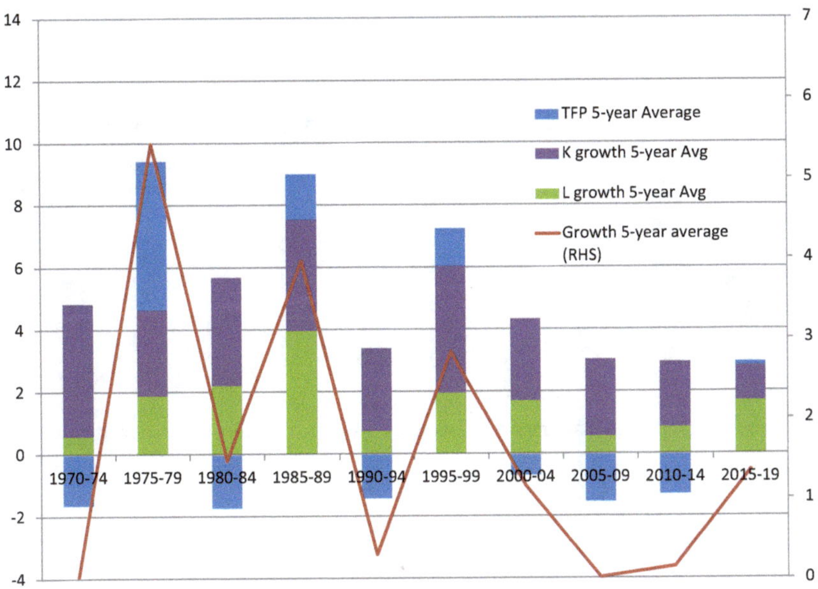

Fig. 3.2 Total factor productivity in tourism-dependent countries, 1970–2019

Growth has slowed during the last decade, reflecting lower commodity prices and lower public investment constrained by the effects of high levels of public debt. TFP has been declining since 2000 and has contributed about −1 percentage points during 2000–2019. The contribution of capital has declined as gross capital formation has slowed. On the other hand, the contribution of TFP to growth in Trinidad and Tobago surged over the period 2000–2015 with a drop off during the last five years. A period of relatively high productivity growth was during 1971–1983, followed by almost 20 years of modest productivity growth. Periods of higher productivity growth have been associated with higher capital investment in the Trinidad and Tobago energy sector. These episodes of investment are usually sparked by upswing in oil prices.

Growth cycles in Guyana and Suriname have been broadly similar, reflecting the broader natural resources base in these countries with a dependence on gold and bauxite. Both countries experienced relatively higher growth during the mid-1970s, 1991–1997 and 2000–2009. On average, Guyana grew about 0.5 percentage points faster than Suriname.

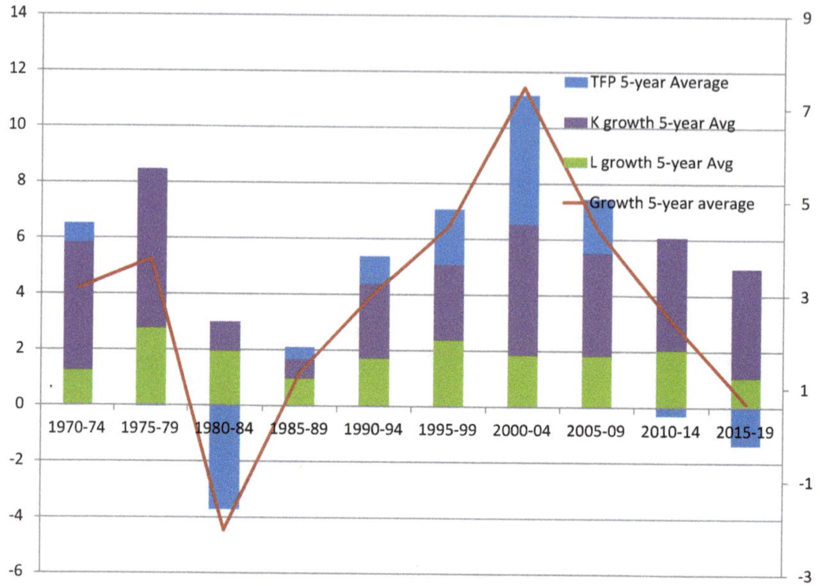

Fig. 3.3 Total factor productivity in commodity-dependent countries, 1970–2019

Growth in TFP appears to be associated with higher capital investment in the natural resources sectors. These spurts of investment, partly financed largely by FDI, tend to follow upswings in commodity prices. The labor contribution to growth in Suriname has been stable like in most other Caribbean countries. On the contrary, labor contribution in Guyana has been more variable perhaps related to the significant outmigration during the 1980s and 1990s culminating in negative population growth during 1989–1993.

In summary, TFP in the Caribbean has been low or declining for most countries. This tendency has exacerbated since 2010 except for Trinidad and Tobago. The contribution of labor to real GDP growth has been broadly stable except for Guyana. The variation in growth has been partly driven by gross capital formation of which FDI constitutes a significant proportion. The decline in TFP is a significant contributor to the decline in growth rates for most of the Caribbean countries. It appears that capital investment has been associated with higher TFP in commodity exporting counties but only modestly so in tourism dependent economies. Some of these issues will be discussed in the following sections.

Information Communications Technology

The decline in TFP in the Caribbean coincides with the rapid expansion of Information Communications Technology (ICT) worldwide. There is growing evidence that the expansion of ICT has contributed significantly to output growth and productivity across all types of states (Hjort & Poulsen, 2019; World Bank, 2016). On the surface, Caribbean countries appear to perform well on the standard indicators of ICT technology penetration, including telephone lines, mobile phones, internet subscriptions, internet service providers (ISP) and broadband connections. The apparently strong ICT penetration raises the question of why ICT has not made a bigger contribution to growth and productivity. Or is it making a significant contribution, but its effects are being swamped by other growth-inhibiting constraints? An attempt to analyze these issues follows in the succeeding sections.

ICT refers to the integrated framework for the efficient use of communications, computer networks and information processing technology. At one level ICT generates innovations and new goods and services like mobile apps, cloud computing, big data analytics, etc., thus contributing directly to real output. At another level, ICT increases the efficiency of production, stimulating innovations across other sectors like banking and finance health, education, transport, etc., helping these sectors to produce goods and services more efficiently and create new goods while also adding to output. The expansion of broadband technology speeds up processing and facilitates production of new and existing services that were hitherto not possible.

There is overwhelming evidence on the contribution of ICT to growth and productivity in developed countries (Jorgenson et al., 2008), Syverson (2011), and Koutroumpis (2009). One of the earliest efforts to link ICT with economic growth was Hardy (1980) who found that there was a strong positive relationship between telephone lines per capita and GDP per capita for the 60 countries he studied. The computer productivity paradox of the early 1990s in the USA gave way to a resurgence in US productivity growth, which had remained stagnant since the 1970s.

ICT has had positive effects on real economic growth in the USA, and productivity more than doubled to 2.8% from 1996 to 2006. However, there is growing evidence that ICT causes labor displacement despite the creation of new jobs. There has been slower wage growth and higher unemployment among less educated workers in the USA and Europe (Acemologu & Autor, 2011; Katz & Margo, 2014). The slower wage growth arises because of the increased demand for graduates as ICT usage expands.

While the evidence on the impact of ICT on economic activity in developing countries is not as voluminous, it is no less convincing. Increased penetration of ICT stimulates growth, increases productivity, and boosts employment and exports. In a cross-section study of 120 developing countries, Qiang and Rossotto (2009) use an endogenous growth model to show that a 10% increase in broadband penetration increases per capita GDP growth by 1.38%. Clarke and Wallsten (2006) estimate that a 1 percentage point increase in internet subscriptions increases exports from low-income countries to developed countries by 3.8 percentage points. In a study using enterprise-level data for Brazil and India, Commander et al. (2011) find that ICT technologies also lead to an increase in exports from these two countries. Contrary to the finding for developed economies, ICT has a net positive impact on employment in developing countries. Hjort and Poulsen (2019), also using enterprise-level data, find that employment among less educated workers and productivity increased with the adoption of fast internet by firms in 12 African countries. They attribute the unexpected increase in the employment of less educated workers to the low educational levels forcing firms to train these workers to undertake the required tasks.

Model and Data

Consistent with the analysis in the *Growth and Productivity* section, a macroeconomic production function is used to estimate the impact on real output. The model is inspired by Koutrumpis (2009) which covered 22 OECD countries. The equation to be estimated is:

$$\log(Y_t) = \alpha_0 + \alpha_1 \log(K_t) + \alpha_2 \log(L_t) + \alpha_3 \log(E_t) + \alpha_4 \log(ICT_t) + \varepsilon_t$$

Where Y_t is real output, K_t is the capital stock, L_t is the labor force, E_t is a measure of the education of the labor force; ICT_t is a measure of ICT penetration; and ε_t is the error term.

Real output, capital stock and labor force are as defined in the section on *Growth and Productivity*, and are from the same sources. The production function is augmented to include education achievement because education enhances the quality of labor and is complementary to the expanded use of ICT in the economy. The World Bank World Development Indicator (WDI) Database has several measures of education but there are innumerable missing observations for the Caribbean countries. The indicator with the most observations that is relevant to the adaption of ICT is the secondary school completion rate. Koutroumpis (2009) uses the proportion of the population with tertiary education, but this data for the Caribbean is almost non-existent. Hjort and Poulsen (2019) find that the percentage of the population that completed primary school was important for the 12 African countries studied. Thus, the secondary school completion rate would seem to be a happy median.

Given the broad range of activities that encompasses ICT, the are several variables which can be potentially used as a measure of ICT penetration. The longest, most consistent series in the WDI database is the number of fixed telephone lines per 100 persons. There is also data with varying degrees of coverage mobile phone subscriptions, ISP per million persons, internet connections and fixed broadband connections. Most recent studies have used fixed broadband connections because it is probably the most consequential development in ICT after the inception of the internet. The high speed of broadband connections facilitates the development of a broader range of services that could not be contemplated before. However, several indicators have been used and this chapter does the same.

Estimation and Results

The equation is estimated using panel regression estimation techniques. With many missing observations, it is an unbalanced panel with the sample runs from 1970 to 2019. There are 13 cross-sections representing the countries for a total (maximum) of 650 observations.

The estimation results given in Table 3.2 are presented in four columns based on different estimation techniques and configuration of independent variables. The first column shows the estimation of the equation,

Table 3.2 Regression results for impact of ICT on growth 1

Variables		*Panel Least Squares (fixed effects)*	*Panel Least Squares (fixed effects)*	*2SLS (fixed effects)*	*GMM (fixed effects)*
Constant	C	2.39***	0.63***	1.21	−1.37***
		(2.78)	(1.31)	(1.26)	(−2.97)
Labor	LT	0.08***	0.31***	0.27***	0.43***
		(0.90)	(6.28)	(2.58)	(8.58)
Capital	KT	0.49	0.34***	0.32***	0.40***
		(10.87)	(13.69)	(6.89)	(16.2)
Fixed telephone lines	FT	0.05***	0.15***	0.19***	0.14***
		(2.86)	(13.05)	(8.19)	(11.84)
Fixed Broadband internet	FBD	0.20***	0.17***		
		(6.49)	(8.93)		
Education	EDU	−0.01			
		(−0.15)			
Summary Statistics					
	R^2	0.99	0.99	0.99	0.99
	Adj. R^2	0.99	0.99	0.98	0.99
	S.E	0.11	0.15	0.16	0.15
	Observations	204	610	593	610

Notes 1/ Bracketed numbers are the t-statistics; Estimated coefficients are significant at *10, **5, ***1% levels, respectively
Source Authors' calculations

using panel least squares, with all the variables included. In this equation, all other variables except labor and education are statistically significant and carry the correct sign. The sign on the labor input is correct but the variable is statistically insignificant. Meanwhile the education variable carries the wrong sign and is statistically insignificant, which could be the result of measurement errors and that the labor variable already embodies some of the effect of education.

In the second column, education is dropped from the equation and estimated using panel least squares regression with cross-section fixed effects. All the variables now carry the correct sign and are all significant at one percent level of significance. In particular, the coefficient on labor input rises and is now statistically significant. The variation in GDP, explained by the equation, is high with an R-squared of 0.99.

To address potential endogeneity between ICT and GDP growth, columns 3 and 4 estimate the equation using two-stage least squares (2SLS) and generalized method of the moments (GMM) estimators. Potential endogeneity arises because as the economy grows, the demand for ICT services rises, reflecting both final consumer demand and intermediate demand by firms to produce goods and services. On the other hand, building out the ICT network generates higher GDP in the current period and the stock of capital in the ICT sector also generates GDP growth in the future. These two estimation methods yield broadly the same results as the panel least square technique, with broadly stable estimates and high explanatory power.

The results show that the usual variables in the production function, capital and labor, are always positive and significant at the one percent level of significance. The coefficients are relatively stable across estimation methods. The education variable does not perform very well, perhaps reflecting the quality of the data. It is statistically insignificant with the incorrect sign. The shortness of the series severely constrains the sample size and limits comparability across the estimates.

Turning to the variables of interest for this chapter, the coefficient for fixed line telephones, representing a broad measure of ICT, is positive and statistically significant across estimation methods. The estimate of the coefficient ranges between 0.14 and 0.19 implying that 10% increase in fixed telephone lines per hundred people is associated with 1.4 percentage points increase in GDP growth. Broadband internet was introduced in the Caribbean between 2000 and 2003. This means that at most there are 20 observations per country. This would be a small sample over which to estimate the coefficients. To better utilize the sample, the broadband variable is treated as a dummy variable which takes the value of 0 before the introduction of broadband in each country and the value of 1 thereafter (Czernich et al., 2009). The coefficient on the dummy variable represents the shift in real GDP growth attributed to the introduction of broadband. The coefficient range of 0.17–0.20 is low compared to 2.7–3.9% higher increase in per capita growth observed by Czernich et al. (2009) in a panel of 25 OECD countries. Hjort and Poulsen (2019) find that the density of night lights (proxy for relative income) increases by 2.4–3.3% with the arrival of broadband internet in the African countries studied. Moreover, they find that relative average incomes begin to increase during the first year after the arrival of broadband and the growth is strongest during the first three years.

Other variables to proxy for ICT were used including the penetration of mobile phones, internet connection and internet ISPs per capita. None of these variables performed as well as the telephone density and broadband penetration. Despite the extremely high penetration of mobile phones, their contribution to growth is insignificant with the wrong sign. This outcome is not surprising as several studies have shown that there is a weak relationship between mobile phone connections and growth (World Bank, 2016). Moreover, mobile connections in many Caribbean countries exceed 100 per 100 people, in some cases approaching 200. This is the legacy of a dysfunctional mobile telephone market with very high interconnection charges between networks that create incentives for consumers to have mobile subscriptions with each service provider at the same time.

Making Sense of It All

This section tries to pull together a few threads from the evidence provided and draws some implications for the role of ICT in growth and productivity in the Caribbean. These inferences include the secular decline in TFP in the Caribbean despite high investment rates, the low ICT impact on growth, the integration of the enterprise-level consideration with the macro perspectives, and the role of regional integration. This discussion takes place against the caveat of the data challenges that the region faces and the need to address these to underpin evidenced-based public policy and private decision-making.

Missing Productivity from Capital Formation

One of the most important issues arising from the evidence presented is that capital accumulation plays a big role in output growth in the Caribbean, however it does not significantly affect productivity. Both the growth accounting and regression analysis capital help explain much of the variation in GDP growth, which is not surprising as many Caribbean countries have investment to GDP ratios averaging between 20 and 30% of GDP annually. The implementation of capital projects creates income in the current period with an investment multiplier close to 1 given high leakages in these small open economies. Going forward, the capital stock facilitates higher output as an input in the production process. What is surprising though is that capital does not appear to lead to higher TFP except in three of the commodity dependent countries.

Conventional economic theory suggests the advanced technology embodied in new investment should increase productivity. Hahn and Mathews (1964) refer to capital accumulation as the vehicle through which new technology is made available to the economy. The new technology combines with existing factors of production to generate greater output. Thus, with such high investment rates, the return in terms of growth is extremely low. Caribbean countries are by nature labor-rich economies, thus the low return cannot be attributed to diminishing returns to capital. So, what explains the low contribution of investment to productivity growth?

One explanation is the impact of natural disasters on capital. The countries are prone to hurricanes, floods, earthquakes and droughts. In *the Growth and Productivity* section, the impact on capital accumulation was discussed but these natural phenomena also affect output directly causing disruption in production and low yield for agricultural output. Adjusting for the impact of hurricanes on capital accumulation reduced the capital stock in some countries by as much as 20% in countries that experienced devastating hurricanes. While the impact on TFP was large for these countries, overall, the difference between adjusted and unadjusted TFP ranged between 0 and 4%. With climate change leading to greater frequency and intensity of natural disasters, this gap could increase over time.

The shift in the structure of production in Caribbean economies could partially explain the slowdown of growth and productivity. Over the period, most Caribbean countries have experienced a huge shift from agriculture to tourism, which has several implications for growth and productivity. First, there was a shift from a sector that largely uses natural capital (land, water, etc.), which is usually not measured, to a sector that required massive investment in buildings. Thus, a moderately growing labor force is now working with a significantly increased amount of measured capital. This explains the higher growth and productivity at the time of the shifts. Second, beyond the installation of the capital, there is not a lot of new technology coming with the construction of hotels. The building might be more comfortable and energy-efficient, but the hotel room still caters for just one guest/family and all the other services remain labor intensive. There is nothing intrinsic in building hotels that make them use complementary factors more efficiently. Put differently, the technology embodied in hotels has not advanced significantly.

Third, the shift to tourism, while lucrative, is a shift to a potentially lower productivity service sector. Baumol (1967) argued that it is more difficult to increase productivity in services sectors than it is in good producing sectors. While this proposition does not hold for every service sector compared to goods production, there is some evidence that this holds in the hospitality sector (Witt & Witt, 1989). The significant challenges in measuring productivity in services sectors are clearly a part of the explanation. Triplet and Bosworth (2000) note that there is no common tendency in the difficulties in measuring productivity in services, but each service activity has its own unique challenges. The drop off in productivity in most Caribbean countries with the shift to tourism bears some evidence to this proposition of lower productivity in the hospitality sector. On the other hand, the countries that have seen some rise in productivity accompanying investment have been commodity exporters (Guyana, Suriname and Trinidad and Tobago) where technology advances, embodied in new investment, have improved efficiency and output growth.

Low ICT Dividend

The region's investment in ICT has not begun to bear fruit yet. The small size of the ICT impact in the Caribbean is reminiscent of the early 1990s in the USA when that country's huge investment in computer technology did not appear to provide the expected bump in productivity until toward the end of that decade (Jorgenson et al., 2008). The slow pick up of productivity could be related to the absence of a critical mass to reap the benefits of ICT investment. Koutroumpis (2009) argued that the slow takeoff of ICT benefits in the OECD countries was related to the initial insufficiency of firms using the new technology. As a critical mass of users came on stream, the spillovers were greater and new industries could be created to service the growing number of firms.

The absence of a critical mass of innovative firms could help explain the delay in reaping the benefits. If this is the case, then the sector should take off as more firms adopt the technology as time goes by. However, it might not be as simple as that. In small economies like the Caribbean, it might be useful to consider whether the individual small domestic markets are large enough to achieve the critical mass needed to sustain a viable set of firms in the ICT sector. Rather than wait to find out, it might be more proactive for the region to take steps to realize the single digital economy, which has languished with the other CARICOM initiatives.[5]

In small economies, government has a critical role to play in the regulation and facilitation of economic activity. Interactions between the public and private sectors can either enhance or hurt economic efficiency. In the Caribbean, the slow pace of government adoption of ICT has probably hurt more than it has enhanced economic efficiency. Many governments have had plans for 'e-Government' for years which have not been implemented. These initiatives would facilitate the delivery of government services. Still, the COVID-19 pandemic found most governments practically unprepared to be a full-service government during the lockdowns to slow the spread of the virus. The pandemic laid bare all the inefficiencies and inconsistencies in government ICT infrastructure. More than a year later, the situation was not much improved. Nevertheless, the pandemic created an opportunity for governments to re-imagine their ICT infrastructure and shift their investment in under-utilized computers systems into a framework for the efficient delivery of government services.

Evidence from Enterprise-level Surveys

The evidence from the limited enterprise surveys broadly complements the macroeconomic analysis. The enterprise surveys reveal an innovation deficit among Caribbean firms, which will be a considerable drag on leveraging ICT for increasing output and productivity. Innovative firms are likely to use more advanced technology and generally have higher productivity (Mohan et al., 2016). This study reveals that only 26% of Caribbean firms are engaged in innovative activity with the highest percentages in Trinidad and Tobago (4%), Suriname (4%) and Guyana (3.5%). Jamaica is a distant fourth with 2.5% of the innovative firms in the Caribbean despite its relative size. This finding is consistent with the higher productivity levels for these commodity producers discussed in the *Growth and Productivity* section and seems to point toward a less than critical mass for ICT usage.

FDI represents a key channel for the transfer of technology to developing countries. Technology could be transferred through several different mechanisms: (i) direct innovation by the foreign firm; (ii) joint

[5] The CARICOM Single Market and Economy includes a protocol for the creation of a single economy in services, but there has been little progress toward this goal.

ventures; (iii) cooperation in innovation with domestic firms; and (iv) competitive pressures exerted by the foreign on the domestic firms forcing them to innovate. Globally, the evidence on the impact of FDI on innovation and productivity has been mixed with evidence consistent with positive, neutral and negative impacts. Regarding the Caribbean, Mohan et al. (2016) find that (i) only a small proportion of foreign-owned firms engage in innovative activity (19% of innovative firms); (ii) decisions of domestic firms to innovate are not driven by competitive pressures from foreign firms; and (iii) domestic firms are more likely to innovate if they use foreign raw material and other inputs. They also find that technical and nontechnical innovation and use of foreign materials have positive and statistically significant effects on productivity.

What Do We Do About It?

Accelerating real economic growth requires harnessing technology to reverse the declining trend in TFP. The evidence provided in this chapter suggests that the slowdown in Caribbean growth over the last three decades is directly related to the decline in TFP, hence reversing the trend in growth implies addressing the factors that reduce productivity. Accordingly, adopting an ICT strategy to facilitate digital transformation and speed up the achievement of a single digital space is key to enhancing productivity and growth.

Far from being a constraint, the small size of the economies is favorable to facilitating digital transformation. The international experience suggests that small, agile and creative economies like Estonia, Singapore and Hong Kong have a decided advantage in appropriating more of the digital dividend by embracing ICT. Furthermore, ICT frees small states from physical constraints—allowing them to increase their market size, to expand production in activities that are not constrained by land space, to better utilize its spectrum resources and to participate in data-related activities that represent the fastest growing sector of the global economy.

Adoption of a strategic ICT framework could increase productivity in several ways:

- Government ICT platform plays a key role in small states. Most governments have plans to implement e-Government that has been fast tracked by the pandemic. However, digitalization of government should go beyond taking existing activities online. It would be necessary to transform business process to eliminate paper, avoid

duplication of data entry and storage and automate government services, thereby increasing productivity of the civil service. A more efficient government creates positive spillover to the private sector and consumers, making them more productive by eliminating wait times and duplicate filling of forms.
- Similarly, leveraging ICT in the private sector would help reduce inefficiencies, lower cost and increase productivity. This would require raising the proportion of firms that are innovative from the currently low 26%.
- Implementing the initiatives envisaged under the Caribbean Single market for services could set the region on a path to a single digital economy. It would create an environment in which Caribbean workers can compete (or collaborate) on a level playing field with their peers in other countries. It would also help establish a digital ecosystem in which innovation can thrive and ideas can be tested.
- A unique digital identification system would be the linchpin for the integration of e-government services, financial intermediation and inclusion and trade and payments.

The envisaged productivity gains could be thwarted by an aging telecoms infrastructure. Boucekkine et al. (2003) argue that since most modern technological advances are embodied in new capital goods, firms need to ensure that they acquire the most up to date computers and communication tools compatible with these systems. Small isolated markets limit the ability to make the investment required to keep pace with fast moving developments. Completing the single market for ICT services by creating a single regulator (or harmonizing regulatory frameworks) will be a good first step. Auctioning regional licenses for firms to operate throughout a larger, integrated market could facilitate investment in modern infrastructure that could increase internet access and reduce roaming charges. This could also help unleash creativity among the region's workforce, foster greater collaboration and create high-quality employment opportunities.

Building resilience to natural disasters could be more easily achieved in an integrated market. Redundancy can be managed at the regional level and traffic routed to other islands if there is mishap in one country. ICT infrastructure is a key part of national resilience that would help these countries to bounce back more easily from natural disasters. ICT resilience requires consideration of the interdependence between the ICT sector and other utilities to minimize the cascading effects of the loss of connectivity. For example, loss of telecommunications could delay the recovery in the energy sector and vice versa. Hardening telecommunications infrastructure is just as important as hardening energy and physical infrastructure to avoid output loss and production delays in the aftermath of hurricanes.

Conclusion

The aim of this chapter is to try to uncover the reasons behind the slow growth and declining productivity experienced by most Caribbean countries over the last three decades. The growth accounting analysis using PWT data and regression analysis of the impact of ICT is complemented by micro data from a 2014 enterprise survey of firms in the 13 Caribbean countries covered in the analysis. The findings that follow should be cognizant of the significant data challenges that these countries face.

Productivity has declined in almost all Caribbean countries since the last significant growth spurt in the 1980s. Adjusting the capital stock for damage caused by natural disasters raises productivity but does not reverse the declining trend. The decline in productivity was greater in tourism dependent economies, perhaps reflecting the shift in the structure of the economies from goods to services production. While the decline in productivity could be partly related to measurement challenges for the service sector, there is not a lot of new technology embodied in the investment in the tourism sector to help increase productivity.

The contribution of ICT to growth is positive but smaller than observed in other groups of countries. The impact of ICT is about one-half of the impact in the OECD and African countries. This distinction could be attributed to a delay in achieving digital benefits because ICT penetration needs to reach a critical mass before the spillover effects can be truly leveraged. A significant innovation deficit among both foreign and domestic firms could also be a motivating factor.

Micro data from enterprise surveys are broadly consistent with the above findings. Only about one-quarter of the nearly 2000 firms surveyed report any basic innovative activity, and foreign-owned firms are less likely to engage in innovative activities than domestic ones. The bulk of the innovative firms is located in three commodity-dependent economies supporting the proposition that innovation and productivity could be higher in goods production than in services.

These findings suggest that encouraging innovation in both the public and private sectors is needed to help reverse the trends in growth and productivity. Regional integration, especially in completing the single digital economy, would be helpful in creating a larger market to facilitate the investment in new ICT technology and help achieve the critical mass needed for leveraging the sector to reignite growth and enhance productivity. Regional integration could also enhance resilience that would help countries recover more quickly from natural disasters.

References

Acemoglu, D., & Autor, D. H. (2011). Skills, tasks and technologies: Implications for employment and earnings. In O. Ashenfelter & D. E. Card (Eds.), *Handbook of labor economics* (Vol. 4, pp. 1043–1171). Elsevier. https://doi.org/10.1016/S0169-7218(11)02410-5

Banerjee, R. (2012). Population growth and endogenous technological change: Australian economic growth in the long run. *Economic Record, 88*(281), 214–228. https://doi.org/10.1111/j.1475-4932.2011.00784.x

Barro, R. J., & Lee, J. W. (1994). Sources of economic growth. *Carnegie-Rochester Conference Series on Public Policy, 40*, 1–46. https://doi.org/10.1016/0167-2231(94)90002-7

Barro, R. J., & Lee, J. W. (2013). A new data set of educational attainment in the world, 1950–2010. *Journal of Development Economics, 104*, 184–198. https://doi.org/10.1016/j.jdeveco.2012.10.001

Baumol, W. J. (1967). Macroeconomics of unbalanced growth: The anatomy of urban crises. *American Economic Review, 57*(2), 415–426.

Bernanke, B. S., & Gürkaynak, R. S. (2002). Is growth exogenous? Taking Mankiw, Romer, and Weil seriously. In B. S. Bernanke & K. Rogoff (Eds.), *NBER Macroeconomics annual 2001* (Vol. 16, pp. 1–72). MIT Press. https://www.nber.org/books-and-chapters/nber-macroeconomics-annual-2001-volume-16/growth-exogenous-taking-mankiw-romer-and-weil-seriously

Boucekkine, R., Del Río, F., & Licandro, O. (2003). Embodied technological change, learning-by-doing and the productivity slowdown. *Scandinavian Journal of Economics, 105*, 87–97. https://doi.org/10.1111/1467-9442.00006

Clarke, G., & Wallsten, S. J. (2006). Has the internet increased trade? Developed and developing country evidence. *Economic Inquiry, 44*(3), 465–484. https://doi.org/10.1093/ei/cbj026

Commander, S., Harrison, R., & Menezes-Filho, N. (2011). ICT and productivity in developing countries: New firm-level evidence from Brazil and India.

Review of Economics and Statistics, 93(2), 528–541. https://doi.org/10.1162/REST_a_00080

Czernich, N., Falck, O., Kretschmer, T., & Woessmann, L. (2009). *Broadband infrastructure and economic growth* (CESifo Working Paper Series No. 2861). SSRN. http://papers.ssrn.com/abstract=1516232

Denison, E. (1962). Sources of growth in the United States and the alternative before us. New York, committee for economic development. *Journal of Economic History, 23*(3), 935–938. https://doi.org/10.2307/2228363

Denison, E., Griliches, Z., & Jorgenson, D. (1972). The measurement of productivity: An exchange of views between Dale W. Jorgenson and Zvi Griliches, and Edward F. Denison. *Survey of Current Business, 52*(5), 3–111.

Dohnert, S., Crespi, G., & Maffioli, A. (Eds.). (2017). *Exploring firm-level innovation and productivity in developing countries: The perspective of Caribbean small states* (IDB Monograph 503). Inter-American Development Bank. https://doi.org/10.18235/0000616

Feenstra, R. G., Inklaar, R., & Timmer, M. P. (2015). The next generation of Penn world tables. *The American Economic Review, 105*(10), 3150–3182. https://doi.org/10.1257/aer.20130954

Gollin, D. (2002). Getting income shares right. *Journal of Political Economy, 110*(2), 458–474. https://doi.org/10.1086/338747

Hahn, F. H., & Matthews, R. C. (1964). The theory of economic growth: A survey. *Economic Journal, 74*(296), 779–902. https://doi.org/10.2307/2228848

Hardy, A. (1980). The role of the telephone in economic development. *Telecommunications Policy, 4*(4), 278–286. https://doi.org/10.1016/0308-5961(80)90044-0

Hjort, J., & Poulsen, J. (2019). The arrival of fast internet in Africa. *American Economic Review, 109*(3), 1032–1079. https://doi.org/10.1257/aer.20161385

Hsieh, C., & Klenow, P. J. (2007). Relative prices and relative prosperity. *American Economic Review, 97*(3), 562–585. https://doi.org/10.1257/aer.97.3.562

Jorgenson, D. W., & Griliches, Z. (1967). The explanation of productivity change. *Review of Economic Studies, 34*, 249–280. https://doi.org/10.2307/2296675

Jorgenson, D. W., Ho, M. S., & Stiroh, K. J. (2008). Retrospective look at the U.S. productivity growth resurgence. *Journal of Economic Perspectives, 22*(1), 3–24. https://doi.org/10.1257/jep.22.1.3

Karabarbounis, L., & Neiman, B. (2014). The global decline of the labor share. *Quarterly Journal of Economics, 129*(1), 61–103. https://doi.org/10.1093/qje/qjt032

Katz, L. F., & Margo, R. A. (2014). Technical change and the relative demand for skilled labor: The United States in historical perspective. In L. P. Boustan, C. Frydman, & R. A. Margo (Eds.), *Human capital in history: The American record* (pp. 15–57). University of Chicago Press. https://doi.org/10.3386/w18752

Koutroumpis, P. (2009). The economic impact of broadband on growth: A simultaneous approach. *Telecommunications Policy, 33*(9), 471–485. https://doi.org/10.1016/j.telpol.2009.07.004

Lee, J. W. (2005). Human capital and productivity for Korea's sustained economic growth. *Journal of Asian Economics, 16*, 663–687. https://doi.org/10.1016/j.asieco.2005.06.009

Leigh, D., Srinivasan K., & Werner, A. (2018). Unleashing Strong, Sustainable and Inclusive Growth in the Caribbean. In Alleyne, T., Otker, I., Ramakrishnan, U., & Srinivasan, K. (Eds.), *Unleashing growth and strengthening resilience in the Caribbean* (pp 1–17). International Monetary Fund.

Loayza, N., Fajnzylber, P., & Calderon, C. (2004). *Economic growth in Latin America and the Caribbean: Stylized facts, explanations, and forecasts*. World Bank. https://doi.org/10.1596/0-8213-6091-4

Mohan, P., Strobl, E., & Watson, P. (2016). Innovative activity in the Caribbean: Drivers, benefits and obstacles. In E. Grazzi & C. Pietrobelli (Eds.), *Firm innovation and productivity in Latin America and the Caribbean: The engine of economic development* (pp. 103–135). Palgrave Macmillan. https://doi.org/10.1057/978-1-349-58151-1_3

Qiang, C. Z., Rossotto, C., & Kimura, K. (2009). Economic impacts of broadband. In The World Bank (Ed.), *2009 Information and communications for development: Extending reach and increasing impact* (pp. 35–50). The World Bank. https://documents1.worldbank.org/curated/en/645821468337815208/pdf/487910PUB0EPI1101Official0Use0Only1.pdf

Ruprah, I., Melgarejo, K. A., & Sierra. R. (2014). *Is there a Caribbean sclerosis? Stagnating economic growth in the Caribbean.* Inter-American Development Bank. https://publications.iadb.org/publications/english/document/Is-There-a-Caribbean-Sclerosis-Stagnating-Economic-Growth-in-the-Caribbean.pdf

Solow, R. M. (1957). Technical change and the aggregate production function. *Review of Economics and Statistics, 39*, 312–320.

Solow, R. M. (1960). Investment and technical progress. In K. J. Suppes & P. Stanford (Eds.), *Mathematical methods in the social sciences* (pp. 89–104). Stanford University Press. https://doi.org/10.2307/1926047

Syverson, C. (2011). What determines productivity. *Journal of Economic Literature, 49*(2), 326–365. https://doi.org/10.1257/jel.49.2.326

Thacker, N., Acevedo, S., & Perrelli, R. (2012). *Caribbean growth in an international perspective: The role of tourism and size* (IMF Working Paper

WP/12/235). International Monetary Fund. https://www.imf.org/en/Publications/WP/Issues/2016/12/31/Caribbean-Growth-in-an-International-Perspective-The-Role-of-Tourism-and-Size-40025

Triplett, J. E., & Bosworth, B. P. (2000). *Productivity in the services sector.* Brookings Institution. https://www.brookings.edu/wp-content/uploads/2016/06/20000112.pdf

Vasilyev, D. (2019). *Reinvigorating growth in Belize* (IMF Working Paper WP/19/24). International Monetary Fund. https://www.imf.org/-/media/Files/Publications/WP/2019/wp1924.ashx

Witt, C. A., & Witt, S. F. (1989). Why productivity in the hotel sector is low. *International Journal of Contemporary Hospitality Management, 1*(2), 28–34. https://doi.org/10.1108/EUM0000000001669

World Bank (1990). *Long-term economic prospects of the OECS countries*. http://documents1.worldbank.org/curated/en/863941468225573002/pdf/multi0page.pdf

World Bank. (2016). *Exploring the relationship between broadband and economic growth.* World Bank Development Report. https://documents1.worldbank.org/curated/en/178701467988875888/pdf/102955-WP-Box394845B-PUBLIC-WDR16-BP-Exploring-the-Relationship-between-Broadband-and-Economic-Growth-Minges.pdf

CHAPTER 4

Estimating the Economic Costs of Noncommunicable Diseases in CARICOM

Samuel Braithwaite

Introduction

"[Y]ou see all of our great athletes. The fastest man in the world. The fastest woman in the world. The second fastest man, and the second fastest woman. And you say, my word, those African people in the Caribbean, they are really fit. The fact is that, that image glosses over the fundamental truth, that the African people in the Caribbean are the unhealthiest people on this planet if we take the criterion of chronic diseases as our measurement. African people in the Caribbean have the highest incidence in the world, of type 2 diabetes and hypertension. In fact, over 60% of all black people in the Caribbean, over the age of 16, have either hypertension, diabetes, or both. Our medical scientists have shown that this is linked directly to the

S. Braithwaite (✉)
University of the West Indies, Kingston, Jamaica
e-mail: samuel.braithwaite@uwimona.edu.jm

C. Cannonier and M. Galloway Burke (eds.), *Contemporary Issues Within Caribbean Economies*, https://doi.org/10.1007/978-3-030-98865-4_4

stress profile experienced by these people during slavery and colonization. And the interesting feature of this is that the same characteristics do not exist in West Africa. And the only other part of the world that has the same pathological conditions are the states of Mississippi and Alabama, in the US, for the same reason."

—Hilary Beckles
"The Meaning of Reparations to Global Africa"
The University of Johannesburg, January 16, 2014

The above excerpt of a speech by Sir Hilary Beckles paints a stark and contrasting picture of the health and athletic prowess of Caribbean peoples. Accordingly, in athletic stadiums around the world, Caribbean athletes are celebrated and envied. However, noncommunicable diseases (NCDs), such as cardiovascular disease and type 2 diabetes, account for more than three-quarters of all deaths in the Caribbean. The Ministry of Health & Wellness, Jamaica, defines NCDs as, "…those diseases that are not transferrable by contact but rather developed through family genetics, degenerative changes or unhealthy lifestyle habits," (Ministry of Health & Wellness, Government of Jamaica, 2021). The full suite of diseases that fall under the umbrella of NCDs in this study are based on the World Health Organization's (WHO) classification, and include but are not limited to cancers, cardiovascular diseases, respiratory diseases, neurological disorders (e.g., epilepsy and multiple sclerosis), and mental and substance use disorders (e.g., depressive disorders and drug addiction). Deaths aside, NCDs are chronic conditions requiring long-term care and significantly reduce the ability of people to fully participate in economic activity, to educate themselves, and to enjoy life. Indeed, apart from the obvious fact that NCDs affect the physical and mental well-being of people, money is needed to treat NCDs; money which could otherwise be used to enhance a person's quality of life. The combination of mortality and morbidity associated with NCDs negatively impacts the prospects of Caribbean countries to attain sustainable economic growth and development.

To better appreciate the rapid growth in the incidence and the prevalence of NCDs, it should be noted that the United Nations did not include any goal for reducing NCDs in its Millennium Development

Goals[1] (*The Economist*, 2007). Rather, the United Nations focused its resources and advocacy on reducing communicable diseases such as HIV/AIDS and Malaria. However, by 2015 the evidence was so overwhelming that it would have been remiss of the United Nations to not include a goal for reducing NCDs in its Sustainable Development Goals (SDGs) framework. The third sustainable development goal is titled, "good health and wellbeing." Target 3.4 (SDG 3.4) of this goal aims to reduce premature mortality from noncommunicable diseases (NCDs) by one-third through prevention and treatment and promote mental health and wellbeing. Caribbean governments have recognized the debilitating impact of NCDs on the wellbeing of Caribbean people and have started initiatives to build awareness, disincentivize harmful behaviors, and promote lifestyle changes to name a few. However, Abdulkadr et al. (2021) suggest that the process has stalled, thereby derailing efforts to achieve SDG 3.4. The necessary preoccupation with battling the COVID-19 pandemic will undoubtedly further stymie initiatives aimed at tackling NCDs. On the other hand, when the impact of COVID-19 is fully assessed, the specter of NCDs will feature largely in that assessment. Indeed, COVID-19 is deadlier for patients who also have NCDs such as cardiovascular disease, diabetes, and obesity.

This chapter contributes to the literature by estimating the economic costs of NCDs for four member countries (Barbados, Guyana, Jamaica and Trinidad and Tobago) of the Caribbean Community (CARICOM). The estimations are done using economic growth (macroeconomic) analysis. The Caribbean Community (CARICOM) is a regional bloc comprising of 15 member countries. The bloc was established by former British Caribbean colonies who viewed regional integration as the best way to ensure their sustainable economic development post-independence. The bloc now includes former non-British colonies. The four CARICOM countries in this study are classified as more developed countries (MDCs) and are the economic and political leaders within the CARICOM community. Excluding Haiti, whose population is approximately 1.5 times that of the rest of the bloc, the four countries studied here account for approximately 75% of the CARICOM population. Therefore, the four CARICOM countries used here form a significant

[1] The Millennium Development Goals (MDGs) was an elaborate 15-year framework for advancing human development in the developing world. It was launched by the UN at its Millennium Summit (September 2000).

portion of the non-Haitian CARICOM population. It is apropos to note that while Haiti is a full member of CARICOM, its perennial economic, political, and social crises have stymied its full participation in CARICOM. In addition to the four CARICOM countries, this chapter also includes two other countries in the hemisphere: Cuba and the United States. Cuba is well known for having an excellent public health system and is famous for sending medical teams (e.g., Henry Reeve International Medical Brigade) to assist countries in need of medical assistance. The United States is the world's largest economy and the world's largest spender on healthcare, in both absolute terms, and as a percentage of GDP when compared to other rich countries (World Bank Data, 2000–2018). In fact, for most of the period 2000–2018, the United States was either in first or second place among all countries in terms of health expenditure as a percentage of GDP.

Socioeconomic Overview

Table 4.1 provides a few indicators which give a snapshot of the socioeconomic situation of the countries examined in this chapter. The second column gives information on the 2020 Human Development Index

Table 4.1 Socioeconomic Indicators

	HDI (2020) & HDI changes (2014–2019)[a]	*GNP per capita rank minus HDI rank*[a]	*2019 per capita income (2010 USD)*[b]	*2019 GDP USD 2010 (millions)*[b]	*Population*[c]	*Life expectancy*[b]
Barbados	58 (−6)	20	$16,100	$4,621	288,000	79
Cuba	72 (2)	45	$6,805	$77,122	11,326,000	79
Guyana	122 (−2)	−10	$6,122	$4,791	786,000	70
Jamaica	101 (−2)	13	$4,874	$14,370	2,960,000	75
Trinidad and Tobago	67 (−1)	−14	$14,921	$20,813	1,398,000	74
United States	17 (−3)	−7	$55,886	$18,349,108	333,102,000	79

Note Sources include [a]Human Development Report 2020; [b]World Development Indicators; and [c]UN Department of Economic & Social Affairs

(HDI) as contained in the UN Human Development Report 2020 (United Nations, 2020). The HDI measures human development along three dimensions: education, health, and income. The second column also includes information on the change in HDI rank of each country for the period 2014–2019. Save for Cuba, every other country has slipped in the rankings, with Barbados recording the largest fall. However, Barbados is still ranked above the other countries, except the United States. It should be noted that movement in the rankings does not necessarily occur because of a country's action or inaction; rather, a country can slip in the rankings, for example, because another country passes it.

The third column is a measure of the difference between a country's Gross National Product (GNP) per capita rank and its HDI rank. The higher the value, the better a country is performing on the HDI relative to what its per capita income would otherwise suggest. The simple rationale here is that since per capita income is often used as a proxy for the quality of life when comparing countries, then it is reasonable to expect little difference between the rankings countries receive in regard to their HDI and GNP per capita ranks. Not surprisingly, Cuba performs well here with regard to the difference between the two (HDI and GDP). In fact, Cuba has the highest difference—between the two rankings—of any of the 189 countries which constitute the 2020 rankings. Cuba's value of 45 means that Cuba's HDI ranking is 45 places ahead of where the per capita income ranking suggests Cuba should be. In other words, contrary to its poor economic outcomes, Cuba is performing creditably well in the social sectors of education and health. Cuba's exceptional performance aside, Barbados and Jamaica are the only other countries in Table 4.1 with positive values. Guyana and Trinidad and Tobago record negative values which means they fail to achieve the standard of living suggested by their incomes. Interestingly, both countries are endowed with significant natural resources; but unlike most CARICOM countries they are plagued by ethnic tensions which for the most part remain just below the surface. Of course, Trinidad and Tobago's negative value must be taken within the context that it is relatively high on the HDI rankings; 55 places above Guyana and 35 places above Jamaica.

Life expectancy follows the path of the HDI more closely as opposed to per capita income, and rightly so as the HDI is designed to capture the overall quality of life. Indeed, save for Trinidad and Tobago, the higher a country's HDI ranking, the higher is its life expectancy.

Methodology and Data

The literature utilizes three approaches to estimating the impact of NCDs: Cost of Illness (COI) methods; economic growth models which focus on the impact of NCDs on human capital and/or labor supply and physical capital; and the full-income method. Traditionally, the COI method was the main approach used in the literature; however, in recent times, economic growth model approaches have gained much traction in the literature. Indeed, the World Health Organization designed the EPIC (Projecting the Economic Cost of Ill Health) model that uses an economic growth model—see Abegunde and Stanciole (2006). Others, such as Chen et al. (2018), have modified the basic EPIC model, adding to its complexity and completeness regarding the economic growth theory. Chen et al. (2018) build on the simple EPIC model by making three modifications: add human capital levels of workers in different age groups; cater for morbidity instead of mortality only; and include a more accurate account of the impact of treatment costs on the accumulation of physical capital.

This research project takes a less sophisticated approach and is best situated somewhere between Abegunde and Stanciole (2006) and Chen et al. (2018) although the methodology used here is guided more by Abegunde and Stanciole (2006) as opposed to Chen et al. (2018). The primary difference between this study and Abegunde and Stanciole (2006) is that morbidity has been catered for alongside mortality. The inclusion of morbidity is explained later in this section. Unlike Chen et al. (2018), this study does not include age specific productivity measures.

The famous Solow-Swan growth model is used to arrive at the projections of real output, Υ. Equation 4.1 is the constant returns to scale Cobb-Douglas function and Eq. 4.2 is the capital accumulation function. Labor inputs, L, grow by a predetermined, per country, constant growth rate.

$$Y_{it} = A_{it} K_{it}^{\alpha} L_{it}^{1-\alpha} \tag{4.1}$$

$$K_{i(t+1)} = sY_{it} - xC_{it} + (1-\delta)K_{it} \tag{4.2}$$

where,
Υ = Real output (GDP)
A = Total Factor Productivity (TFP)
K = Capital accumulation

L = Labor inputs
α = Elasticity of Υ with respect to K
$1 - \alpha$ = Elasticity of Υ with respect to L
i = Countries
t = Year (time period)
s = Savings rate
C = Cost of treating illness
X = Proportion of C funded from savings
δ = Depreciation

Table 4.2 provides more details on the parameters and variables used in the growth model. The capital share ($\alpha = 0.40$) and depreciation rate ($\delta = 0.05$) parameters are chosen in keeping with Chen et al. (2018). The values of the capital share and depreciation parameters are assumed to be the same for all the countries in this study. Assuming the same parameter values for capital share and depreciation across all countries allows for greater focus on other parameters, such as saving rates and cost of healthcare. While it is certainly better to have country specific parameter values, the dearth of studies on developing countries makes this difficult to achieve. It should be noted that Schündeln (2012), analyzing data from Indonesia, supports the use of the same depreciation rate for different countries.

Table 4.2 Data and data sources

Variables and parameters	*Sources*
Total factor productivity (A)	Calibrated (country specific values)
Capital accumulation (K)	Calibrated (country specific values)
Capital share (α)	Chen et al., (2018)
Depreciation rate (δ)	Chen et al., (2018)
Gross domestic product (Y)	World Bank Group (constant 2010 USD) 2019 GDP (millions of USD)
Medical cost (% of savings) (χ)	Assumed to be equal to the savings rate
Savings rate (% of GDP) (s)	World Bank (gross savings—% of GDP)—2019 country specific values
Total medical expenditures (C)	World Bank Group (% of GDP)—2018 country specific values
Working age population (L)	UNDESA age 15–65 (2020 and 2030 data)

A country's initial capital stock and total factor productivity (TFP) are obtained by calibrating the model to obtain the actual level of real GDP for the year 2019 and the average GDP growth rate for the period 2010–2019. For each country, a singular average rate of growth is used to calibrate the model. The average growth rates are rounded to the nearest whole number. In cases where the average growth rate is negative, or equivalent to zero after rounding, a growth rate of 1% is used. The period 2010–2019 is an ideal period to obtain each country's average growth rate as the GDP data is based on 2010 prices and 2019 is the starting point for the analysis.

The level of medical expenditure is determined by using the World Bank's estimates of what percentage of GDP represents total health expenditure on goods and services for a specific year. The year 2018 is the most recent year of estimates available. This estimate of health expenditure excludes capital health expenditures on items such as buildings, machinery, and stocks of vaccines for emergency use or disease outbreaks. Every method of estimation, or every estimate, comes with benefits and costs. Abdulkadri et al. (2009) use the Cost of Illness (COI) approach (microeconomic approach) to ascertain the economic burden of diabetes and hypertension on The Bahamas, Barbados, Jamaica, and Trinidad & Tobago. The COI approach allows for more precise estimation of costs, especially when seeking to look at specific illnesses; however, obtaining the data, especially for developing countries, requires much effort and resources. A cost which is arguably not generally outweighed by the return (benefit). The COI approach seeks to capture information on personal medical care and non-medical costs associated with the illness (direct costs) and indirect costs (e.g., loss of income due to ill health). According to Chen et al. (2018), an advantage of the COI is that it is easy to interpret as the monetary resources that could be saved by avoiding a particular disease. A drawback of this approach is that it ignores the effect of disease morbidity and mortality on the accumulation of human and physical capital. See Chen et al. (2018) for a more fulsome comparison of alternative methods for assessing the economic burden of diseases. The estimates of health expenditures used here are derived from a simple and straightforward method and the data needed are easily accessible. In keeping with the approach taken by Chen et al. (2018), the savings rate and the percentage of savings attributable to medical expenses are assumed to be equal. Country specific savings rates are obtained from the World Bank Group.

Table 4.3 Parameter/variable values

	BRB	*CUB*	*GUY*	*JAM*	*TTO*	*USA*
Savings rate (% of GDP [2019])[a]	16.9%	16.8%	16.8%	22.9%	16.9%	18.7%
Medical expenditures (% of GDP [2018])[a]	6.6%	11.2%	5.9%	6.1%	6.9%	16.9%
Average GDP growth rate (2010–2019)[a]	1.0%	2.0%	4.0%	1.0%	1.0%	2.0%
Working age population						
2020 est. (thousands)[b]	192	7,723	513	2,000	957	215,143
Growth rate[c]	−0.7%	−0.8%	0.3%	0.2%	−0.1%	0.1%
Growth rate (DALYs)[c]	−1.3%	−1.3%	−0.4%	−0.2%	−0.7%	−0.5%
Growth rate (NCD DALYs)[c]	−1.2%	−1.2%	−0.2%	−0.1%	−0.6%	−0.4%

Sources [a]World Bank Group, [b]UNDESA and [c]Author's Calculations (2020–2030 average)

A crucial and simplistic assumption is made to derive the medical costs of NCDs. Total medical costs are adjusted by the percentage of disability-adjusted life years (DALYs) attributable to NCDs (2019) (see Table 4.3). This percentage is generally lower than the percentage of total deaths attributable to NCDs and is therefore a conservative and arguably more reasonable gauge of the percentage of total healthcare costs attributable to NCDs. To better appreciate the argument for using the percentage of DALYs attributable to NCDs, it is useful to note that using the percentage of deaths attributable to NCDs is likely to overstate the healthcare costs resulting from NCDs. Indeed, many illnesses are treatable but do come at a cost. Moreover, in high-income and middle-income countries, where NCDs are more prevalent, many forms of other illnesses are easily treatable given the access to medicine and proper healthcare facilities, but they come at a cost—a cost that is likely to be underestimated if percentage of deaths attributable to NCDs is used as a proxy for obtaining the medical expenditures to treat with NCDs, and by extension the medical expenditures on communicable and other diseases. The WHO combines communicable diseases (e.g., infectious and parasitic diseases) with maternal, perinatal, and nutritional conditions. Surely, the medical costs for treating these illnesses and conditions are substantial and are very likely to be more than what the percentage of deaths from these illnesses and conditions indicate.

Controlling for mortality and morbidity is crucial to estimating the economic health burden of NCDs. This chapter includes both issues by using country specific data on DALYs. According to the WHO, the economic cost of diseases cannot be fully assessed by only looking at the number of deaths (morbidity), rather a fulsome appreciation of the burden of disease also requires the inclusion of mortality. The DALYs is "[a] time-based measure that combines years of life lost due to premature mortality (YLLs) and years of life lost due to time lived in states of less than full health, or years of healthy life lost due to disability (YLDS). One DALY represents the loss of the equivalent of one year of full health" (World Health Organization, 2021, para.1).

The growth rate of the working age population is calculated over the period 2020–2030, as per UNDESA estimates. The average growth rates for each country are calculated and applied for each year. These rates work seamlessly for the analysis covering the 2019–2030 period. These same averages are also used for the analysis covering the period 2019–2050. The working age population is adjusted to cater for morbidity and mortality.

For inclusion into the simple economic growth framework used here, the DALYs are converted to an approximate number of persons. To this end, DALYs for the age groups in the working age population are used. For example, in the 15–49 age group, the DALYs number is divided by 77, which is the difference between 92 and 15; 92 is the life expectancy used in the WHO's calculation of DALYs and 15 is the lower number in the range (15–49). Using the lower number in the range gives a more conservative number as opposed to say the midpoint in the range. The converted DALYs numbers are then added together to arrive at an aggregate value, this aggregate value is then written as a percentage of the working age population and then subtracted from the growth rate of the working age population. The outcome is a growth rate of the working age population adjusted for the DALYs. This exercise is done for two scenarios—NCDs only and all causes of death and illness. The two growth rates generated are then used to arrive at the two "status quo" scenarios—GDP with costs for all diseases or illnesses, and GDP incorporating the costs of NCDs only. These scenarios are compared with the "counterfactual" scenario. In the counterfactual scenario it is assumed that the disease burden is completely removed and therefore has no effect on GDP.

Results and Analysis

For the period spanning from 2000 to 2019, NCDs have become a relatively greater burden globally. Part of the story is that across the globe much effort has been made to fight communicable diseases, such as malaria. Concurrently, as global incomes rise, caloric intake increases and work life becomes more sedentary, ultimately leading to increases in the prevalence and incidence of NCDs. Notwithstanding the increase in the prevalence and incidence of NCDs, COVID-19 reminds us that we remain vulnerable to communicable diseases. Interestingly, rising incomes not only increase the prevalence and incidence of NCDs but also mean more disposable income for travel and increased travel increases the probability of the spread of infectious diseases. Infectious diseases need not be as contagious as COVID-19 but could be as deadly, and those infected patients who also have NCDs (comorbidities) could suffer a more debilitating illness, causing additional strain on healthcare systems. In sum, rising incomes arguably promote a confluence of communicable and noncommunicable diseases. The developing world is least able to deal with these issues, on top of the perennial issues which plague them and for which insufficient resources are available to resolve the issues.

Of the countries in Table 4.4, Guyana more closely aligns with the

Table 4.4 Noncommunicable diseases relative to all causes of illnesses

	Average annual deaths[a]	*NCD deaths (% of total)*			*NCD DALYs (% of total)*		
		2000 (%)	*2010 (%)*	*2019 (%)*	*2000 (%)*	*2010 (%)*	*2019 (%)*
Barbados	2,646	84	86	88	76	81	83
Cuba	90,676	81	84	84	78	82	83
Guyana	6,302	63	69	74	52	60	65
Jamaica	17,483	80	83	87	69	73	78
Trinidad and Tobago	10,420	79	81	86	70	73	79
United States	2,603,159	88	89	90	84	85	86
Global	53,300,000	61	67	74	48	55	64

Source Institute for Health Metrics and Evaluation. [a]Average of deaths from all causes for the years 2000, 2010 and 2019 (author's calculations)

global situation. This is not surprising given that developing countries account for approximately 70 percent of the world's population, and communicable diseases are relatively more important there than in developed countries. As an example, Guyana is a large country covered primarily by thick tropical rainforest in which trees and other vegetation are cleared for human activity (i.e., gold mining). Malaria, for example, has been known to thrive in such conditions of deforestation and human activity. The other CARICOM countries, which are small islands, are less prone to such conditions.

Table 4.5 presents the primary results of this chapter. The analysis covers the periods 2019–2030 and 2019–2050. For each period, four bits (columns) of information are provided. First, estimates of the economic cost of all diseases are given. These costs are given in terms of the total loss for the entire period relative to 2019 GDP. Additionally, the total cost (total loss) is also given relative to the total GDP for the entire period. This latter measure is akin to the average per annum percentage

Table 4.5 Country estimates for 100% reduction of disease burden

	2019–2030				*2019–2050*			
	All diseases[a]	*NCDs*[a]	*Total burden of NCDS (USD millions)*	*Cost per capita (USD)*	*All diseases*[a]	*NCDs*[a]	*Total burden of NCDS (USD millions)*	*Cost per capita (USD)*
Barbados	45% (4%)	37% (3%)	$1,718	$5,967	297% (8%)	246% (7%)	$11,345	$39,391
Cuba	58% (4%)	49% (4%)	$37,698	$3,328	356% (10%)	300% (8%)	$231,322	$20,423
Guyana	67% (5%)	47% (3%)	$2,266	$2,884	514% (11%)	374% (8%)	$17,925	$22,806
Jamaica	35% (3%)	28% (2%)	$3,997	$1,350	245% (7%)	197% (5%)	$28,335	$9,572
Trinidad and Tobago	43% (3%)	35% (3%)	$7,192	$5,145	293% (8%)	239% (7%)	$49,754	$35,589
United States	78% (6%)	67% (6%)	$12,348,300	$37,070	497% (12%)	430% (11%)	$789,349	$236,969

Author's Calculations. [a]Estimates of percentage loss are based on the total loss relative to 2019 GDP, and in parenthesis, total loss relative to total GDP for the entire period (2019–2030 or 2019–2050)

cost and is therefore naturally smaller than the estimate of the total cost as a percentage of 2019 GDP. The second set of estimates utilizes the same approach taken for the first set of estimates but only for NCDs. The third set of estimates presents the dollar value (USD 2010) of the total economic burden of NCDs for the entire period. The final estimates are concerned with representing the total economic burden relative to the size of the population (per capita economic burden).

In both periods and for every metric, save for the absolute total burden of NCDs, Jamaica records the lowest cost (burden) relative to the other countries examined here. The United States, on the other hand, consistently ranks at the top of the list for both periods and for every metric. This is not surprising given that the United States is a world leader in healthcare expenditure. The stories for Barbados, Cuba, Guyana, and Trinidad and Tobago are mixed. Of the four countries for the period 2019–2030, Guyana has the highest percentages for all diseases but Cuba has the highest percentages for NCDs. Cuba and Guyana are followed by Barbados and Trinidad and Tobago, respectively. Regarding cost per capita, for the same four countries and the same period, Barbados records the highest per capita cost followed by Trinidad and Tobago, Cuba and Guyana. It is interesting to note that the per capita cost rankings of these four countries are positively related to their relative performance on the HDI. In fact, if Jamaica is omitted there is a strong positive relationship between the HDI and the performance of the other countries assessed here. Indeed, Guyana's HDI ranking is the lowest of all the countries assessed but Jamaica records the lowest per capita cost. For the period 2019–2050, Guyana stands at the top of the list this time regarding the percentage cost (loss) for all diseases and for NCDs. As before, Guyana's surpassing Cuba aligns with its relatively higher growth rate which is compounded over a longer period than was the case in the other period (2019–2030). Guyana is followed by Cuba, Barbados, and Trinidad and Tobago. As it pertains to the other period, Barbados has the highest per capita cost followed by Trinidad & Tobago, Guyana, and Cuba.

Another way to assess the per capita cost of NCDs is to look at it relative to per capita income. It can be shown mathematically that this is equivalent to the total loss for the period (2019–2030 or 2019–2050)

Table 4.6 Estimates of 100% reduction of NCDs disease burden: Jamaica

	Total disease burden (USD billions)	*% of initial GDP*	*Per capita loss (USD)*	*% of Total GDP (full period)*
2019–2034 (Author's Calculations—Jamaica)	$7.04	49%	$3,520	2%
2015–2030 Bloom et al. (2018)	$18.45	105%	$6,306	N/A
2019–2054 (Author's calculations—United States)	$99,239	541%	$297,924	11.00%
2015–2050 Chen et al. (2018)	$94,500	569%	$265,000	10.85%

relative to 2019 GDP.[2] The United States remains at the top for both periods, while Jamaica, with the largest population of the CARICOM countries, retains the lowest relative per capita cost. However, Cuba and Guyana, which were below Barbados and Trinidad and Tobago in terms of per capita cost, are now above both countries. This jump is reflective of the lower per capita incomes of both countries and underscores the greater NCD burden both countries face when considering their broader economic situation. Of course, the estimates for Guyana should be taken with caution as that country became an oil producer in late 2019.

Given the simple estimation approach used in this chapter, it is useful to compare the results with more sophisticated studies. Table 4.6 contains the estimates for the United States obtained here and in the study by Chen et al. (2018). The results compare somewhat favorably. The estimations have different start and end years, but there is overlap and both periods cover 36 years. The higher dollar values of the disease burden, in terms of total and per capita costs, for the period 2019–2054 are understood as they are percentages of a larger GDP. In both cases GDP is based on constant 2010 USD. Table 4.6 also presents the estimates for

2
$$\frac{\text{Per Capita Total Loss}}{\text{Per Capita Income}} = \frac{\text{Total Loss}}{\text{2019 Population}} \div \frac{\text{2019 GDP}}{\text{2019 Population}}$$
$$= \frac{\text{Total Loss}}{\text{2019 Population}} \times \frac{\text{2019 Population}}{\text{2019 GDP}} = \frac{\text{Total Loss}}{\text{2019 GDP}}$$

Jamaica. The estimates for Jamaica obtained here do not compare favorably with the estimates of Bloom et al. (2018). This study provides a more conservative estimate of the economic burden of NCDs in Jamaica.

At this juncture, it is apropos to provide a brief discussion on the sensitivity of the estimates to different parameters values. This discussion should provide context for the differing estimates among the countries studied here. Generally, changes in any of the parameter values will impact the estimates, however, some parameters are of greater importance. The United States aside, Guyana's estimates of the economic burden as a percentage GDP are the highest (Table 4.5). The best explanation for this significant difference can be attributed to Guyana's larger average GDP growth rate. Of the countries studied, Guyana has the highest average GDP growth rate. This higher growth rate magnifies the yearly differences between the status quo GDP and the counterfactual GDP by a larger number than what obtains for the other countries. Not surprisingly, the differences are more pronounced for the period 2019–2050 as opposed to the shorter period, 2019–2030.

Average GDP growth rates aside, the other parameters that significantly impact the estimates are the parameters for the growth rates of the working age populations, especially those rates that have been adjusted to cater for NCDs only or for "all illnesses/diseases." The estimates for Jamaica, vis-à-vis the other countries, allow for a better appreciation of the sensitivity of the estimates to these parameters. To be specific, Jamaica records the lowest declines (negative growth rates) in both categories for all the countries explored (Table 4.3). These low negative growth rates reduce the differences between the working age populations used to estimate the status quo GDP and the counterfactual GDP; therefore, the economic value of the health burden will be lower relative to the other countries—*ceteris paribus*. It should be noted that the estimates for Jamaica would have been even lower if the country had a savings rate on par with its other Caribbean counterparts. However, while Jamaica's savings rate is about six percentage points (23–17%) higher than the other Caribbean countries, a change in its savings rate will not lead to a commensurate percentage point change in its estimates for the period 2019–2030. In addition to the relative insensitivity of the estimates to changes in the savings rate, the estimates are also relatively insensitive to changes in the percentage of medical costs attributable to NCDs.

Conclusion

This chapter contributes to the literature on the economic burden of noncommunicable diseases by providing estimates for a few CARICOM countries (Barbados, Guyana, Jamaica, and Trinidad and Tobago) within a simple macroeconomic framework. Cuba and the United States are also included for comparison purposes. Not surprisingly, the estimates of the economic burden of noncommunicable diseases are lower for the CARICOM countries relative to the estimates for the United States, whether in absolute or relative (percentage) terms. The estimates for the United States in this study compare favorably with those of the United States in at least one other academic study. Comparisons with the United States aside, this study contributes to the view that NCDs present a clear and present danger to the sustainable economic development of CARICOM states, which are already burdened by low growth, high debt, migration, and climate disasters. Further, increases in the movement of people, occasioned by rising incomes and the rapid dissemination of information, increases the chances of the spread of infectious diseases, diseases which may not develop into a pandemic on the level of COVID-19 but could be potent enough to increase the number of deaths and worsen the morbidity levels of people with NCDs.

While this study does not delve into the efficacy of alternative intervention measures, and therefore does not suggest which types of interventions are more effective, it provides evidence of the economic burden of NCDs. Surely, even in the absence of country specific analysis of alternative intervention measures, governments of CARICOM countries can create initiatives within their current budgets to build awareness about NCDs and how to prevent and manage them. To date, Barbados, Guyana, Jamaica, and Trinidad and Tobago have national NCD strategic plans. These plans cover various lengths of time over the period from 2013 to 2021 and would have been informed by the Port of Spain Declaration (2007) and the stellar efforts of the WHO. In 2013, the WHO provided a framework (Global Action Plan [GAP] 2013–2020) of nine voluntary global targets for governments around the world to follow in the fight against NCDs (World Health Organization, 2013) . The GAP 2013-2020 targets are to be achieved by 2025 as a result of the implementation of policy initiatives between 2013-2020. Abdulkadr et al. (2021) examine the progress of 16 Caribbean countries, 14 of which are members of CARICOM. Save for the United States, all the countries in this chapter are examined by Abdulkadr et al. (2021). The study concludes that based on current trends, many Caribbean countries are not likely to achieve the GAP 2013–2020 targets and SDG 3.4. Of the Caribbean countries examined in this chapter, as Abdulkadr et al. (2021) note, only Barbados and Trinidad and Tobago are on track to meet the GAP 2013–2020 targets and SDG 3.4. Cuba, Guyana and Jamaica are all unlikely to meet both sets of targets. In all of the five Caribbean countries studied here, the lowering of mortality from NCDs remains a major concern. Of course, the continuing onslaught of the COVID-19 pandemic is very likely to disrupt the global fight against NCDs; therefore, those countries which were on track to meet the two sets of targets, as of 2019, could see their progress stalled.

Governments, of course, cannot do this on their own. Civil society and the private sector have crucial roles to play. The private sector, as an employer of labor and as the main producer of foods, beverages, and medications, has a crucial role to play in reducing the incidence and prevalence of NCDs. Research and development initiatives will have to be geared toward producing newer, more wholesome products and for improving the conditions under which labor works. As a less obvious example, it is becoming increasingly important for firms to pay attention to how they can develop initiatives for dealing with the full spectrum of mental health illnesses among their staff. Civil society, by their nature, can play a supportive role by targeting specific demographics, such as children. Indeed, according to Abdulkadr et al. (2021), the rising levels of childhood obesity are a major cause for concern. A future of healthy and highly productive workers requires a generation of healthy children today.

References

Abdulkadr, A., Floyd, S., Mkrtchyan, I., Marajh, G., Gonzales, C., & Cunningham-Myrie, C. (2021). *Addressing the adverse impacts of non-communicable diseases on the sustainable development of Caribbean countries*. Studies and Perspectives Series—ECLAC Subregional Headquarters for the Caribbean, No. 100 (LC/TS.2021/4-LC/CAR/TS.2021/2). Economic Commission for Latin America and the Caribbean. https://repositorio.cepal.org/bitstream/handle/11362/46642/1/S2000964_en.pdf

Abdulkadri, A., Cunningham-Myrie, C., & Forrester, T. (2009). Economic burden of diabetes and hypertension in CARICOM states. *Social and Economic Studies, 58*(3–4), 175–197.

Abegunde, D., & Stanciole, A. (2006). *An estimation of the economic impact of chronic noncommunicable diseases in selected countries*. World Health Organization. https://www.who.int/chp/working_paper_growth%20model29may.pdf

Bloom, D. E., Chen, S., & McGovern, M. E. (2018). The economic burden of noncommunicable diseases and mental health conditions: Results for Costa Rica, Jamaica, and Peru. *Revista Panamericana de Salud Pública/Pan American Journal of Public Health, 42*(e18). https://doi.org/10.26633/RPSP.2018.18

Chen, C., Kuhn, M., Prettner, K., & Bloom, D. (2018). *The macroeconomic burden of noncommunicable diseases in the United States: Estimates and projections*. PLoS One, *30*(11), e0206702. https://doi.org/10.1371/journal.pone.0206702

Ministry of Health & Wellness, Government of Jamaica. (2021). *The noncommunicable disease and injury prevention unit*. https://www.moh.gov.jm/programmes-policies/chronic-non-communicable-diseases/

Schündeln, M. (2012). Appreciating depreciation: Physical capital depreciation in a developing country. *Empirical Economics, 44*(3), 1277–1290. https://doi.org/10.1007/s00181-012-0592-2

The Economist. (2007, August 9). *The maladies of affluence*. Retrieved July 2021, from https://www.economist.com/international/2007/08/09/the-maladies-of-affluence

United Nations. (2020). *Human development report 2020*. United Nations. http://hdr.undp.org/en/2020-report/download

United Nations, Department of Economic and Social Affairs, Population Division. (n.d.). *World population prospects 2019*. https://population.un.org/wpp/

World Health Organization. (2013). *Global action plan for the prevention and control of noncommunicable diseases* 2013–2020. World Health Organization. https://www.who.int/publications/i/item/9789241506236

World Health Organization. (2021). *The global health observatory*. Retrieved July 2021, from https://www.who.int/data/gho/indicator-metadata-registry/imr-details/158

CHAPTER 5

Taxes and Fiscal Sustainability in Caribbean Countries

Jeetendra Khadan and Inder Ruprah

Introduction

The moniker often invoked to describe the Caribbean is low economic growth-high debt economies. Today, commodity-dependent economies have shared these two interrelated characteristics since the end of the world commodity boom, and for a longer time, tourism-dependent economies. In this chapter, the main fiscal problems of the region that underlie these two characteristics are reviewed, with particular emphasis on the role of taxes.

The COVID-19 pandemic has, to a large extent, accentuated these two characteristics and the underlying fiscal problems in the region.[1]

[1] The exception is Guyana, which, in 2020, became an oil exporter.

J. Khadan
World Bank, Washington, DC, USA

I. Ruprah (✉)
Independent Consultant, Washington, DC, USA

C. Cannonier and M. Galloway Burke (eds.), *Contemporary Issues Within Caribbean Economies*, https://doi.org/10.1007/978-3-030-98865-4_5

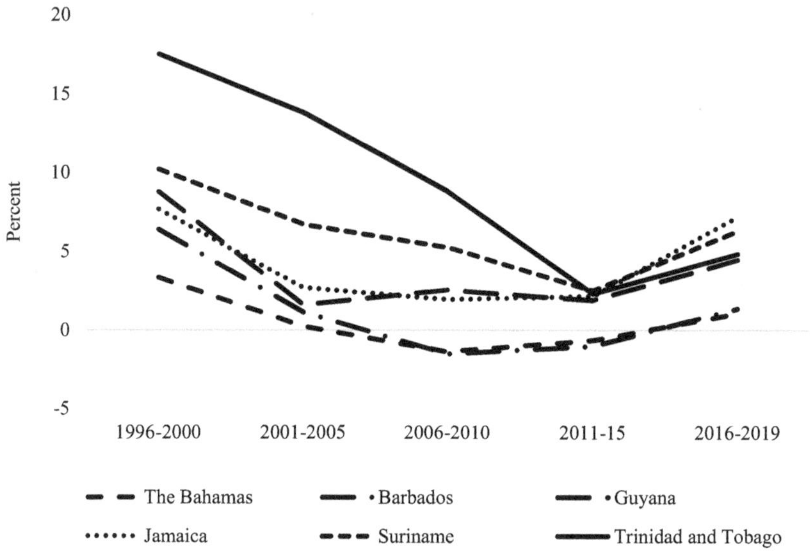

Fig. 5.1 Falling Economic Growth 5-year Averages (*Source* World Economic Outlook, April 2021)

Considerable uncertainty surrounds COVID-19. What is certain is that fiscal deficits will rise due to increased COVID-19-related expenditure and revenue fall due to the combined effects of discretionary tax measures that reduce tax liabilities and fall in economic activity. To finance the rising fiscal deficit, public debt will be higher.[2] In addition, it will worsen two other existing problems, with the first being high current expenditure with low capital expenditure. Countries may further shift their public spending away from the less urgent but more profitable capital expenditure projects. The second is that governments may turn to the state-owned enterprises searching for funds worsening their already bad finances.

Figures 5.1 and 5.2 show the overall underlying problem. In Fig. 5.1, the five-year economic growth averages show a steady decline for

[2] For a description of specific fiscal measures taken by countries see: Fiscal Monitor Database of Country Fiscal Measures in Response to the COVID-19 Pandemic: https://www.imf.org/en/Topics/imf-and-covid19/Fiscal-Policies-Database-in-Response-to-COVID-19

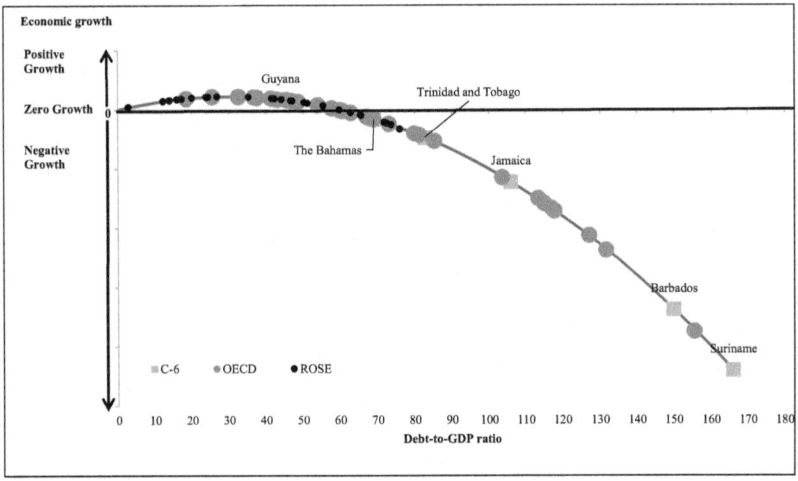

Fig. 5.2 The dark side: debt and economic growth (*Note* C6 = The Bahamas, Barbados, Guyana, Jamaica, Suriname, and Trinidad and Tobago; OECD = Organisation for Economic Co-operation and Development; ROSE = Rest of small economies. *Source* Authors estimates from World Economic Outlook, April 2021)

the Caribbean. The Caribbean development model, primarily based on tourism and financial services for some countries and commodities for others—high export concentration—is no longer delivering. Figure 5.2 shows that the Caribbean countries, excluding Guyana, are on the dark side of the relation between economic growth and public debt to GDP ratio (i.e., where the marginal and average effect of debt/GDP on economic growth is negative[3]). Public debt and fiscal deficits are not only high but face sustainability challenges in the medium to long term. Khadan (2019a) finds that a less than unity long-run relationship (i.e., revenues rise less than an increase in expenditures) between government revenues and spending supports a "weak" fiscal sustainability position for Caribbean countries.

[3] For the debt-economic growth relation, in Fig. 5.2, we use the estimated coefficient found in Greenidge et al. (2012).

Negative Loops

The standard narrative found in the literature explaining these two features typically involves feedback loops between large adverse external shocks—both natural and economic—that are not fully offset given domestic macroeconomic imbalances combined with severe structural economic constraints.[4] Negative external shocks include the loss of preferential trade access to European markets, the decline of bilateral and multilateral official aid, and increasingly frequent and more intense natural disasters and economic shocks from the world economy. Caribbean economies have not been able to insulate themselves from such shocks fully. Such inability is partially due to their large chronic macroeconomic imbalances (the twin deficits of a fiscal and current account of the balance of payments) and high public debt burdens that, when combined, successfully constrain countercyclical fiscal policy in response to shocks. Partly this is because the countries have low policy buffers, both domestic and external, to mitigate the economic shocks. But there are deeper problems—fiscal multipliers are smaller for small economies (Ilzetzki et al., 2012; Khadan, 2019b), and long-run tax revenue buoyancy is lower than unity. Ilzetzki et al. (2012) found that where the debt of the central government exceeded 60% of GDP, as is the case of most Caribbean countries, the impact of a fiscal multiplier was not statistically different from zero and was negative (and statistically different from zero) in the long run. Hence, the bang for the buck of increased fiscal expenditure is low. Khadan's (2019b) finding of a less than unity long-run tax buoyancy implies that expansionary fiscal policies are not self-financing. Combined, they result in a vicious cycle—an external shock leading to an attempt at compensatory expansionary budgetary policy does not lead to more than proportionate effect on tax revenue. Hence, it has a long-term deficit-increasing impact, consequently increasing debt and putting downward pressure on growth. Simultaneously, with income increasingly used for interest payments, these limitations have contributed to a squeeze in spending on infrastructure that has impeded private sector activity.

However, macroeconomic imbalances hinder response and weaken political and economic institutions, where the former leads to a "wait and see" policy response and the latter leads to inadequate implementation issues. Hence, most analyses place the public sector and public policy as

[4] See IMF (2013a), Ruprah et al. (2014), and Beuermann and Schwartz (2018).

the root of the problematic "loop" dynamics or as part of the solution in breaking the loop. Among the structural factors often listed to account for economic stagnation and the high volatility is an inadequately diversified economic structure—i.e., high concentration in few exports and export markets. Further, the policy has locked the countries into that structure and an unfriendly business environment that prevents a dynamic private sector from being formed through tax expenditures.

Inadequate diversification poses a problem for tourism economies as their motors of growth are fading. The peculiarity of tourism export services is that they are consumed within the confines of the exporting country. In principle, this feature of tourism provides opportunities for taxes. In practice, tourism is lightly taxed. Tourism is an industry of numerous subsectors; thus, it is difficult to define precisely what constitutes a tourism service and how to tax it. Some Caribbean countries, particularly tourism-dependent ones, also have an offshore sector. Offshore financial centers (OFCs or tax havens) play a significant role in the Caribbean. OFCs in the Caribbean are mainly booking centers for intra-group funding. They are small by international standards; however, they are relatively large concerning the size of host economies.

Both activities, tourism and OFCs, may no longer be the sources of growth. First, the maturity of the tourist sector in the Caribbean partially explains the decline in average spending per visitor. According to Butler (1980), tourist destinations follow a lifecycle from birth to maturity to old age and finally a reduction (the "Butler S-curve"). Based on the tourist area lifecycle, tourist destinations experience increasing difficulty attracting tourists, despite marketing efforts, because of the negative utility of over-utilization of resources (see Greenidge & Whitehall, 2000; Whitehall & Craigwell, 2006). The maturity of a destination alters the demand for the tourism product irrespective of price-income factors. This process eventually leads to decline unless rejuvenation occurs. The second is international initiatives that will undermine tax havens. One hundred thirty countries have agreed on a global minimum tax backed by the USA as part of a worldwide effort to keep multinational firms from dodging taxes by shifting their profits to countries with low rates. The agreement attempts to address challenges presented by a globalized and increasingly digital world economy in which profits can be relocated across borders and companies can earn online profits in places with no taxable headquarters. Under the deal, countries could tax their companies' foreign earnings up to 15% if they go untaxed through subsidiaries in other countries. The agreement also provides for taxing a portion of the profits of the largest global companies in countries where they do business online but may have no physical presence. The proposal would remove the incentive to use accounting and legal schemes to shift profits to low-rate countries where they do little or no business since the gains would be taxed at home anyway. The proposal to tax companies with revenue but no physical presence would require countries to sign up for a multilateral convention. In contrast, the minimum corporate tax could be adopted voluntarily by each government through national legislation.

Tax Problem

The tax problem can be viewed from both the aggregate and structure viewpoints. At the aggregate level, what has often been emphasized in the literature is the (i) tax revenue to expenditure ratio that is below unity and falling (see Fig. 5.3) and (ii) tax to GDP ratio has high volatility.

Table 5.1 shows that Caribbean countries have higher volatility and a

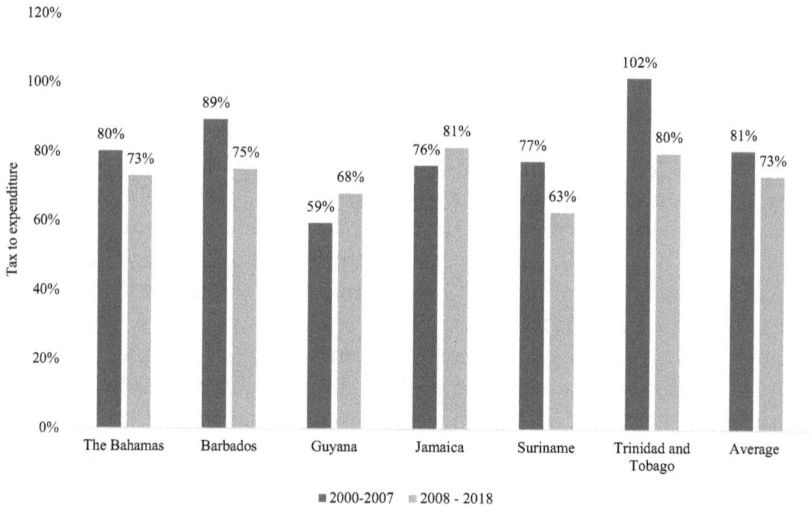

Fig. 5.3 Tax to expenditure (*Source* Authors estimates from World Economic Outlook, April 2021)

Table 5.1 Economic growth and tax revenues

Economic growth			*Tax revenue*		
1980–2019	*SD*	*Mean*	*1990–2019*	*SD**	*Mean*
The Bahamas	2.97	1.83	The Bahamas	2.52	12.52
Barbados	2.95	0.9	Barbados	1.56	26.99
Guyana	4.53	1.92	Guyana	2.26	27.58
Jamaica	2.53	1.28	Jamaica	2.29	25.64
Suriname	5.55	1.28	Suriname	3.46	22.64
Trinidad and Tobago	5.55	2.43	Trinidad and Tobago	3.02	27.67
ROSE	1.59	4.05	ROSE	2.05	34.24

Source Authors estimates from World Economic Outlook, April 2021

lower mean of the percentage change in real GDP growth when compared to the rest of the small economies[5] (ROSE). Commodity-exporting countries, Guyana, Suriname, and Trinidad and Tobago have higher volatility than tourist-dependent countries, The Bahamas, Barbados, and Jamaica. Table 5.1 shows that GDP and revenue to GDP volatility, excluding Barbados, are higher for the Caribbean than the volatility's mean value for ROSE. Government revenue volatility is higher for commodity-dependent countries relative to tourist-dependent ones.[6]

The tax structure is measured by the share of significant taxes in total tax revenue. The composition matters partly because different taxes affect economic growth differently in addition to the composition's effect on volatility, tax buoyancy, and automatic stabilizers. There are other issues related to the composition of taxes. Tanzi and Zee (2001) argue these issues that involve both efficiencies—whether the tax enhances or diminishes the overall welfare of those taxed—and equity, such as whether the tax is fair to everybody (see World Bank, 2009). Regarding economic growth, the common wisdom, at least as held by the IMF in its adjustment programs, is a hierarchy of taxes. From bad to less bad, as noted in an issue of the IMF's Fiscal Monitor (IMF 2013b),

> …corporate income taxes have the most negative effect, followed by labor income taxes, then consumption taxes, and finally property taxes. In line

[5] A small country is one with a population size of less than 3 million.

[6] For the impact of revenue volatility, see Talvi and Végh (2005).

> with this "growth hierarchy,"... a revenue-neutral rebalancing that reduces income taxes while increasing consumption and property taxes is associated with faster long-term growth. (p. 31)

However, Xing (2012) found that

> ...the "tax and growth ranking" is not robust under different assumptions about heterogeneity across countries hence of the long-run and short-run coefficients in the underlying econometric model. Evidence for significant tax structure effects depends on long-run parameter homogeneity restrictions, underlying pooled mean group estimation, which are found to be invalid. (p. 379)

A similar caution to the IMF's orthodoxy is supported by Mcnabb (2018).

The tax structure also matters regarding the volatility of tax revenue (Table 5.2). Different taxes have different volatilities, and within the general observation, volatility is high in the Caribbean due to a narrow tax base reflecting an undiversified economy. Not only is higher volatility often associated with a lower mean value of the revenue to GDP ratio but revenue volatility exacerbates the capacity of the Ministry of Finance and tax authorities to generate reliable forecasts. This feature often contributes to fiscal instability as revenue outcomes differ from programed ones. Table 5.3 shows volatility, measured by the standard deviation for the period 1990 to 2018, of selected revenue items—VAT (value-added tax) has higher volatility than CIT (corporate income tax) except in the case of Trinidad and Tobago. Generally, SSC (social security contributions) has the lowest volatility.

Table 5.2 The volatility of selected revenue items

	SSC	*CIT*	*VAT*
The Bahamas	0.43	NR	1.68
Barbados	0.93	0.99	3.71
Guyana	0.58	0.57	2.89
Jamaica	0.44	0.49	1.77
Trinidad and Tobago	0.72	5.08	0.51
ROSE	1.48	0.41	1.06

Note SSC = Social security contributions, CIT = Corporate income tax, VAT = Value added tax, ROSE = Rest of small economies.
Source Authors using OECD, Global Revenue Statistics Database

Common Underlying Contributory Factors

Several common contributory factors underlie the inadequacy of tax revenue in the region. We can invoke the shadow economy, the perverse effects of tax expenditures, the inadequacy of tax administration, amnesties, and international tax issues. These common problems play a critical role in the "negative feedback loops" discussed previously.

Shadow Economy

The first issue is the shadow economy. Activities included in the shadow economy (see OECD, 2017) are underreported business income, unreported sources of income, inflated costs, including the inflation of tax deductibles and false invoices, moonlighters, cross-border fraud, money laundering, distance selling, non-registered firms (i.e., firms not registered with tax authority but that maybe with other public agencies), and phoenix companies (i.e., firms created to become insolvent when taxes are due). Informal activities in a shadow economy are not just a "mum and pop" corner shop. The ramifications of the shadow economy include (i) the direct loss of tax revenue and the indirect loss that undermines trust in the tax system and the norms supporting voluntary tax compliance; (ii) the distortion of competition through lower costs due to non-compliance of firms compared to their registered counterparts; and (iii) the exploitation of workers due to lack of contractual protection. The extent of these problems for the Caribbean depends on the size of the shadow economy.

As a principal economic activity, service is the largest and increasing sector of the Caribbean economy—personnel services, hospitality (restaurants, cafes, hotels), retail, tourism, real estate, internet, freelancers, and professionals. Further, the definition of shadow economy facilitates the inclusion of changes that further undermine tax compliance, namely the increasing use of sophisticated technology (e.g., apps for false invoices), cross-border fraud, the rapid growth of the sharing economy, and the gig economy. The gig economy is when individuals offer their services on a part-time basis to firms. The sharing economy is when individuals take advantage of underutilized assets they possess and rent them to people who need them.

Awasthi and Engelschalk (2018) suggest that the higher the level of the shadow economy (as a proportion of the official GDP), the lower is the tax revenue (tax revenue to GDP). The correlation coefficient is −0.278, a decrease in one percentage point in the shadow economy's size (S.E.'s GDP to official GDP) increases revenue (revenue to GDP) by 0.278. The S.E.'s GDP is related negatively to governance. A one percentage point increase in regulatory quality and control of corruption reduces the size of the shadow economy's GDP by 0.6435 and 0.6763%, respectively. The direct effect on tax revenue to GDP is 1.473 of regulatory quality and 2.8 of control of corruption.

Estimates of the shadow economy suggest it comprises one-third of the economy (see Table 5.3) (Medina & Schneider, 2017; Peters, 2017; Veletin, 2008). The official figure of the relatively high tax to GDP ratio of 21% falls to a low of 16% once the shadow economy is taken into account (i.e., revenue to official plus shadow economy's GDP). For the countries in the sample, the average tax revenue loss is 33% of official tax revenue. Tax to public expenditure increases from 68 to 91% when tax lost is added to tax revenue.

Table 5.3 The shadow economy: size and revenue loss

	Size of informal sector (% of GDP)							
	Medina and Schneider (2017)	*Veletin (2008)*	*Peters (2017)*	*Tax to official GDP*	*Tax to official plus shadow GDP*	*Tax loss to tax revenue*	*Tax to expenditure*	*Tax plus tax loss to expenditure*
The Bahamas	34	15.9	20–30	0.16	0.12	0.34	0.67	0.9
Barbados				0.28	0.21	0.35	0.83	1.11
Guyana	32	37	29–40	0.22	0.17	0.32	0.65	0.86
Jamaica	33	35	35–44	0.27	0.2	0.33	0.89	1.15
Suriname	32	n.a	35–45	0.12	0.29	0.32	0.47	0.62
Trinidad and Tobago	34	24	26–33	0.2	0.15	0.34	0.98	0.77
Average				0.21	0.16	0.33	0.68	0.91

Source Authors compilation from Medina and Schneider (2017), Peters (2017), and Veletin (2008)

The shadow economy plays a critical role in the negative feedback loops. When the urgent need for revenue increases due to an external shock, authorities respond with quick tax policy changes that do not solve the structural problems but raise revenue in the short term and perpetuate a perverse vicious cycle. The response is typically an increase in tax rates and/or the introduction of distortive taxes. The increase in the tax burden on taxpayers gives an additional impetus for agents to operate below the radar. Hence, the informal economy grows—a growth that consequentially reduces tax revenue, a shortfall that lowers the quality of public services, and retards economic growth (see Awasthi & Engelschalk, 2018; Elgin & Birinci, 2016).

Tax Expenditure

The second feature leading to the tax problems is tax expenditure. The Caribbean widely uses tax expenditures rather than reducing the rates applied to different taxes. Tax expenditures are defined as foregone tax revenue. Those government expenditures are carried out through tax legislation and practices that reduce or defer taxes for some taxpayers. Tax expenditures do not appear in the annual budgetary appropriation process. Hence, they are not as scrutinized by parliament and citizens as is direct spending. Tax expenditures appear to be tax cuts rather than spending as they transfer funds through a tax subsidy. Thus, it is easier to spend through tax expenditures, particularly in the Caribbean, as they can be authorized at the ministerial level. Political expediency may be the reason for choosing tax expenditures instead of direct spending. However, the concern is that the tax expenditures negatively affect tax revenue and budget and tax policies, which adversely affect the transparency, efficiency, and equality of the fiscal systems but without the expected positive effect on the economy. Tax expenditures also make the tax system less transparent and more difficult to administer. Further, particularly in the Caribbean, they are directed at stagnant sectors, locking the Caribbean into low economic growth.

In the Caribbean, tax expenditures are directed at a few sectors, mainly tourism and manufacturing (Van Parys & James, 2010). Many Caribbean countries also grant corporate income tax exemptions to offshore banking and insurance companies.[7] The official raison d'être is to promote these sectors, mainly through influencing their decision of which country to locate. Typically, a package of exemptions is crafted to include corporate income tax holidays, exemptions from value-added tax, and customs duties. Tax holidays, for five to 25 years, are typical. In the case of The Bahamas, since there are no corporate or personal income taxes, the incorporation of offshore corporations implies an automatic zero income tax rate and no tax expenditures since the no income tax rule applies to locals and foreign taxpayers. Thus, tax expenditures are the preferred tool in the race to the bottom, rather than the more typical reduction of tax rates, particularly for corporate taxes.

Further, most Caribbean countries use tax expenditures to bypass the common tariff system. Caribbean countries are the members of CARICOM, a customs union, and unlike most customs unions worldwide, members of CARICOM can give import duty relief from the

[7] The Bahamas became popular tax haven in the 1990s after passing legislation that enabled the incorporation of offshore corporations and IBCs, becoming one of the preferred tax havens for residents of the United States and European countries. The Bahamas provides offshore banking, registration of offshore companies, registration of ships, and offshore trust management. Offshore companies are not required to submit any accounting records to tax authorities. The Bahamas is a tax haven, with no tax liability at all for offshore companies or individual offshore bank account holders on income earned outside of the jurisdiction.

common external tariffs of CARICOM. These tax exemptions allow particular investors not to pay customs tariffs and VAT, where such exemptions can be up to 100% of potential tax liability. For example, a reduced VAT rate on tourism-related services is applied to hotel accommodation, tour operators, and restaurants. Additionally, employment credits and property tax exemptions are also frequently used to complement the tax exemptions.

There are seven main drawbacks of tax expenditures (Brixi et al., 2004). First, it reduces the tax base—the sizeable informal sector already compresses the tax base. Second, tax expenditures are less transparent than direct subsidy programs. The latter is in the budgets approved by parliament, while the former is not. Tax expenditures thus allow spending that is outside of the parliament-approved budget. Third, tax expenditures encourage corruption as discretionary exemptions encourage government officials to grant exemptions in exchange for a bribe. Fourth, tax expenditures create horizontal inequities across taxpayers as taxpayers with similar incomes pay different levels of taxes. Fifth, tax expenditures accrue disproportionally to middle-high income households, thereby worsening income inequality, and by reducing revenue, they limit the government's ability to finance poverty–inequality–reducing programs. Sixth, tax expenditures reduce domestic competition as they give the privileged firms an unfair advantage. Seventh, tax expenditures are not necessarily instruments to attract direct foreign investments as many firms report the tax incentives were not a crucial variable in their location decision. These seven disadvantages show the mechanisms of how tax expenditure operates and contributes to the negative loops that characterize the Caribbean economies' development.

Tax Administration

The third issue is problematic tax administration. The existing tax system faced by taxpayers reflects tax laws, and those laws are implemented in practice. How a tax system is administered affects its yield, incidence, and efficiency; in that sense, "tax administration is tax policy" (Casanegra de Jantscher, 1990, p. 179). In which case, it is "misguided … to reform the tax structure while ignoring tax administration" (Bird, 1989, p. 315) and that it is critical to guarantee that "changes in tax policy are compatible with administrative capacity" (World Bank, 1991, p. 51). This point is not trivial given the proportion of total government revenue that the Caribbean tax administrations administer (see Fig. 5.4).

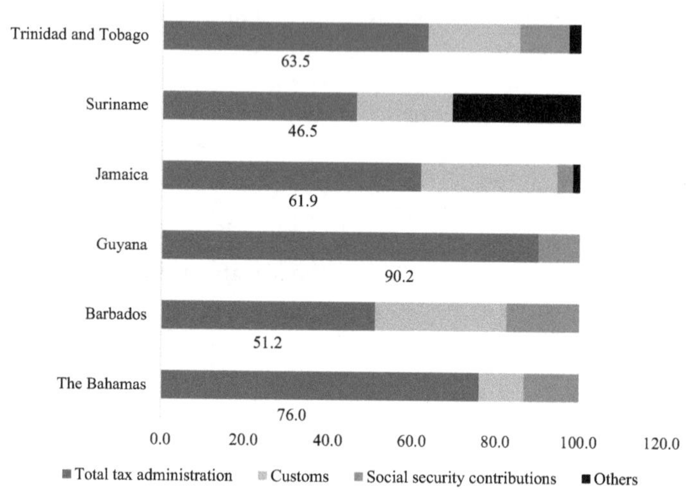

Fig. 5.4 Revenue by tax administration (*Source* Author's elaboration using IDB—Inter-American Center of Tax Administrations database 2019 and Ministry of Finance of Suriname reports [Howel & Reyes-Tagle, 2018])

A proxy for the efficiency of tax administration could be the ratio between the administrative cost of collection and the revenue (taxes and customs) collected. Figure 5.5 shows the Caribbean average is above Latin America, with Trinidad and Tobago being the only country below. Muyangwa et al. (2017) identified several deficiencies in Trinidad and Tobago's tax system. The flaws are low integrity in the taxpayer registration database, underdeveloped compliance risk management practices, limited use of electronic services for filing and payment, limited use of non-audit initiatives to promote voluntary compliance, delays in processing taxpayer accounting transactions, lack of impact assessment of compliance management interventions, a flawed value-added tax refund process, weak revenue accounting systems, shortage of technical staff, a weak internal audit function, and an inadequate external assurance capacity undermined by confidentiality provisions. Similar challenges exist in other Caribbean countries (see Reyes-Tagle et al., 2021). The case of Trinidad and Tobago could be taken as *prima facie* evidence of inefficient and ineffective tax administrations. However, given fixed costs, this could also be partly due to the unavoidable effect of the countries' small size.

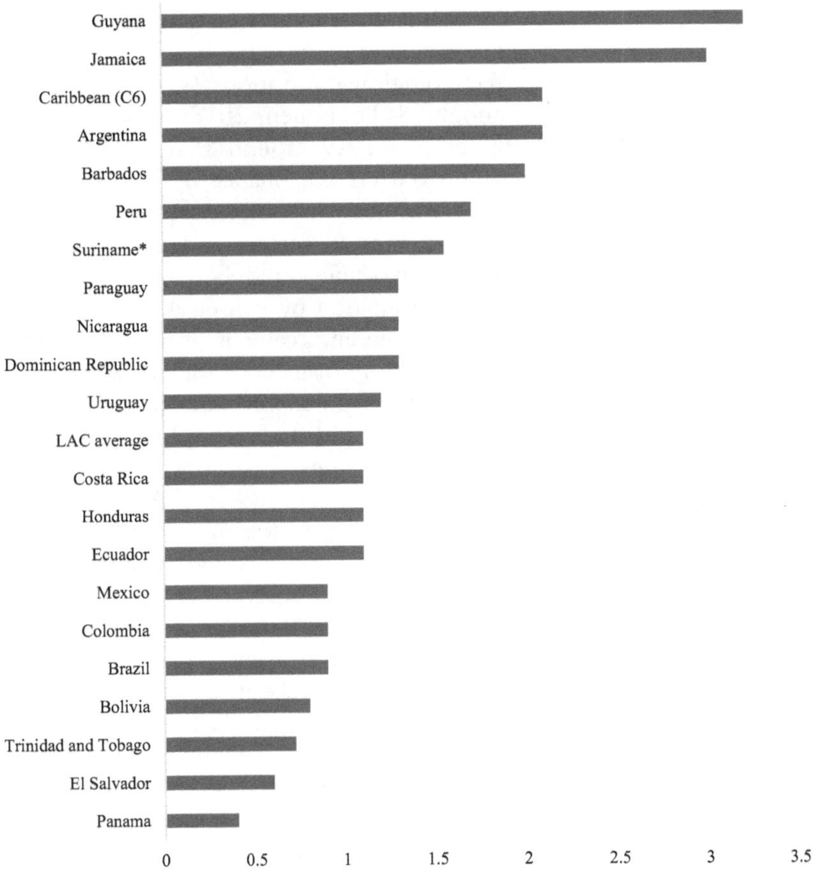

Fig. 5.5 Administrative Costs (as a percent of revenue) (*Source* Authors calculations from Arias (2016); Revenue Administrations in Latin American and the Caribbean. For Suriname the average is for the period 2015–2016 while for the rest of the countries is for 2007–2011)

For example, software and equipment cost the same independently of the size of the number of taxpayers.

Digitalization of tax authorities can improve tax compliance, reduce inefficiencies in the tax system, and improve transparency. Early evidence on introducing technological innovations to tax administrations shows encouraging results. The few available studies found increases in tax compliance, payments by some firms and sectors, and higher tax revenues after tax authorities adopt technological innovations (see Bellon et al., 2019; Fan et al., 2020; Okunogbe & Pouliquen, 2018; Mascagni et al., 2021). For example, Bellon et al. (2019) found that the introduction of e-invoicing in Peru improved tax compliance by up to 5% after the first year of adoption. They noted that the increase in compliance mainly was among small firms and in sectors with higher rates of non-compliance—implying that e-invoicing could be lowering compliance costs for taxpayers. Another evaluation by Fan et al. (2020) found that adopting new technology increased enforcement of the value-added tax. They estimated that technological reforms contributed to 27.1% of VAT revenues and 12.9% of total government revenues over five years. More recently, Mascagni et al. (2021) found that technological adoption had a highly positive impact on tax revenues in Ethiopia—tax revenues increased by at least 12% for income taxes and 48% for VAT. Okunogbe and Pouliquen (2018) similarly found evidence for e-filing in Tajikistan.

However, the digital transformation of tax administrations in Caribbean countries has been constrained by several factors. In a review of tax systems in Caribbean countries, Reyes-Tagle et al. (2021) found that the most common factors contributing to weak I.T. systems for tax authorities are (1) incomplete view of taxpayers at a national level; (2) outdated platforms with no upgrade options; (3) lack of modules for risk management and auditing; (4) inadequate revenue accounting environment; (5) inadequate management information reports; (6) existing systems do not provide sufficient information to assess debt management practices; (7) lack of interoperability with other government systems or the tax system; (8) frequent system failures; and (9) a lack of essential taxpayer services. Slow progress on the adoption of digital technologies has contributed to a lack of transparency and governance issues, organizational inefficiencies, data integrity issues, and operational ineffectiveness, all of which undermine the economic and social objectives of tax policies.

Radian (1980) distinguishes between the extent to which tax revenue is attributable to enforcement—i.e., the active intervention of the administration, rather than compliance, such as the relatively passive role of the tax administration as the recipient of revenues generated by societal features. The reflexive part is when tax administrations tend to be passive recipients of funds rather than active collectors—i.e., "tellering" instead of "collecting." To a large extent, Caribbean tax administrations are generally more akin to "tellering" than "collecting" due to a lack of capacity of Caribbean tax administrations to take a more proactive role and due to different factors ranging from the environment of trust in public institutions to outdated and complex legal frameworks to institutional arrangements within the administrations. These factors have delayed necessary reforms for so many years and hindered the efficient fulfillment of tax functions.

Fiscal Institutions and Frameworks

Strong institutions are necessary to safeguard fiscal sustainability. Institutions, in general, consist of both informal constraints (sanctions, customs, traditions, and codes of conduct) and formal rules (constitutions, laws, and property rights) of the game that shape the incentive structure for human interaction and decision making (North, 1991). Consequently, institutions and their evolution, to a large extent, determine countries' progression or decline. The literature has well documented the importance of institutions to development (see Beuermann & Schwartz, 2018). Fiscal institutions—the budget process's mechanisms, rules, and procedures—can help countries improve the quality of decisions and fiscal performance (see Alesina & Perotti, 1999 and Fabrizio & Mody, 2006). Wright et al. (2017) found that Caribbean countries would find great difficulty overcoming their fiscal and debt challenges unless binding rules to establish greater fiscal discipline, reduce procyclicality, and improve fiscal transparency and budget credibility are enforced. The fiscal framework covers the procedures and institutions responsible for planning and implementing budgetary policies. The main components of fiscal frameworks are numerical fiscal rules, independent fiscal councils; procedures for the preparation, approval, and implementation of budget plans; and medium-term budgetary frameworks.

A few Caribbean countries have been moving in the right direction to strengthen fiscal institutions and fiscal frameworks. Jamaica has made substantial and sustained progress in upgrading its fiscal framework in recent years with the support of IMF programs and international financial institutions. Underlying its progress has been the efforts to strengthen the country's fiscal responsibility framework, which established the central government and public bodies' procedures and numerical fiscal rules.

Jamaica's fiscal framework also includes mechanisms to strengthen transparency and control of budgetary operations, including a fairly detailed risk analysis. Barbados and the Bahamas have recently taken steps to strengthen their respective fiscal responsibility frameworks. In the case of Barbados, updates to its financial management and audit act in 2019 now require the annual budget preparation to be in the context of a rolling medium-term fiscal framework. It is expected that Barbados will continue to strengthen legislation in public financial management, procurement, fiscal statistics, and the management of the public debt and introduce a numerical fiscal rule in 2021. The Bahamas also introduced a fiscal responsibility law in 2018 that aims to introduce numerical fiscal rules, strengthen transparency requirements, and establish an independent fiscal council.

Apart from Sovereign Wealth Funds (SWFs), the commodity-dependent countries of the Caribbean are lagging in establishing solid fiscal frameworks. SWFs are an essential element of the fiscal framework in commodity-dependent countries as they help mitigate fiscal risks associated with volatility in revenue flows, smooth consumption, and increased savings. The three commodity-dependent countries in the Caribbean—Guyana, Suriname, and Trinidad and Tobago—have either established or are establishing an SWF. However, recent evidence has shown that the effectiveness of SWFs can be undermined by the degree of commodity dependence as higher dependence on one commodity reduces the efficacy of the SWF (Balin, 2009) and the quality of institutions (Asik, 2013; Frankel et al., 2012). Further research by Giles et al. (2021) also found that the success of SWFs appears to be associated with broader institutional quality, especially fiscal institutions. However, commodity-dependent countries in the Caribbean are far behind in developing robust fiscal frameworks and improving the quality of fiscal institutions (Beuermann & Pecha, 2018). For example, Trinidad and Tobago do not have a credible medium-term fiscal framework, numerical fiscal rules, and an independent fiscal council to support the implementation of fiscal policy. While Suriname has a medium-term fiscal framework, it lacks credibility, and there is no significant analysis of fiscal risks or no independent external scrutiny of it. The country has yet to operationalize its Savings and Stability Fund after its parliament approved it in 2017. Guyana, a recent oil exporter, established a Natural Resource Fund in 2019 and has only recently begun to address significant institutional weaknesses, including strengthening its medium-term fiscal framework, budgetary processes, procurement, and transparency as well as governance challenges (see Khadan & Baxter, 2018).

What to Do?

There is generally a low effective tax burden for many Caribbean countries but high statutory tax rates. The narrow tax base is partly due to a complex system of exemptions, incentives, deductions, allowances, and discretionary waivers—i.e., tax expenditures, compounded by a large informal sector. Tax reform implies enlarging the tax base by reducing tax expenditures, including the informal sector, into the tax system, changing statutory rates, and strengthening tax administrations and customs.

The road to take is relatively straightforward. If a political commitment to reform and public buy-in can be obtained, the country can take the road. On this road, tax reform should pursue four objectives: (1) broaden the tax bases; (2) reduce statutory rates and tariffs consistent with a responsible fiscal situation; (3) simplify the tax system, including reducing tax expenditures to facilitate compliance, enforcement and transparency; and (4) strengthen tax administration where the pursuance of these objectives is within the umbrella goals of increasing tax revenue towards obtaining the required primary fiscal balances to reduce public debt and simultaneously creating a pro-growth with equity tax policy environment.

If done correctly, pursuing digital transformation of tax and customs administrations can benefit Caribbean countries. The pandemic has undoubtedly highlighted the importance of digital platforms and I.T. systems to support the work of tax authorities and address other long-standing challenges. Countries that have moved many of their operations online are expected to accelerate the digital transformation of tax administration in the coming years, given the pandemic experience (see OECD, 2021). However, Caribbean countries are lagging in digitalizing their tax administration processes and operational procedures. There are few examples of Caribbean tax administrations moving towards paperless processes, and they often fall short due to gaps in legal requirements. For instance, taxpayers in Guyana, Suriname, and Trinidad and Tobago can use electronic filing and payment because tax administrations in those countries do not have the legal power to enact such requirements. Thus, e-filing is not mandatory.

Furthermore, legal constraints on using available technology limit digital enforcement practices. For example, in some Caribbean countries, e-communications (e-notices, e-notifications, and e-mails) are not considered legal for tax enforcement purposes (Reyes-Tagle et al., 2021). This result implies that for Caribbean countries to be successful on the digital path, they must first address gaps and constraints in the current legal and operational frameworks. Only then will I.T. infrastructure and management and performance frameworks ensure a smooth transition of tax administrations to the digital era succeed.

Beyond tax reform, there is a need to strengthen fiscal institutions to restore and safeguard debt sustainability. As discussed in this chapter, Caribbean countries' fiscal positions face sustainability challenges from medium to long term. For tax reform to effectively support fiscal sustainability efforts, Caribbean countries should strengthen their fiscal institutions. For the commodity-dependent countries of Guyana and Trinidad and Tobago that have established SWF (Sovereign Wealth Fund), there is scope for adjusting the rigid rules of those SWFs into financing or quasi-financing type funds with flexible rules to achieve more integrated and effective asset-liability management (see Ossowski, 2021). SWFs alone may not necessarily contribute to greater fiscal discipline but should be complemented by strengthening the broader fiscal and public institutions. Caribbean countries should continue to implement and improve vital fiscal elements: numerical fiscal rules; independent fiscal councils; effectively functioning budgeting cycles and procedures; and medium-term budgetary frameworks, contributing to more sustainable fiscal policies in Caribbean countries.

Conclusion

This chapter examined the main macroeconomic challenges—low economic growth and high debt—for countries in the Caribbean, emphasizing the role of taxes. Even before the pandemic, most Caribbean countries were experiencing decades of low and volatile economic growth, with some countries being among the most indebted in the world. The pandemic has, to a large extent, accentuated the growth and fiscal problems in the region.

The complex economic history in the Caribbean has been linked to the countries' vulnerability to external shocks, including recurring natural disasters and commodity price shocks and the absence of adequate solid economic institutions. In terms of the latter, we identified several challenges the tax system faces to deliver on economic and social objectives. These challenges include a relatively large shadow economy, the perverse effects of tax expenditures, the inadequacy of tax administration, amnesties, and international tax issues. These problems are common across most countries and play a critical role in the "negative feedback loops."

Finally, we suggest that if a political commitment to reform and public buy-in can be obtained, then the path to tax reform in particular and the strengthening of fiscal institutions, in general, are relatively straightforward. For tax reform, we suggest that Caribbean countries should pursue four key objectives: (1) broaden the tax bases; (2) reduce statutory rates and tariffs consistent with a responsible fiscal situation; (3) simplify the tax system, including reducing tax expenditures, to facilitate compliance, enforcement and transparency; and (4) strengthen tax administration where the pursuance of these objectives is within the umbrella goals of increasing tax revenue towards obtaining the required primary fiscal balances to reduce public debt and simultaneously create a pro-growth, with equity, tax policy environment. Furthermore, given the poor state of tax administration across the region, including the lack of digitalization of basic processes and operations, it is suggested that pursuing digital transformation of tax and customs administrations can provide significant benefits for Caribbean countries. However, Caribbean countries would need to ensure that all the necessary legal and operational frameworks and I.T. infrastructure are established to support the region's tax administrations in the digital era. Tax reforms will need to be supported by more vital fiscal and public institutions if the region is to restore growth and debt sustainability.

References

Alesina, A., & Perotti, R. (1999). Budget deficits and budget institutions. In J. Poterba & J. von Hagen (Eds.), *Fiscal institutions and fiscal performance* (pp. 13–36). University of Chicago Press. https://www.nber.org/books-and-chapters/fiscal-institutions-and-fiscal-performance

Arias, L. (2016). *The revenue administrations in latin America and the Caribbean 2011–2013*. The Inter-American Center of Tax Administrations (CIAT).

Asik, G. A. (2013). *Stabilization funds in oil-rich countries and fiscal policy: (A) cyclicality*? London School of Economics.

Awasthi, R., & Engelschalk, M. (2018). *Taxation and the shadow economy: How the tax system can stimulate and enforce the formalization of business activities* (Policy Research Working Paper 8391). The World Bank. http://hdl.handle.net/10986/29603

Balin, B. J. (2009). *Sovereign wealth funds: A critical analysis* (Working Paper Series). Johns Hopkins University, School of Advanced International Studies (SAIS). https://doi.org/10.2139/ssrn.1477725

Bellon, M., Chang, J., Dabla-Norris, E., Khalid, S., Lima, F., Rojas, E., & Villena, P. (2019). Digitalization to improve tax compliance: Evidence from VAT e-Invoicing in Peru (Working Paper 231). International Monetary Fund. https://ssrn.com/abstract=3496709

Beuermann, D., & Pecha, C. (2018). Trust and institutions in Caribbean countries. In M. J. Schwartz and D. W. Beuermann (Eds.), *Economic institutions for a resilient Caribbean* (pp. 185–201). The Inter-American Development Bank. https://doi.org/10.18235/0003053

Beuermann D., & Schwartz, M. (2018). *Nurturing institutions for a resilient Caribbean*. Inter-American Development Bank. https://doi.org/10.18235/0001333

Bird, R. (1989). The administrative dimension of tax reform in developing countries. In M. Gillis (Ed.), *Tax reform in developing countries* (pp. 314–346). Duke University Press. https://www.dukeupress.edu/tax-reform-in-developing-countries

Brixi, H., Valenduc, C., & Swift, Z. (2004). *Tax expenditures shedding light on government spending through the tax system: Lessons from developed and transition economies*. The World Bank.

Butler, R. W. (1980). The concept of tourism area cycle of evolution: Implications for management of resources. *Canadian Geographer, 24*(1), 5–12. https://doi.org/10.1111/j.1541-0064.1980.tb00970.x

Casanegra de Jantscher, M. (1990). Administering the VAT. In M. Gillis, C. Shoup & G. Sicat (Eds.). *Value added taxation in developing countries* (pp. 171–179). The World Bank. https://digitallibrary.un.org/record/62986?ln=en

Elgin, C., & Birinci, S. (2016). Growth and informality: A comprehensive panel data analysis. *Journal of Applied Economics, 19*(2), 271–292. https://doi.org/10.1016/S1514-0326(16)30011-3

Fabrizio, S., & Mody, A. (2006). Can budget institutions counteract political indiscipline? *Economic Policy, 21*, 689–739.

Fan, H., Liu, Y., Qian, N., & Wen, J. (2020). *Computerizing VAT invoices in China* (NBER Working Paper No. 24414). National Bureau of Economic Research. https://www.nber.org/papers/w24414

Frankel, J. A., Vegh, C. A., & Vuletin, G. (2012). On graduation from fiscal procyclicality. *Journal of Development Economics, 100*(1), 32–47.

Giles, L., Gauto, V., & Khadan, J. (2021). Enhancing fiscal sustainability in resource-rich Caribbean countries. In M. J. Schwartz & D. W. Beuermann (Eds.). *Economic institutions for a resilient Caribbean* (pp. 297–337). The Inter-American Development Bank. https://doi.org/10.18235/0003053

Greenidge, K., & Whitehall, P. (2000). Tourism maturity and demand. In A. Maurin & P. Watson (Eds.), *Empirical studies in Caribbean economy* (pp. 161–189). Caribbean Centre for Monetary Studies.

Greenidge, K., Craigwell, R., Thomas, C., & Drakes, L. (2012). *Threshold effects of sovereign debt: Evidence from the Caribbean* (IMF Working Paper No. 12/157). International Monetary Fund. https://www.imf.org/external/pubs/ft/wp/2012/wp12157.pdf

Howell, H., & Reyes-Tagle, G. (2018). *Fiscal strengthening for economic growth program (SU-L1050) institutional capacity assessment*. Inter-American Development Bank.

Ilzetzki, E., Mendoza, E., & Végh, C. (2012). How big (small?) are fiscal multipliers? *Journal of Monetary Economics, 60*(2), 239–254.

International Monetary Fund (IMF). (2013a). Caribbean small states: Challenges of high debt and low growth. *Policy Papers*, 2013(0111). International Monetary Fund. https://doi.org/10.5089/9781498342261.007

International Monetary Fund (IMF). (2013b). *Fiscal monitor: Taxing times.* International Monetary Fund. https://www.imf.org/en/Publications/FM/Issues/2016/12/31/~/media/Websites/IMF/imported-flagship-issues/external/pubs/ft/fm/2013/02/pdf/_fm1302pdf.ashx

Khadan, J. (2019a). Fiscal sustainability in the Caribbean: An econometric analysis. *Research in Applied Economics, 11*(2), 1–25.

Khadan, J. (2019b). Tax buoyancy in the Caribbean: Evidence from heterogenous panel cointegration models. *Research in Applied Economics, 11*(4), 36–48.

Khadan, J., & Baxter, S. (2018). *Strengthening Guyana's fiscal framework in anticipation of an oil boom* (Policy Brief IDB-PB-290). Inter-American Development Bank. https://doi.org/10.18235/0001164

Mascagni, G., Mengistu, A., & Woldeyes, F. (2021). Can ICTs increase tax compliance? Evidence on taxpayer responses to technological innovation in Ethiopia. *Journal of Economic Behavior & Organization, 189*, 172–193.

Mcnabb, K. (2018). Tax structures and economic growth: New evidence from the government revenue dataset. *Journal of International Development, 30*(2018), 173–205.

Medina, L., & Schneider, F. (2017). *Shadow economies around the world: What did we learn over the last 20 years?* (IMF Working Paper 18/17). International Monetary Fund. https://doi.org/10.5089/9781484338636.001

Muyangwa M., Miller N., Bonner T., & van den Bosch, R. (2017). *Tax administration diagnostic assessment tool performance assessment report for*

Trinidad and Tobago. International Monetary Fund. https://www.finance.gov.tt/wp-content/uploads/2018/03/TADAT-December-2017-Report-on-Trinidad-and-Tobago-BIR-Performance.pdf

North, D. C. (1991). Institutions. *Journal of Economic Perspectives, 5*(1), 97–112.

OECD (Organization for Economic Co-operation and Development). (2017). *Shining light on the shadow economy: Opportunities and threats*. OECD Publishing. https://www.oecd.org/tax/crime/shining-light-on-the-shadow-economy-opportunities-and-threats.pdf

OECD (Organization for Economic Co-operation and Development). (2021). *Tax administration: Digital resilience in the COVID-19 environment*. OECD Publishing. https://read.oecd-ilibrary.org/view/?ref=1092_1092163-3s4b6i4lda&title=Tax-Administration-Digital-Resilience-in-the-COVID-19-Environment&_ga=2.162126396.1677442946.1635700742-1375029183.1616354716

Okunogbe, O., & Pouliquen, V. (2018). *Technology, taxation, and corruption: evidence from the introduction of electronic tax filing* (Policy Research Working Paper No. WPS 8452; Impact Evaluation series). The World Bank. http://hdl.handle.net/10986/29862

Ossowski, R. (2021). Sovereign wealth funds in resource-rich Caribbean countries. In M. J. Schwartz & D. W. Beuermann (Eds.), *Economic institutions for a resilient Caribbean* (pp. 241–295). The Inter-American Development Bank. https://doi.org/10.18235/0003053

Peters, A. (2017). *Estimating the size of the informal economy in Caribbean states* (IDB Technical Note No. 1248). Inter-American Development Bank. https://doi.org/10.18235/0000791

Radian, A. (1980). *Resource mobilization in poor countries-implementing tax policies*. New Transaction Books.

Reyes-Tagle, G., Silvani, C., & Ospina, L. (2021). The nuts and bolts of revenue administration in the Caribbean. In M. J. Schwartz & D. W. Beuermann (Eds.), *Economic institutions for a resilient Caribbean* (pp. 43–93). Inter-American Development Bank. https://doi.org/10.18235/0003053

Ruprah I., Melgarejo, K., & Sierra, R. (2014). *Is there a Caribbean sclerosis? stagnating economic growth in the Caribbean*. Inter-American Development Bank.

Talvi, E., & Végh, C. (2005). Tax base variability and procyclical fiscal policy in developing countries. *Journal of Development Economics, 78*, 156–190.

Tanzi, V., & Zee, H. (2001). *Tax policy for developing countries*. International Monetary Fund.

Van Parys, S., & James, S. (2010). The effectiveness of tax incentives in attracting investment: Panel data evidence from the CFA Franc zone. *International Tax and Public Finance, 17*, 400–429. https://doi.org/10.1007/s10797-010-9140-1

Veletin, G. (2008). *Measuring the informal economy in Latin America and the Caribbean* (Working Paper No. 08/102). International Monetary Fund. https://www.imf.org/en/Publications/WP/Issues/2016/12/31/Measuring-the-Informal-Economy-in-Latin-America-and-the-Caribbean-21898

Whitehall, P., & Craigwell, R. (2006). *Does tourism potential influence tourism demand in the Caribbean*. Research Department, Central Bank of Barbados.

World Bank. (1991). Tax Administration and tax reform: Reflections on experience. In Javad Khalilzadeh-Shirazi & Anwar Shah (Eds.), *Tax policy in developing countries* (pp. 38–56). World Bank.

World Bank. (2009). *A handbook for tax simplification*. The World Bank.

Wright, A., Grenade, K., & Scott-Joseph, A. (2017). *Fiscal rules: Towards a new paradigm for fiscal sustainability in small states* (IDB-WP-780). IDB Working Paper Series. Inter-American Development Bank.

Xing, J. (2012). Tax structure and growth: How robust is the empirical evidence? *Economics Letters, 117*(1), 379–382.

CHAPTER 6

Employment and Earnings Disparity: A Comparison of "Belongers" and "Non-Belongers" in the Turks and Caicos Islands

Amos C. Peters

Introduction

Although immigrants possess a variety of skills and useful attributes that contribute to the diversity of the host country, they are often stigmatized, discriminated against, and blamed for many of the problems in the host country. In general, there is a sense among many native-born residents that immigrants do not "belong." A large amount of literature has documented the labor market outcomes of immigrant populations (Borjas, 1994). However, because most migration corridors flow from the global

A. C. Peters (✉)
UCLA Institute of the Environment and Sustainability, California, USA
e-mail: amos.c.peters@gmail.com

C. Cannonier and M. Galloway Burke (eds.),
Contemporary Issues Within Caribbean Economies,
https://doi.org/10.1007/978-3-030-98865-4_6

South to the global North, these studies focus primarily on immigrant–native differentials in the United States and other developed countries. Peters and Sundaram (2015) offered three reasons that researchers should extend this literature by studying immigrant outcomes in developing host countries: (1) immigrant inflows to developing countries continue to rise as these countries transform their economies into engines of wealth and opportunity; (2) labor markets in developing countries are often characterized by labor market frictions that can aggravate issues related to labor market discrimination and impede the assimilation of foreign-born populations into the host country; and (3) developing countries frequently experience skills shortages, which can result in differential opportunities for immigrant labor, often by country of origin.

This study attempts to address this gap in the literature by analyzing the labor market outcomes of immigrants and natives in a developing small island state and seeks to identify and explore earnings and employment disparities by immigrant status, and among immigrants by country of birth. Turks and Caicos Islands (TCI) present an interesting case for studying this issue. TCI is a small British Overseas Territory (BOT) located southeast of The Bahamas and 190 miles north of Haiti. It comprises 40 islands and cays, six of which are permanently inhabited.[1] In 2016, the territory's population was just over 37,000 (Morlachetti, 2017). As early as the 1990s, TCI experienced dramatic increases in economic activity because of the rapid expansion of the tourism and offshore financial sectors. This economic transformation resulted in a substantial increase in the population, fueled largely by immigration from neighboring countries. The population of TCI is projected to reach 61,457 by 2027 (ECLAC, 2016). ECLAC's (2016) estimates suggest that net migration will account for 68% of this projected increase while the rate of natural increase will account for 32% of the growth.

Few countries experience population growth so dramatically driven by immigration, and even fewer have populations that are majority foreign-born. Further, in TCI the native-born population's resentment of immigrants is exacerbated by a complex and opaque system of naturalization that categorizes TCI "citizens" as Belongers and "non-citizens" as non-Belongers. Thus, TCI offers a unique case for studying migration and labor market outcomes. Using data from the 2012 Survey of

[1] Grand Turk (the capital), Salt Cay, South Caicos, Middle Caicos, North Caicos, and Providenciales.

Living Conditions, a component of the TCI Country Poverty Assessment survey, this study estimates standard earnings and employment equations to determine the existence and extent of labor market disparities by nativity in TCI.

Migration Sources

With a relatively high per capita income—currently over US$25,000—the Turks and Caicos Islands are among the richest nations in the Caribbean. In the 1990s, the TCI economy experienced a dramatic transformation as the tourism industry began to expand rapidly. Tourism expansion and the emergence of an offshore financial service sector stimulated a massive construction boom and, in turn, very high levels of economic growth (Thomas-Hope, 2011). As a direct result of the substantial increase in economic activity, the demand for labor increased. Higher-level positions were filled mainly by North Americans and the British, while Haitian migrant labor began to fill the demand for workers with lower-level skills (Thomas-Hope, 2011). The neighboring countries of the Dominican Republic and Haiti were sources of cheap labor at the onset of TCI's economic expansion and remain the primary sources of immigrant labor. Haiti is the poorest country in the Western Hemisphere and is only 190 miles from TCI. Given the large income differential between Haiti and TCI and the close proximity of the two countries, they form a natural migration corridor.

The Haiti–TCI migration flow has posed considerable challenges for TCI because migrants are entering a country with an extremely small population. The labor market has become highly segmented as migration flows in excess of labor demand have caused many migrants to take temporary and/or casual jobs, thus increasing the poverty level among the Haitian-born population. The Government of the Turks and Caicos (2000) found that TC Islanders often feel sandwiched between lowly paid Haitians willing to work in menial jobs and highly paid expatriates from North America and Europe who are more likely than native-born residents to have high-quality skills and training. This sentiment as well as the growing pressure that high levels of migration (particularly illegal migration) have placed on public services and infrastructure, have reduced social cohesion and contributed to environmental deterioration. Illegal migration, inadequate housing, overcrowding, environmental deterioration, and overburdened social services have led to negative perceptions of

Haitian immigrants, whom many native-born residents blame for most of the islands' problems (Thomas-Hope, 2011).

These negative perceptions, typically fueled by the arrival of undocumented Haitians attempting to enter TCI illegally, have given rise to discriminatory treatment and exploitation of vulnerable groups within the Haitian community (Thomas-Hope, 2011). For example, Thomas-Hope (2011) found that on the islands of Grand Turk, Providenciales, and South Caicos, 34.2%, 39.7%, and 40.0% of Haitian immigrants, respectively, felt either very welcome or somewhat welcome, suggesting that the majority of Haitian immigrants felt either unwelcome or not very welcome. Using a case study approach, Brown (2002) documented the experiences of Haitian migrants in TCI. He described the experiences of these migrants being physically present in TCI but living as aliens as "living in a place of 'inbetweenity'." The accounts Brown (2002) provided contain common themes of poverty, discrimination, and stigmatization of Haitians.

The scenario is complicated by an inadequacy of legal and administrative systems to regularize the status of persons born in TCI to foreign-born parents. TCI citizenship is not granted solely on birthplace and is not easily acquired by adults. Children born in TCI to parents who are not Belongers automatically inherit the nationality of their parents. If the parents are undocumented immigrants, then the children are too, which creates additional complications related to accessing education and other social services. Further, in several cases, even Haitian parents who were legal immigrants had great difficulty regularizing their children and the grounds for refusal were unclear (Thomas-Hope, 2011). Morlachetti (2017) conducted a comprehensive review of child migrants and the issue of statelessness and found that notwithstanding TCI's ratification of the Convention relating to the Status of Stateless Persons, the process of regularizing children born in TCI to migrant parents, and even the process of these children officially obtaining the same nationality status as their parents, is complex. Thus, children often remain without any nationality for long periods of time.

Data and Empirical Approach

The study used data from the 2012 Survey of Living Conditions, a component of the Turks and Caicos Islands Country Poverty Assessment survey conducted by the National Assessment Team (NAT)[2] and the Caribbean Development Bank. These data are the most recent[3] and comprehensive source of information available on labor market outcomes, in particular outcomes disaggregated by nativity. The final sample, after excluding children under the age of 15 and adults 66 years and older, consists of 1,142 TCIslanders.

Labor Market Outcomes

Two variables measure labor market outcomes. The first is the monthly earnings of working-age individuals (15–65 years old). This variable is continuous and transformed into natural logarithms. The second variable is a categorical measure of employment status, equal to 1 if the individual is employed either full-time or part-time, and equal to 0 otherwise.

Explanatory Variables

The key explanatory variables are Belonger status and non-Belonger status by country of birth. According to the Immigration Department of the Ministry of Border Control and Employment, a Belonger is an individual who is free from immigration restrictions in relation to the amount of time they may remain in the islands, having acquired Belonger status under the relevant law. Belonger status is acquired by a person who:

- was born in the Islands, and at the time of his birth at least one of his parents had Belonger status;
- was born outside the Islands and (i) at least one of his/her parents had Belonger status at the time of his birth; and (ii) at least one of his/her parents was born in the Islands;
- was born outside the Islands and lawfully adopted in the Islands by a person who had Belonger status at the time of his adoption;

[2] The NAT comprises both the government of the Turks and Caicos Islands and non-governmental organizations.

[3] A labor force survey was conducted in 2017 but the raw data are not publicly available.

- has been granted a Certificate of Belonger Status by the Governor for having made a significant social or economic contribution to the development of the islands.
- is the dependent child of a person to whom any of the foregoing paragraphs apply; or
- is the spouse of a Belonger who has made an application to the Governor in Cabinet, and has lived with his/her spouse for a period of five consecutive years.

The status of the British Overseas Territories as colonies of the United Kingdom entails legal distinctions that do not exist in independent countries. An individual can be a British Overseas Territories Citizen (BOTC) but not a Belonger and vice versa. Belonger status does not confer nationality and BOTC status does not confer freedom from immigration restrictions. In brief, Belonger status confers all the rights associated with citizenship, including the right to vote, except nationality, which can only be granted by the United Kingdom.

The Belonger variable is categorical and equal to 1 if the individual reports Belonger status and 0 otherwise. In addition, a set of three categorical variables were created to reflect Belonger status and country of birth, focusing on TCI and Haiti since most of the migrant population is from Haiti. The three variables are Belonger-Haiti (equal to 1 if the individual reports Belonger status and country of birth as Haiti and 0 otherwise), Belonger-TCI (equal to 1 if the individual reports Belonger status and country of birth as TCI and 0 otherwise), and Belonger-Other (equal to 1 for all respondents not included in the previous two categories who report Belonger status and 0 otherwise).

The analysis controls for demographic and socioeconomic characteristics that are likely to be related to earnings and employment outcomes, including age, educational attainment, marital status, household size, gender, and the island of residence.

Summary Statistics

Table 6.1 presents summary statistics for TCI Belongers and non-Belongers. The data show that on average Belongers earn more and have a higher likelihood of being formally employed than non-Belongers. Belongers report average monthly earnings of US$1,587.13 compared with US$1,213.48 for non-Belongers. Among working-age Belongers,

Table 6.1 Summary statistics, aggregated

	Belongers	*Non-Belongers*
Individual-level characteristics		
Monthly earnings (in US$)	1587.13	1213.48
	(1791.76)	(1803.50)
Employed	0.70	0.66
	(0.46)	(0.47)
Age (range: 15–65)	35.99	37.19
	(13.72)	(10.23)
Male	0.46	0.50
	(0.50)	(0.50)
Married	0.41	0.48
	(0.49)	(0.50)
Household size	3.72	2.99
	(1.89)	(1.96)
Highest level of education completed		
No schooling	0.01	0.04
	(0.10)	(0.18)
Primary	0.08	0.13
	(0.27)	(0.33)
Lower secondary	0.13	0.12
	(0.34)	(0.37)
Upper secondary	0.45	0.42
	(0.50)	(0.49)
Tertiary	0.30	0.23
	(0.46)	(0.42)
Island of residence		
Providenciales	0.63	0.81
	(0.48)	(0.39)
Grand Turk	0.25	0.12
	(0.43)	(0.32)
North Caicos	0.05	0.04
	(0.23)	(0.19)
South Caicos	0.06	0.03
	(0.23)	(0.16)
Salt Cay	0.00	0.00
	(0.07)	(0.06)
Middle Caicos	0.01	0.00
	(0.09)	(0.05)

Note Standard deviations are in parentheses

70% were employed compared with 66% among non-Belongers. Given that the two groups have very similar age and gender profiles, the source of this variation likely lies in the educational characteristics of each group. Educational attainment is generally high in TCI, with 30% of Belongers and 23% of non-Belongers having completed some post-high school education.

Table 6.2 presents descriptive statistics disaggregated by Belonger/non-Belonger status and country of birth. Haitian-born individuals constitute a substantive proportion of both the Belonger and non-Belonger populations. Among both Belongers and non-Belongers, the labor market attributes of those born in Haiti are distinct from those of people born in TCI. Among Belongers, the Haitian-born population earns an average of US$1,340.32 per month compared with US$1,493.78 for the TCI-born population, an 11.45% wage differential. Haitian-born Belongers have an employment rate of 78%, which is significantly higher than the 66% employment rate of TCI-born Belongers. The earnings gap is likely due to differences in several individual characteristics by country of birth. TCI-born Belongers are more educated than Haitian-born Belongers, with 30% of the former group reporting tertiary-level educational attainment compared with 22% of the latter group. In addition, Table 6.2 reveals an important gender differential—men account for 48% of TCI-born Belongers but only 38% of Haiti-born Belongers. Finally, the geographic distributions of the respective populations differ. TCI-born Belongers are much more evenly distributed across the Turks and Caicos Islands, with 60% living in Providenciales, 26% living in Grand Turk, and 7% living in North Caicos. In contrast, Haitian-born Belongers are much more concentrated in Providenciales, with 78% living in Providenciales, 10% living in Grand Turk, and 8% living in South Caicos.

Non-Belongers also display a significant degree of within-group variation by country of birth. On average, TCI-born non-Belongers earn US$513.90 per month compared with US$716.12 per month for Haitian-born non-Belongers. This differential might be due to the large difference in average age by country of birth. TCI-born non-Belongers have an average age of 21.12 compared with 37.53 for Haitian-born non-Belongers. Haitian-born non-Belongers have an employment rate of 59% compared with a rate of 33% for TCI-born non-Belongers. Both TCI-born and Haitian-born non-Belongers are geographically concentrated in Providenciales (94 and 80%, respectively).

Table 6.2 Summary statistics disaggregated by place of birth

	Belongers				*Non-Belongers*			
	TCI	*Haiti*	*Dom. Rep*	*Other*	*TCI*	*Haiti*	*Dom. Rep*	*Other*
Individual-level characteristics								
Monthly earnings (in US$)	1493.78	1340.32	1645.30	2118.41	513.90	716.12	945.00	2280.44
	(1330.22)	(1635.82)	(1428.41)	(3106.55)	(657.44)	(676.02)	(761.82)	(2808.75)
Employed	0.66	0.78	1.00	0.75	0.33	0.59	0.80	0.80
	(0.47)	(0.42)	(0.00)	(0.44)	(0.49)	(0.49)	(0.40)	(0.40)
Age (range: 15–65)	35.59	37.47	30.74	36.99	21.12	37.53	34.67	39.12
	(14.29)	(12.60)	(11.8)	(12.07	(7.64)	(9.97)	(6.59)	(10.40)
Male	0.48	0.32	0.37	0.50	0.72	0.50	0.44	0.47
	(0.50)	(0.47)	(0.53)	(0.50)	(0.46)	(0.50)	(0.50)	(0.50)
Married	0.38	0.56	0.60	0.41	0.05	0.50	0.30	0.53
	(0.49)	(0.50)	(0.54)	(0.50)	(0.22)	(0.50)	(0.46)	(0.50)
Household size	3.82	3.64	2.84	3.33	7.02	3.00	2.38	2.73
	(1.90)	(2.25)	(1.44)	(1.54)	(3.26)	(1.93)	(1.73)	(1.30)
Highest level of education completed								
No schooling	0.02	0.00	0.00	0.00	0.00	0.05	0.02	0.01
	(0.12)	(0.00)	(0.00)	(0.00)	(0.00)	(0.22)	(0.15)	(0.09)
Primary	0.08	0.13	0.12	0.04	0.09	0.20	0.06	0.03
	(0.27)	(0.34)	(0.35)	(0.20)	(0.30)	(0.40)	(0.23)	(0.16)
Lower secondary	0.14	0.18	0.12	0.07	0.28	0.17	0.16	0.01
	(0.34)	(0.39)	(0.35)	(0.26)	(0.46)	(0.37)	(0.37)	(0.11)
Upper secondary	0.43	0.43	0.76	0.51	0.32	0.44	0.53	0.35
	(0.50)	(0.50)	(0.47)	(0.50)	(0.48)	(0.50)	(0.50)	(0.48)
Tertiary	0.30	0.22	0.00	0.34	0.24	0.06	0.19	0.57
	(0.46)	(0.42)	(0.00)	(0.48)	(0.44)	(0.24)	(0.39)	(0.50)

(continued)

Table 6.2 (continued)

	Belongers				*Non-Belongers*			
	TCI	*Haiti*	*Dom. Rep*	*Other*	*TCI*	*Haiti*	*Dom. Rep*	*Other*
Island of residence								
Providenciales	0.60	0.78	0.56	0.63	0.94	0.80	0.71	0.85
	(0.49)	(0.42)	(0.54)	(0.49)	(0.25)	(0.40)	(0.46)	(0.36)
Grand Turk	0.26	0.10	0.35	0.29	0.06	0.10	0.23	0.12
	(0.44)	(0.31)	(0.52)	(0.46)	(0.25)	(0.30)	(0.43)	(0.33)
North Caicos	0.07	0.02	0.00	0.03	0.00	0.05	0.01	0.03
	(0.25)	(0.14)	(0.00)	(0.18)	(0.00)	(0.22)	(0.12)	(0.16)
South Caicos	0.06	0.08	0.08	0.04	0.00	0.04	0.03	0.00
	(0.23)	(0.28)	(0.31)	(0.19)	(0.00)	(0.19)	(0.19)	(0.07)
Salt Cay	0.01	0.00	0.00	0.00	0.00	0.00	0.01	0.00
	(0.07)	(0.06)	(0.00)	(0.00)	(0.00)	(0.05)	(0.08)	(0.06)
Middle Caicos	0.01	0.01	0.00	0.01	0.00	0.00	0.00	0.00
	(0.10)	(0.09)	(0.00)	(0.07)	(0.00)	(0.07)	(0.00)	(0.00)

Note Standard deviations are in parentheses. Population weights are applied

There are also differences in education by Belonger/non-Belonger status within country of birth for Haitians. Among those born in Haiti, Belongers and non-Belongers have markedly different education profiles. Only 6% of Haitian-born non-Belongers have tertiary education, which is substantially lower than the 22% of Haitian-born Belongers with this level of education. Further, 42% of the former group have less than a high school education compared with 31% of the latter group. In contrast, among those born in TCI, the educational profiles of Belongers and non-Belongers are similar, suggesting that the differences in the labor market characteristics of these groups might be driven largely by age.

Figure 6.1 shows educational attainment by country of birth for the full focal sample (Belongers and non-Belongers). The modal educational category for those born in TCI, Haiti, and Jamaica is upper secondary education. In addition, a significant number of Haitians reported lower secondary or primary level education as the highest level completed, while a significant proportion of TCI-born individuals have completed some type of post-secondary education. The modal educational attainment level for individuals born in other countries, the majority of whom are from North America and the United Kingdom, is a bachelor's degree.

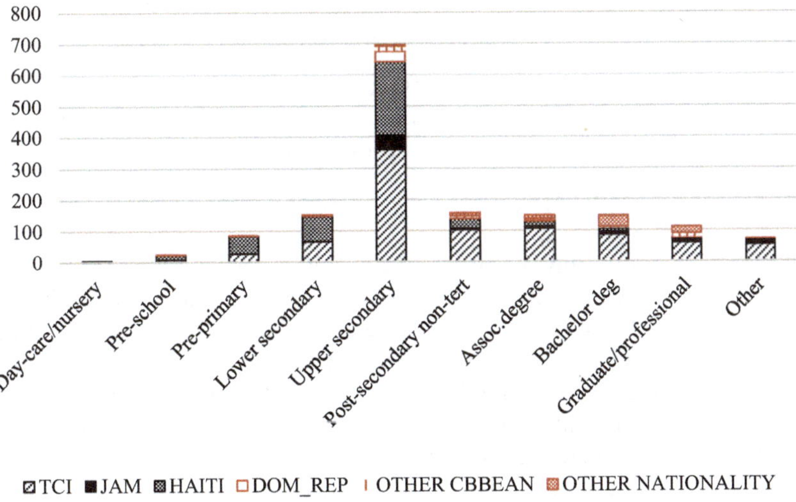

Fig. 6.1 Educational attainment by nationality

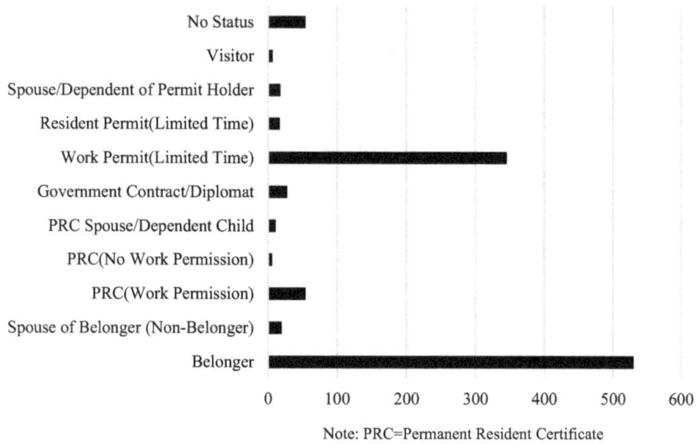

Fig. 6.2 Residence status in the Turks and Caicos Islands

Figure 6.2 shows the distribution of the residence status in the sample. The modal groups are Belongers and individuals with limited-time work permits.

Empirical Approach

This study focuses on two outcomes: earnings and employment. To determine the relationship between immigration status and monthly earnings, a standard Mincer wage equation was estimated as follows:

$$W_i = \beta_0 + \beta_1 \text{BELONGER}_i + \delta_1 D_i + \delta_2 S_i + \delta_3 \text{ISLAND}_i + u_i \quad (6.1)$$

where W_i is monthly earnings, $\text{BELONGER}_i$is a set of categorical variables that denote immigration status, D_i is a vector of individual demographic characteristics, S_i is a vector of individual and household socioeconomic factors, and ISLAND_i is a categorical variable that indicates island of residence. The disturbance term, u_i, includes unobservable characteristics such as motivation, ability, and family background. All models were estimated using ordinary least squares. The employment model was estimated using the following specification:

$$\text{EMPL}_i = \beta_0 + \beta_1 \text{BELONGER}_i + \delta_1 D_i + \delta_2 S_i + \delta_3 \text{ISLAND}_i + u_i \quad (6.2)$$

where $EMPL_i$ is the probability of employment, and all other variables are as previously defined. OLS linear probability models were used to estimate the probability of employment.

Results

The results of models that estimate the relationship between Belonger status and the two labor market outcomes—monthly earnings and employment—are presented first. Next, the results of disaggregated models that estimate the relationship between Belonger status by country of birth and the same labor market outcome variables are reported.

The results in Table 6.3 show that Belonger status has a positive and statistically significant effect on earnings. Belongers earn 29.1% more than their non-Belonger counterparts after controlling for all observable characteristics. This disparity is quite sizeable and reflects a substantial benefit for Belongers. Adding the control variables did little to reduce the income disparity, which is only slightly smaller in the multivariate results than in the descriptive statistics (30.8%). This pattern could indicate that discrimination against non-Belongers is responsible for a large part of the disparity. The results also show a statistically significant and sizeable gender gap in income. Models 1–3 show that men earn between 14.1 and 14.6% more than women. After controlling for occupation, the gender gap widens to 20.9%, a result that strongly suggests gender discrimination in the Turks and Caicos Islands labor market. As expected, completing tertiary education has a positive and significant impact on earnings in the first three models. After controlling for occupation, the coefficient for tertiary education remains positive but is no longer statistically significant, indicating a high correlation between tertiary educational attainment and occupational category. The skills coefficient is also suggestive of such a correlation as individuals engaged in skilled labor earn more than those engaged in unskilled labor. In addition, individuals with skills training to improve their job performance have higher monthly earnings than those without such training. The coefficients for the island of residence reflect patterns of development and urbanization in the Turks and Caicos Islands. Those who live in Providenciales and Grand Turks have significantly higher earnings than those living in North Caicos (the reference category).

Table 6.3 Multivariate model of earnings and employment by Belonger status

	Earnings				*Employment*		
	(1)	*(2)*	*(3)*	*(4)*	*(5)*	*(6)*	*(7)*
Individual-level characteristics							
Belonger status	0.360***	0.345***	0.326***	0.291***	0.0648**	0.0574*	0.0524*
	(0.0622)	(0.0611)	(0.0608)	(0.0654)	(0.0301)	(0.0299)	(0.0297)
Age (log)	1.712	1.587	0.736	2.325	5.700***	5.689***	5.534***
	(2.208)	(2.200)	(2.207)	(2.063)	(0.694)	(0.690)	(0.685)
Age squared (log)	– 0.182	–0.168	–0.0498	–0.276	–0.785***	–0.786***	–0.764***
	(0.315)	(0.314)	(0.315)	(0.290)	(0.102)	(0.101)	(0.100)
Male	0.143**	0.146**	0.141**	0.209***	0.0539*	0.0522*	0.0504*
	(0.0595)	(0.0594)	(0.0577)	(0.0567)	(0.0308)	(0.0306)	(0.0305)
Married	0.0543	0.0449	0.0245	0.0537	–0.0115	–0.0171	–0.0234
	(0.0622)	(0.0627)	(0.0606)	(0.0566)	(0.0340)	(0.0338)	(0.0339)
Educational attainment							
Primary	–0.386*	–0.400**	–0.413**	–0.403**	0.133	0.127	0.124
	(0.199)	(0.197)	(0.194)	(0.169)	(0.126)	(0.127)	(0.127)
Lower secondary	–0.0161	–0.0466	–0.0569	–0.180	0.108	0.0931	0.0907
	(0.180)	(0.179)	(0.176)	(0.159)	(0.125)	(0.125)	(0.125)
Upper secondary	0.179	0.125	0.0922	–0.0369	0.269**	0.236**	0.228*
	(0.160)	(0.160)	(0.157)	(0.153)	(0.117)	(0.119)	(0.119)
Tertiary	0.737***	0.648***	0.523***	0.214	0.430***	0.369***	0.323***
	(0.167)	(0.171)	(0.168)	(0.159)	(0.117)	(0.119)	(0.120)
Training		0.136**	0.131**	0.122**		0.106***	0.101***
		(0.0630)	(0.0610)	(0.0557)		(0.0330)	(0.0326)
Skilled			0.407***	0.215**			0.180***
			(0.0829)	(0.103)			(0.0244)

	Earnings				*Employment*		
	(1)	*(2)*	*(3)*	*(4)*	*(5)*	*(6)*	*(7)*
Occupational Dummies				Yes			
Island of residence							
Providenciales	0.494***	0.500***	0.512***	0.431***	-0.0380	-0.0357	-0.0320
	(0.0897)	(0.0888)	(0.0886)	(0.0898)	(0.0407)	(0.0403)	(0.0400)
Grand Turk	0.270***	0.276***	0.300***	0.231**	0.0398	0.0404	0.0460
	(0.0990)	(0.0978)	(0.0970)	(0.0982)	(0.0429)	(0.0427)	(0.0426)
South Caicos	−0.606***	−0.594***	−0.543***	−0.640***	0.0718	0.0776	0.0925*
	(0.155)	(0.153)	(0.153)	(0.157)	(0.0527)	(0.0526)	(0.0526)
Salt Cay	−0.0173	−0.0201	0.0103	0.0214	−0.0100	−0.0114	−0.00115
	(0.191)	(0.181)	(0.173)	(0.161)	(0.112)	(0.110)	(0.109)
Middle Caicos	−0.522***	−0.533***	−0.493***	−0.451**	0.0246	0.0197	0.0317
	(0.155)	(0.160)	(0.159)	(0.206)	(0.138)	(0.136)	(0.136)
Constant	2.433	2.694	4.225	2.106	−9.862***	−9.817***	−9.546***
	(3.875)	(3.860)	(3.863)	(3.686)	(1.189)	(1.183)	(1.176)
Observations	741	741	741	656	1,072	1,072	1,072
R^2	0.340	0.346	0.370	0.461	0.207	0.217	0.228

Robust standard errors in parentheses. Reference categories: No Schooling and North Caicos
*** $p < 0.01$, ** $p < 0.05$, * $p < 0.1$

Belonger status is also associated with the probability of employment. Table 6.3 shows that Belongers have a 5.2–6.5% higher probability of being employed than non-Belongers.

Age (which can be viewed as a crude proxy for experience) has the expected inverted-U relationship with employment. Men have a 5.0–5.4% higher probability of being employed than women, but this effect is only significant at the $p < 0.10$ level. The highest levels of educational attainment, particularly completing upper secondary and tertiary-level education, have large and statistically significant positive relationships with the probability of employment. Both, having a skilled job and having training, are associated with a higher probability of being employed.

The results reported in Table 6.3 offer initial support for the hypothesis that there are labor market advantages associated with Belonger status. However, these models mask fundamental migration issues. Thus, additional analyses disaggregated by Belonger status and country of birth were conducted. The two major country of birth groups are the Turks and Caicos Islands and Haiti. Other migrants come from the Dominican Republic, other Caribbean countries, the United Kingdom, the United States, and Canada. Because of the small sample size, these other countries were grouped into an "Other" category. Table 6.4 presents the results of these disaggregated models. The dominant group, Belongers born in TCI, is the reference category. The results show that after controlling for all available observables, there is no statistically significant difference between the earnings of Belongers born in Haiti and Belongers born in TCI. Further, there is no statistically significant difference between the earnings of Belongers born in other countries and TCI-born Belongers. In Models 3 and 4, the coefficients for Belonger/Haiti and Belonger/Other are negative, whereas in Models 1 and 2, the coefficient for Belonger/Other is positive. All non-Belonger groups have statistically significant negative coefficients. These results are robust to the inclusion of all available observable characteristics. Focusing on Model 4, relative to Belongers born in TCI, non-Belongers born in TCI earn 70.5% less, while non-Belongers born in Haiti earn 48.1% less, and non-Belongers born in other countries earn 20.9% less. The results for the independent variables are comparable to those presented in Table 6.2.

When the country of birth is controlled, the effect of Belonger status on the probability of employment diminishes and is no longer statistically insignificant. Belongers born in Haiti and other countries have

Table 6.4 Multivariate model of employment and earnings by Belonger status and country of birth

	Earnings				*Employment*		
	(1)	*(2)*	*(3)*	*(4)*	*(5)*	*(6)*	*(7)*
Individual-level characteristics							
Belonger/Haiti	−0.135	−0.117	−0.0675	−0.162	0.0978	0.109	0.126*
	(0.130)	(0.130)	(0.128)	(0.121)	(0.0782)	(0.0760)	(0.0760)
Belonger/other	0.0345	0.0161	−0.0140	−0.112	0.0577	0.0505	0.0379
	(0.131)	(0.130)	(0.137)	(0.154)	(0.0519)	(0.0496)	(0.0488)
Non-Belonger/TCI	−0.614***	−0.652***	−0.650***	−0.705***	−0.127	−0.139	−0.136
	(0.197)	(0.178)	(0.192)	(0.213)	(0.110)	(0.109)	(0.107)
Non-Belonger/Haiti	−0.573***	−0.556***	−0.516***	−0.481***	−0.0712*	−0.0613	−0.0480
	(0.0746)	(0.0740)	(0.0731)	(0.0750)	(0.0414)	(0.0410)	(0.0411)
Non-Belonger/other	−0.179**	−0.164**	−0.168**	−0.209***	0.000880	0.00848	0.00439
	(0.0714)	(0.0710)	(0.0694)	(0.0697)	(0.0393)	(0.0393)	(0.0389)
Age (log)	1.184	1.018	0.356	1.890	5.543***	5.489***	5.318***
	(2.109)	(2.102)	(2.115)	(1.966)	(0.725)	(0.717)	(0.714)
Age squared (log)	−0.113	−0.0922	−0.000259	−0.218	−0.764***	−0.759***	−0.735***
	(0.300)	(0.299)	(0.301)	(0.276)	(0.106)	(0.105)	(0.104)
Male	0.141**	0.145**	0.145**	0.198***	0.0572*	0.0561*	0.0557*
	(0.0588)	(0.0587)	(0.0574)	(0.0571)	(0.0310)	(0.0308)	(0.0306)
Married	0.0705	0.0605	0.0379	0.0625	−0.0101	−0.0161	−0.0243
	(0.0609)	(0.0614)	(0.0600)	(0.0568)	(0.0341)	(0.0339)	(0.0340)
Educational attainment							
Primary	−0.389*	−0.403*	−0.414*	−0.430**	0.131	0.124	0.119
	(0.219)	(0.217)	(0.213)	(0.168)	(0.127)	(0.127)	(0.127)
Lower secondary	−0.0687	−0.0977	−0.103	−0.240	0.102	0.0877	0.0856
	(0.203)	(0.201)	(0.196)	(0.158)	(0.125)	(0.125)	(0.126)

(continued)

Table 6.4 (continued)

	Earnings				*Employment*		
	(1)	*(2)*	*(3)*	*(4)*	*(5)*	*(6)*	*(7)*
Upper secondary	0.0756	0.0246	0.00429	−0.123	0.254**	0.222*	0.217*
	(0.187)	(0.186)	(0.180)	(0.153)	(0.118)	(0.119)	(0.119)
Tertiary	0.534***	0.451**	0.362*	0.0867	0.398***	0.338***	0.300**
	(0.194)	(0.196)	(0.191)	(0.160)	(0.119)	(0.121)	(0.122)
Training		0.132**	0.132**	0.126**		0.106***	0.103***
		(0.0607)	(0.0591)	(0.0539)		(0.0331)	(0.0327)
Skilled			0.356***	0.182*			0.181***
			(0.0811)	(0.102)			(0.0265)
Occupational Dummies				Yes			
Island of residence							
Providenciales	0.499***	0.504***	0.514***	0.444***	−0.0439	−0.0413	-0.0378
	(0.0883)	(0.0874)	(0.0871)	(0.0879)	(0.0407)	(0.0404)	(0.0401)
Grand Turk	0.246**	0.254***	0.279***	0.217**	0.0334	0.0344	0.0415
	(0.0976)	(0.0966)	(0.0961)	(0.0966)	(0.0426)	(0.0425)	(0.0426)
South Caicos	−0.557***	−0.546***	−0.508***	−0.628***	0.0709	0.0760	0.0893*
	(0.148)	(0.147)	(0.148)	(0.153)	(0.0532)	(0.0532)	(0.0531)
Salt Cay	0.0309	0.0256	0.0434	0.0318	−0.00963	−0.0116	−0.00262
	(0.166)	(0.158)	(0.155)	(0.148)	(0.115)	(0.113)	(0.111)
Middle Caicos	−0.497***	−0.509***	−0.479***	−0.462**	0.0271	0.0228	0.0349
	(0.136)	(0.138)	(0.139)	(0.193)	(0.143)	(0.141)	(0.141)
Constant	3.913	4.230	5.389	3.311	−9.507***	−9.395***	−9.104***
	(3.695)	(3.683)	(3.697)	(3.507)	(1.236)	(1.223)	(1.218)
Observations	742	742	742	657	1,073	1,073	1,073
R^2	0.372	0.377	0.395	0.480	0.212	0.222	0.233

Robust standard errors in parentheses. Reference categories: Belonger/TCI, No Schooling, and North Caicos
$^{***}p < 0.01$, $^{**}p < 0.05$, $^{*}p < 0.1$

positive coefficients and in Model 4 the coefficient for Belonger/Haiti indicates a statistically significant 12.6% higher probability of employment than Belongers born in TCI. All non-Belonger groups have negative coefficients (i.e., they are less likely to be employed than TCI-born Belongers).

Figure 6.3 is a pictorial representation of the results of Models 3 and 7 in Table 6.4. Figures 6.4 and 6.5 show the education–earnings and education–employment gradients, respectively, for the six Belonger/country of birth groups. The gradients were computed using the predicted values of the dependent variable at the grand mean of each independent variable across education levels.

Figure 6.4 shows that across all educational categories except no schooling, the education–earnings gradient is positive, meaning that higher levels of education are associated with higher earnings for all Belonger/Country of Birth groups. The notable exception is that an extremely small group of individuals (under 1% of the sample in most

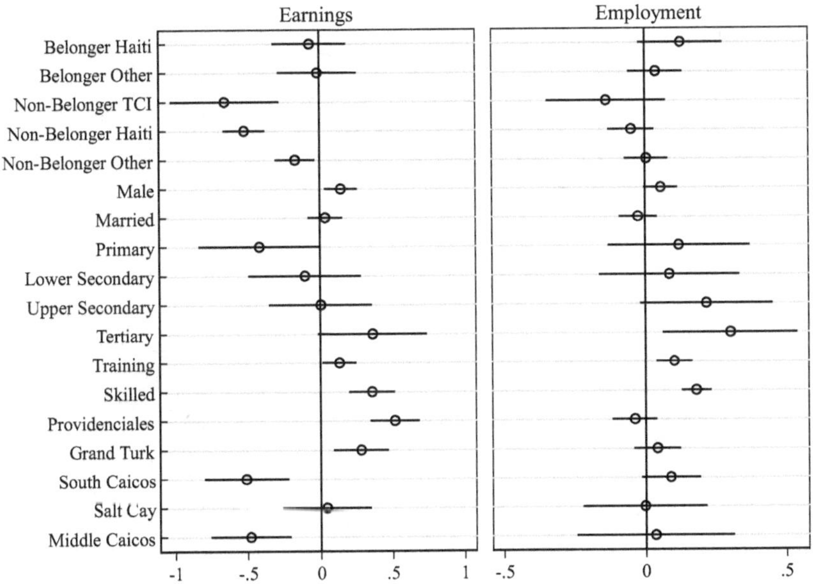

Fig. 6.3 Results of Models 3 and 7 (Belonger/Haiti and Belonger/other): earnings and employment

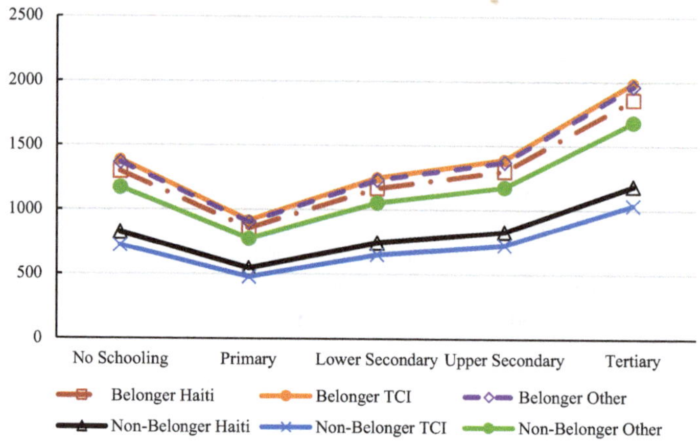

Fig. 6.4 Education–earnings gradients by Belonger status and country of birth

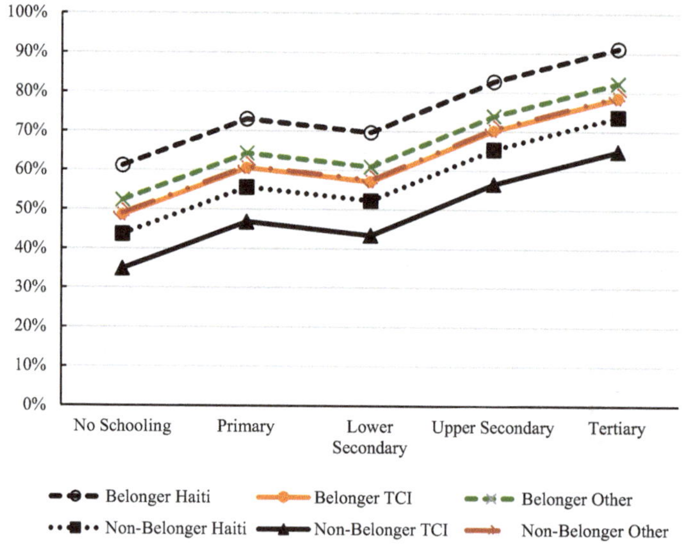

Fig. 6.5 Education–employment gradients by Belonger status and country of birth

cases) with no formal education outperform those whose highest level of educational attainment is primary or lower secondary, perhaps due to the fact that this group is dominant in the informal sector, where skills (and earnings) are not as directly linked to formal education as obtained in the formal sector. Belongers born in TCI are at the top of the earnings distribution followed by Belongers born in other countries; however, these two groups are statistically indistinguishable. The third group in the earnings hierarchy is Belongers born in Haiti. The groups at the bottom of the hierarchy are all non-Belongers. Non-Belongers born in other countries outperform non-Belongers born in Haiti, who, in turn, outperform non-Belongers born in the TCI. Average monthly earnings diverge at higher levels of education, a pattern that is highly suggestive of differential returns to education across groups. The main divergence is between one category consisting of Belongers born anywhere and non-Belongers born in other countries (i.e., not Haiti or TCI) and a second category consisting of non-Belongers born in Haiti and TCI. The latter two groups have a much flatter education–earnings trajectory than their counterparts.

Figure 6.5 shows that the education–employment gradient is positive for all groups, indicating that higher employment probabilities are associated with higher levels of education. Across all educational categories, Belongers outperform non-Belongers. In the hierarchy of employment probability, Belongers born in Haiti are most likely to be employed, followed by Belongers born in other countries and then Belongers born in TCI. Non-Belongers born in other countries and Belongers born in TCI come next and are indistinguishable.

Non-Belongers born in Haiti have the fifth-lowest probability of employment across all levels of education. Finally, non-Belongers born in TCI have a much lower probability of being employed than any other group. There is no discernible convergence or divergence across educational categories, which suggests persistent and structural differences in employment by Belonger status/country of birth group.

Discussion and Conclusion

This chapter examined the impact of Belonger status and country of birth on labor market outcomes in the Turks and Caicos Islands. The key findings suggest that there are labor market advantages associated with Belonger status. Belongers are more likely to be employed and earn more, on average, than non-Belongers. Controlling for observable characteristics (such as age, gender, marriage, education, training and skills, and the island of residence) widened the Belonger–non-Belonger gaps in both earnings and employment relative to the corresponding raw mean differentials. A pay gap between two groups of individuals can usually be explained by differences in education, training, and experience but in this instance after accounting for such differences, the pay gap between Belongers and non-Belongers increases. Under these conditions, if a Belonger and non-Belonger had identical years of education, training, and experience (among other endowments), their labor market rewards would differ. This pattern suggests there are differential returns to key observable characteristics such as education. Any number of interpretations can be assigned to this phenomenon, for example, it could indicate differences in the quality of education which is not directly observed in the data or it could also support the existence of discrimination in the labor market. In addition, there are also notable gender gaps in both wages and employment.

A subsequent analysis that disaggregated Belongers and non-Belongers by country of birth also showed a Belonger earnings advantage that increased with higher levels of educational attainment. This divergence is indicative of a labor market characterized by differential returns to education, especially with respect to non-Belongers from Haiti and non-Belongers born in TCI, many of whom have Haitian heritage. Country of birth was more important for earnings at higher levels of education than at lower levels of education, which suggests the existence of frictions in the labor market or "brain waste." Non-Belongers of Haitian origin or their children TCI-born children TCI who have high levels of education are in lower paying jobs compared with Belongers and their non-Belonger counterparts from other origin countries. The earnings hierarchy suggests that two groups—those born in Haiti and those born in TCI who have Haitian parents and are non-Belongers—have a clear labor market disadvantage. While acquiring Belonger status greatly improves earnings, Haitian-born Belongers appear to have lower earnings than Belongers born in other countries, although these results are not statistically robust. The findings for employment follow a similar pattern—Belongers have an employment advantage relative to non-Belongers. However, the hierarchy of employment probabilities differs from the hierarchy of earnings. Belongers who were born in Haiti are more likely to be employed than any other group. Within Belonger status, there seems to be a preference for foreign-born workers. Mirroring the earnings results, non-Belongers who were born in TCI are considerably less likely to be employed than any other group.

TCI is a small labor market with unique characteristics. It is dominated by immigrant and expatriate labor (members of both groups are foreign-born). Immigrants are largely from neighboring Caribbean countries, in particular Haiti, which accounts for the largest immigration stream. Expatriates are mostly from the United Kingdom, the United States, and Canada. Because being born in TCI does not confer Belonger status if neither parent is a Belonger, these migration patterns have given rise to a group of people who were born in TCI to Haitian parents but do not have Belonger status, a group that is somewhat akin to Dreamers in the United States.[4] The evidence presented in this chapter suggests that this group is subject to significant labor market disadvantages. These results are consistent with the work of Morlachetti (2017), who identified a pattern of discrimination against TCI-born children of non-TC Islander parents. He related this discrimination to the TCI constitution, which, notwithstanding its guarantee of fundamental rights and freedoms without distinction of any kind, provisions for equal protection under the law, and protections against discrimination, allows for different treatment with respect to "persons who are not Turks and Caicos Islanders." Moreover, Morlachetti (2017) found that a significant proportion of children from the Dominican Republic and Haiti were excluded from school, whether due to discriminatory practices (which are strictly prohibited by the Education Ordinance) or an overburdened education system.

Relative to Belongers born in TCI, Haitian immigrants are more likely to be employed and yet earn less, whereas expatriates earn more. Overall, the results indicate that Belonger status offers persistent advantages and that in TCI, labor market rewards are not well aligned with skills or human capital accumulation. This finding suggests a high degree of labor market segmentation and the possible existence of discriminatory practices in the TCI labor market.

[4] Dreamers were born outside the United States and migrated illegally as children.

References

Borjas, G. (1994). The economics of immigration. *Journal of Economic Literature, 32*(4), 1667–1717.

Brown, D. (2002, July1–3). *Inbetweenity: Marginalisation, migration and poverty among Haitians in the Turks and Caicos Islands* [Conference Paper]. The Society for Caribbean Studies Annual Conference Papers, Volume 3 (S. Courtman, Ed.), University of Warwick, UK. http://community-languages.org.uk/SCS-Papers/olv3p14.PDF

Economic Commission for Latin America and the Caribbean [ECLAC]. (2016, July 20). *The development of population projections for the Turks and Caicos Islands 2012–2027* (LC/CARL.501). https://www.cepal.org/en/publications/40406-development-population-projections-turks-and-caicos-islands-2012-2027

Government of the Turks and Caicos. (2000). *TCI draft final poverty assessment report*. Author.

Morlachetti, A. (2017). *Study on children in situations of migration and statelessness in the Caribbean UK overseas territories*. UNICEF Office for the Eastern Caribbean Area. https://www.unicef.org/easterncaribbean/media/1236/file/ECA-Statelessness-in-the-OTs-Report-doc-2017.pdf

Peters, A., & Sundaram, A. (2015). Country of origin and employment prospects among immigrants: An analysis of south-south and north-south migrants to South Africa. *Applied Economics Letters, 22*(17), 1415–1418.

Thomas-Hope, E. (2011). *The characteristics and impact of Haitian migration in the Turks and Caicos Islands*. International Organisation for Migration.

CHAPTER 7

Exchange Rate and Inflation Dynamics, and Monetary Policy in Haiti

Yves Nithder Pierre

Introduction and Background

Inflation is relatively strong and persistent in Haiti, a small and open developing country with deep-rooted economic, political, and social problems contributing to its weak growth and low saving rates over the last 40 years. Indeed, since the late 1990s, the Haitian economy has presented two high inflation episodes experienced from 1995 to 1998 and 2003 to 2006 with an average rate of 17.3% and 23.2%, respectively. The inflation process is fed by a permanent monetary expansion, which is consistent with standard theory and linked to the monetization of government budget deficit. In parallel, the monetary effect is amplified and somewhat distorted by many other factors such as inflation inertia, price-setting behavior in the stagnating economy and by the effects of

Y. N. Pierre (✉)
Central Bank of Haiti (BRH), Money and Economic Analysis Department, Port-au-Prince, Haiti
e-mail: yves-nithder.pierre@brh.ht

C. Cannonier and M. Galloway Burke (eds.),
Contemporary Issues Within Caribbean Economies,
https://doi.org/10.1007/978-3-030-98865-4_7

changes in relative prices. Regarding the effects of relative prices, the most significant ones are those associated with the pass-through of foreign exchange (FX) rate on the consumer price index (CPI) which is the main gauge of overall price in the economy.

The money creation derived from central bank financing of the fiscal deficit has become chronic in Haiti and has resulted in an environment of high liquidity. During the 1980s, the country has suffered the economic consequences of numerous shocks, including political instability, which have led to a persistent decline in economic activity and exports revenue. In addition, the government kept implementing some infrastructure projects that began in 1979, requiring substantial budgetary outlays which have significantly worsened the country's fiscal position through outsized budget deficits.[1] In parallel, a significant decrease in external financing was recorded due to noncompliance with some conditionalities. As a matter of fact, the World Bank's initially postponed the second disbursement under the Economic Recovery Credit approved in 1987 and then the credit was canceled in September 1988 (International Monetary Fund (IMF) Staff Report for the Haiti Article IV Consultation, 1989). Monetary financing has increased as a result of tax revenue shortfalls and a decline in external financial assistance without appropriate adjustments in public expenditures. Although central bank lending to the government should have been a certain amount and temporary as imbedded in the law, it has been used over years.[2] Thus, the central bank balance sheet expanded and government spending resulted in a steady expansion and sustained liquidity inflows in domestic currency in the financial system, that have been affecting prices and foreign exchange rate level in a context of structural impediments to private credit growth.[3] Figure 7.1 illustrates the fact that for many years, liquidity in the banking system has been driven mostly by the credit to central government.

[1] The government launched many projects including a Fishing Project (SPIA), an edible oil Project SODEXOL and a Sugar Plant Darbonne.

[2] In the law of August 17th, 1979, creating the central bank of Haiti, the Bank of Republic of Haiti (BRH), the articles 41, 43, and 45 clearly express that the central bank can lend to the government. However, such advances may not exceed 20% of the amount of the tax revenue collected during the previous year. In addition, they must be repaid within 180 days.

[3] In 2018, the private credit-deposit ratio was 39%. In terms of GDP, private credit accounted only for 16.5%.

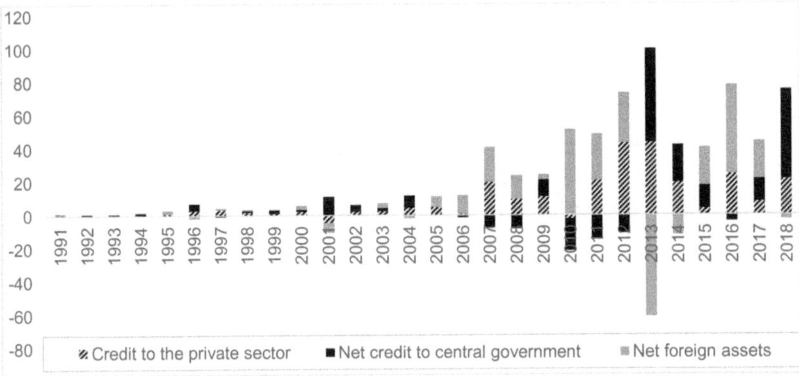

Fig. 7.1 Sources of liquidity in the Haitian financial system (Growth Decomposition of M3, in percent). *Source* Bank of Republic of Haiti (BRH) and author's calculations

In the second half of the 1980s, fiscal dominance coupled with the decline in export and tourism revenue, and administrative measures on export receipts led to the collapse of the fixed exchange rate regime through a widening of the discount on the Haitian currency, the Gourde in the parallel market.[4] Since 1919, the Gourde (HTG) was pegged to the US dollar at the fixed rate of 5.00 gourdes for US 1.00 dollar. In the late 1980s, in the context of falling foreign exchange reserves, maintaining the fixed parity became more and more unsustainable while the spread between the informal black-market rate and the official rate kept widening. By 1991, the authorities adopted a flexible foreign exchange rate regime, around five years after Haiti had embarked on a major program to liberalize its trade regime. While those policies were welcomed as critical steps toward economic modernization and sound macroeconomic management, they also created new challenges. As a matter of fact, all those changes did not prevent the country from low

[4] The authorities indicated to commercial banks their intention to raise the surrender requirement on export receipts from 50 to 75% in order to increase in resources channeled to the Central Bank and make it possible to support higher imports of essential commodities at the official rate, and contain price increases (IMF Staff Report for the Haiti Article IV Consultation, 1989, p.17).

growth and they revived inflation along with volatile economic environment. Such context has resulted in an increased demand for imports. In terms of gross domestic product (GDP), total imports grew steadily to reach 58.5% in 2018 compared to 33.4% in 2000, as the main factor fueling the demand for foreign exchange transactions. In addition to this growth, the rise in precautionary FX demand along with the expectations associated with exchange rate upward appreciation trend that have set the tone for the dollarization process of the economy, which has strengthened over years. Before 2010, the dollarization of deposits averaged 52% but afterward it rose to almost 60%.[5] The strengthening of the dollarization phenomenon put a strain on monetary policy measures in the fight against inflation.

As most of the central banks, the Bank of Republic of Haiti (BRH)'s primary mission is to maintain price stability while creating conditions for economic growth and development. Before the financial liberalization in 1994, the BRH set the interest rates on liabilities and assets in the banking system along with the bank's reserves requirement ratio to manage liquidity in the banking system.[6] The established interest rate ranges were periodically adjusted to take into account liquidity coefficients, inflation, and foreign interest rates. By 1996, the central bank introduced indirect monetary policy instrument called "BRH bonds" that were accessible to the banks, then to non-banking financial institutions (starting in 2008). It is a short-term liquidity management instrument which has three maturities: 7, 28, and 91 days while the interest rates on the 91-day BRH bond are usually considered as the central bank interest rate to influence the financial system and the rest of the economy. Since 1996, the BRH bonds and the rates on them were used along with FX interventions and banks' reserves requirements as the main instruments to keep inflation under control in the environment of high liquidity that was prevalent over many years. Coupled with that, the country's financial system featured a weak interbank market and issued few government

[5] The opposite situation has occurred regarding the dollarization of portfolios. It has reduced, coming from 53% before 2010 to less than 41% afterwards, as a result of administrative and policy measures by the central bank, which have increased the cost of lending US dollar.

[6] In 1993, the Central bank decided to remunerate the excess banks' reserves for better liquidity management. A decision lasted less than 6 months (Bank of Republic of Haiti—Annual Report, 1993, p.49).

securities along with no secondary market. Additionally, Lebelon and Augustin (2014) found that "the monetary policy framework of BRH has also used the nominal exchange rate as a policy instrument to have inflation under control and prevent second round inflationary effects in the country, especially in the period of inflation spikes in food items" (p. 24). This study also indicated that such policy was put in place because of the openness of the economy and the significant exchange rate pass-through to inflation.

This chapter empirically analyzes the exchange rate and inflation dynamics and the effectiveness of monetary policy as well as its main impediments in fighting inflation from 1996 to 2018. This period follows a 73-year fixed exchange rate regime that was formally abandoned in 1991. Furthermore, as distinctive feature, it has the use of *BRH bonds* as the main monetary policy instrument by the Central Bank of Haiti to manage liquidity in the financial system. The section on inflation developments considers the inflation developments over the period under review. In the following section, the major sources of inflationary pressures (drivers) are examined. Based on the estimated model, the last section investigates the effects—and their strength—on the dynamics of inflation in Haiti. The modeling approach analyzes the monetary policy power. It also highlights the bottlenecks in the transmission mechanism that limit the effects on price level, including the indirect impact of monetary policy through different channels including the foreign exchange rate is one. The discussion in this section is followed by the concluding remarks.

Inflation Developments

Over the last 25 years, Haiti alongside Venezuela and Argentina has recorded the highest inflation rates in the Western Hemisphere.[7] The 12-month inflation rate is considered as the "headline" inflation. As shown in Table 7.1, the rate reached 14.6% in September 2018, following an upward trend that began at the end of 2014. In fact, except for the fourth quarter of 2013, inflation has been rising steadily since the January 2010 earthquake from an annual average ranging from 6.2% to 9.5% over the period ending in fiscal year 2018. Changes in the overall price level

[7] According to the World Bank database, the annual inflation rate in Venezuela averaged almost 80% from 2010 to 2016 (October 2019)

Table 7.1 Selected countries: macroeconomic performances

	Inflation (Percent, End of period)			*GDP growth (percent)*			*External current account balance (Percent of GDP)*		
	2016	*2017*	*2018*	*2016*	*2017*	*2018*	*2016*	*2017*	*2018*
Haiti	12.5	15.4	14.6	1.5	1.2	1.5	−1	−4	−4
Argentina	…	24.8	40.5	−1.8	2.9	−2.6	−2.7	−4.9	−3.7
Dominican Republic	1.7	4.2	4.1	6.6	4.6	6.4	−1.1	−0.2	−1.6
Jamaica	1.7	5.2	3.5	1.5	0.7	1.2	−2.7	−2.8	−2.9
Latin America and Caribbean	4.6	5.9	6.8	−0.6	1.3	1.2	−1.9	−1.5	−1.6
United States	1.6	2.2	2.1	2.2	2.2	2.9	−2.3	−2.3	−2.5

Source World Bank Database and *Institut Haïtien de Statistique et d'Informatique (IHSI)*. October 2019

have reached double-digit since the end of 2010 for the actual annual average of 13.7%, far ahead of the United States' 2.5%, and the average Caribbean at 4.5% (with Jamaica at 4.9%, Dominican Republic at 4.4%, and Trinidad & Tobago at 2.7%).[8] It is the second time that the inflation rate has remained this high for such a long period since the adoption of the floating exchange rate in 1991. The first was from 2002 to 2008 and was marked by a number of factors including rising oil prices, depreciation of local currency, and domestic markets disruption owing to protracted political instability.

The headline inflation rate dropped sharply at the end of the 1990s with the implementation of an IMF/World Bank-sponsored program that was introduced at the end of the 1992–1994 embargo. This program was also funded through the involvement of other technical and financial partners including the Inter-American Development Bank (IDB) and the Organization of American States (OAS).[9] This three-year structural adjustment program committed foreign financial and technical assistance to Haiti to a large-scale modernization program. The main features of this

[8] World Bank database: October 2019.

[9] Many competent Haitian-American professionals were given incentives by international technical and financial partners to come back and take part in the implementation of that program, called Camdessus-Preval Initiative (Buss, 2009).

program were privatization of public enterprises (which can be considered as the main sources of deficit financing); progressive elimination of public sector deficits through tight fiscal policies; and a major review of retail oil prices administration toward more price flexibility. In addition, there was the adoption of indirect monetary policy instrument along with the abolition of floors and ceilings on interest rates.

By 1998, following the derailment of the structural adjustment program, the inflation rate increased markedly when central bank financing replaced foreign financing to maintain the fiscal expansion that was underway. Moreover, subsequent currency depreciation has fuelled inflationary pressures along with rising foreign oil prices. Inflation accelerated at the turn of the twentieth century, approaching 20% and fed by monetary expansion, was aggravated by a major correction in the foreign exchange market. For the entire period of 1998–2000, inflation tended to (fall) rise whenever base money grew (slowed) faster than the CPI.

From 2002 to 2008, inflation has been quite volatile and erratic, driven by sharp currency depreciation and rising oil prices. For instance, a low rate of 8% in March 2002 was followed six quarters later by a high of more than 40% (in September 2003) and with a high of close to 20% in September 2008, preceding a low of −4.7% in September 2009. In fact, between September 2002 and March 2003, the Haitian Gourde gradually lost 53.3% of its value against the US dollar. The impact was severe on the economy, especially for consumers, owing to the fact that the currency depreciation abruptly fed through to consumer prices. Accordingly, annual inflation jumped from 14.8% in September to 37% in December 2002 before reaching 42.5% in March 2003, the highest rate over the last 40 years (the embargo period not included). However, the inflation rate then gradually declined to 8% after 14 quarters. In 2008, despite a stable foreign exchange rate, inflationary pressures increased as a result of high oil prices and decline in domestic supply due to the environmental shocks that hit the country (Descieux & Divers, 2017). The inflationrate jumped from 13.6% in March 2008 to 19.8% in September 2008, leading to violent protests against the increasing cost of living.

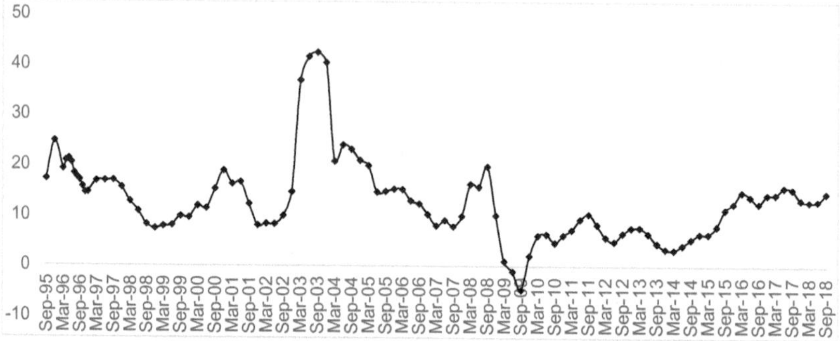

Fig. 7.2 CPI inflation (12-month variation, percent). *Source* Institut Haitien de Statistique et d'Informatique (IHSI)

Regarding the "underlying" or "core" inflation, which shows the basic trend of price movements, the central bank of Haiti estimates this indicator on a monthly basis using the exclusion method.[10] Items, such as those in food and energy group, are excluded because of their volatility. Additionally, efforts have been made by the central bank to find a better measure of this policy-relevant indicator. Jean Baptiste and Augustin (2010) found that "both exclusion method and limited influence method contain information about future values of headline inflation" (p. 32). However, in the case of Haiti, this research suggested that the exclusion method provides better results with respect to the statistical parameters used. Although the long-term means of the two measures converge, it is not sure that the "core" measure has been completely shielded of the effects of the headline inflation. According to the study by Cayemitte and Georges (2010), "both headline and core inflation series show approximately similar trends, while almost faithfully reflecting the reversal movements that occur in the observed inflation" (p. 48).

Like most countries, the headline inflation rate in Haiti is the 12-month change of the consumer price index (CPI) (see Fig. 7.2), which

[10] It is the most popular method used in many countries is the exclusion method, which simply excludes a fixed, pre-specified list of volatile CPI components (typically food and energy items) whose short-term behavior tends to diverge from that of the underlying price trend (Guinigundo, 2004, p. 38).

Table 7.2 Structure of the Haitian Consumer Price Index (CPI)

Groups		*Weights (%)*	*Consumption expenditures on locally produced (%)*	*Consumption expenditures on imported (%)*
1	Food and Alcohol products	50.35	52.75	49.03
2	Clothing	6.86	4.24	20.7
3	Rent/energy	11.05	11.77	4.37
4	Home furniture and maintenance	4.70	5.65	6.78
5	Health	2.90	3.37	3.94
6	Transportation	13.74	12.17	9.02
7	Entertainment/education/leisure	5.84	8.49	2.04
8	Others	4.56	1.55	4.12
	Total	100.00	100.00	100.00

Sources "Indice des Prix à la Consommation. Base 100 en Août 2004". IHSI, MEF. July 2005

is compiled every month using an arithmetic mean. The CPI is calculated as a Laspeyres index, which was updated in 2005, and covers 140 items broken into 8 groups with fixed weights adding up to 100, as shown in Table 7.2. The weights are derived from the 2000 comprehensive *Household Consumption Budget Survey* (EBCM-2000). Among the distinctive features of the Haiti's new CPI is the addition of two new price indexes to the main one—a locally produced goods price index and an imported goods prices index. All three have been produced and published on a common reference base August 2004 = 100. Information is gathered simultaneously but separately for the three aggregates but the *Institut Haitien de Statistique et d'Informatique* (IHSI), the collecting agency, has yet to publish the weight of each group (in total consumption expenditures) in the global CPI index.[11] Table 7.2 illustrates that food, clothing, and transportation make up 79% of consumption expenditures on imported goods but less than 70% of consumption expenditures on domestically produced goods. For data collecting purpose, the whole

[11] The Haiti collecting data agency (IHSI) changed this feature in the beginning of 2019 by introducing a new CPI using the 2012 comprehensive *Household Consumption Budget Survey* (EBCM-2012). Compared to the former index, the new is now a linear combination of the locally produced goods price index and the imported goods prices index while all three are based on the fiscal year 2017–2018. It's one of the main changes occurred within the new CPI along with having 12 groups instead of 8.

country is divided into 5 economic regions: Metropolititan Area, Rest West, North, Transversal, and South.[12]

Sources of Inflationary Pressures

Money Supply

Monetary stance remains the main determinant of inflation, consistent with standard theory, albeit with lags. Figure 7.3 shows how the erratic base money growth tends to pull up and down the inflation rate over the period under study (i.e., money is running faster than prices when inflation is rising and slower otherwise). From September 1997 to September 2018, the average money supply growth was 14.1% while the average GDP growth was only 1.2%. By the end of 2013, there was a steady upward trend in money supply along with the inflation rate. This period corresponds to the decline in external budgetary support, which implied a rise in monetary financing. Between 2013 and 2018, monetary financing growth averaged almost 98%. In 2018, it reached 24.34 billion gourdes (approximatively 372.1 million US dollars), which was the highest level since the creation of the central bank. In percent of GDP, it went from 0.65% GDP in 2013 to 4% in 2018.

The volatility of money base growth points to a critical feature of the monetary policy framework—the deficit financing constraint which makes it impossible to target other monetary aggregates or inflation measures.

The "fiscal dominance" issue makes it harder to anticipate the inflation outcomes and is conducive to exagerated inflation expectations in order for agents to be on the safe side (loss minimizing behavior). As a result, in an environment where price and wage settings are far from competitive, inflation tends to be persistent as it is difficult for monetary policy to be credible (Redifer & Hartelius, 2007).

Inflation Persistence

Current inflation in Haiti appears to be quite sensitive to past inflation, ceteris paribus. Autocorrelation is indeed significant over many quarters. This inertia or sluggishness can be explained also by past policies,

[12] The Metropolitan Area represents Port-au-Prince (the Capital) and its surrounding areas.

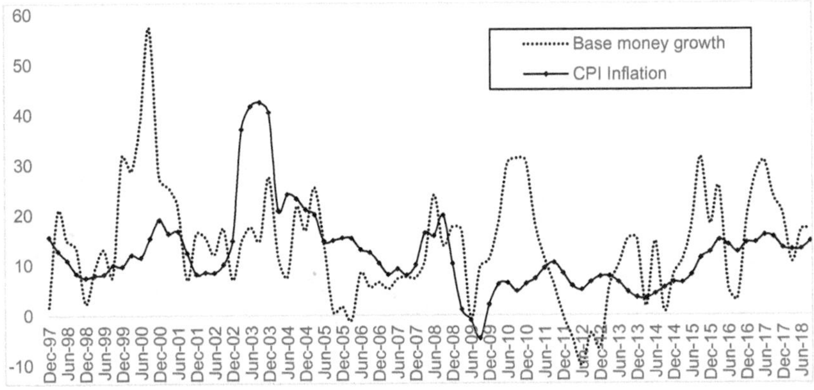

Fig. 7.3 CPI inflation and base money growth (% 12-month). *Source* BRH and IHSI

substantial imperfections in the structure of the economy, inflation expectations, preexisting contracts, etc. (Justinville, 2008). Agénor (2002) has explained the "strong degree of persistence in developing countries" by the "lack of confidence in the policymakers' commitment to or ability to maintain low inflation" (p. 101).

Money and inflation inertia—or inflation persistence—however, are not the only drivers of the headline inflation rate. Relative price changes—or "shocks"—have been found to exert significant and lasting effect on the CPI or headline inflation. In Haiti, for instance, it has been shown that there exists a positive, although weak, causal relationship between inflation and the variance and the dissymetry of relative prices over a 24-month period ending in 1998, and that this relation is not less strong than the causal relationship between money and inflation (Dubois, 1999) (Fig. 7.4).

Oil Prices

More than money growth, the exchange rate changes seem to move the CPI rates up and down, reflecting a significant pass-through from import prices to overall consumer prices. Adding to the strength of the pass-through is the effect of individual prices—like retail oil prices—on the price index through the exchange rate, as in Figure 5, along with the

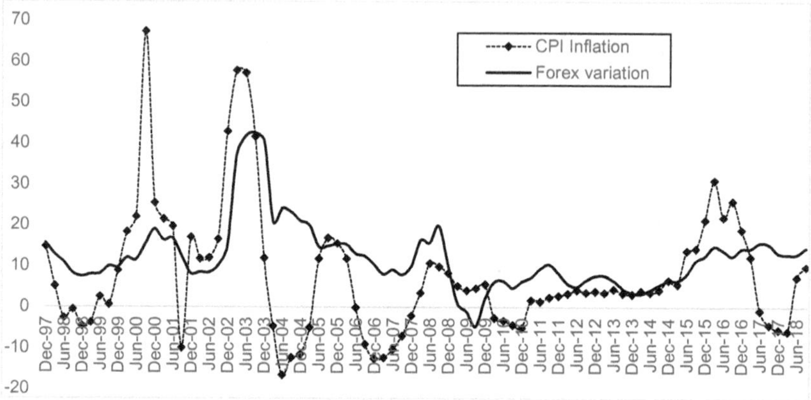

Fig. 7.4 CPI inflation and foreign exchange (12-month variation, percent). *Source* BRH and IHSI

> more subtle effect of financial dollarization on exchange rate variability.[13] In a recent study, Kavila and Le Roux (2016) concluded that "exchange rate pass-through to prices plays a greater role in economies that are highly dollarized than elsewhere" (p. 113).

The March 1995 law which regulates the price formation of petroleum products, states that retail prices of gasoline, gasoil, and kerosene, must be adjusted upward or downward whenever the cost, insurance, and freight (CIF) prices in local currency rise or fall by at least 5%. Therefore, the adjustment must occur whenever the algebraic sum of changes in the US$ CIF prices and the exchange rate is $\geq$ or $\leq$5%. Although the adjustments have not been automatic, the effect is evident on the CPI.

On several occasions, the government decided to stop the adjustment mechanism and subsidize the retail price of petroleum products to alleviate the adverse impact of their rise on the cost of living.[14] Such administrative price-setting measures usually resulted in the government accruing large subsidy bills to compensate local gas stations' owners

[13] The reasons for increased exchange rate volatility are discussed in IMF (1999).

[14] Oil prices subsidies have been effective from 1999 to 2003 and from 2011 to 2017 although prohibited as intended in the March 1995 law.

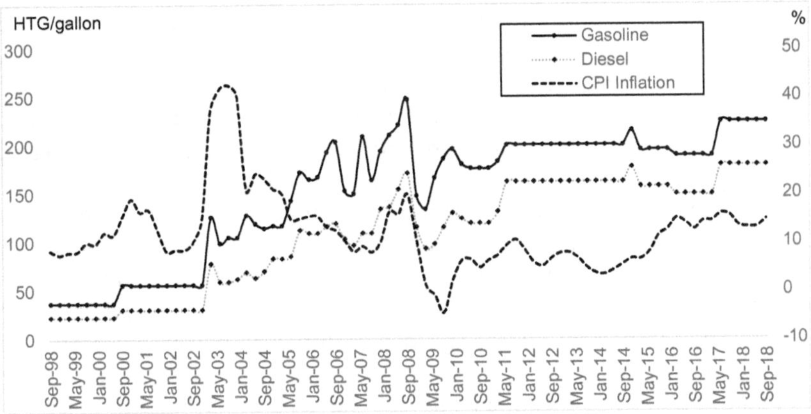

Fig. 7.5 CPI inflation (percent) and domestic gasoline and diesel prices (HTG/gallon). *Source* IHSI and Ministry of Economy and Finance (MEF)

for lost income, which leads to loss of revenues in terms of taxes. Additionally, in the periods where the oil spot prices rise continuously on the international market along with no adjustment of the retail prices, the government actually proceeds with direct transfers to the gas station owners that go beyond the loss of tax revenue. Such decisions have led to an increase in the fiscal deficit as well as its financing by the central bank.

Currency Depreciation

Exchange rate pass-through to consumer's prices seems to be the main factor that explains most of the inflation dynamics in Haiti (Parkin, 1994). This empirical evidence contradicts somewhat standard anticipated inflation theory (Fig. 7.5). Per Parkin (1994):

> Other things equal, the higher the expected rate of inflation, the higher the level of market interest rates, the higher the rate at which wages rise and the faster the rate of currency deperciation. Furthermore, these effects will all be one on one. An x percent higher anticipated inflation will be asociated with x percent higher nominal interest rates, with wages rising x percent faster and with currency depreciating x percent faster. (p. 294)

In other words, consistent with the monetary approach to the exchange rates, inflation implies currency depreciation (Buteau, 2008), not the other way around as suggested in the exchange rate pass-through theory.

The conventional monetary theory does not exclude relative price effects (like exchange rate pass-through) on absolute prices to the extent that they are temporary. In his famous 1974 article, Milton Friedman argued that it is essential to distinguish changes in *relative prices* from changes in *absolute prices*. The special conditions that drove up the prices of oil and food required purchasers to spend more on them, leaving less to spend on other items. Did that not force other prices to go down or rise less rapidly than otherwise? Thanks to delays in adjustment, the rapid rises in oil and food prices may have temporarily raised the rate of inflation somewhat. He also added that the basic source of inflation leads to faster growth in the quantity of money than in output. It follows that an accommodative monetary policy in the form of permanent growth of the monetary base (irrespective of output growth) will not allow "...other prices to go down or rise less rapidly" (Friedman, 1974, p. 73) and therefore, will transform a temporary change in relatives prices into a permanent change in absolute prices.

Modeling Approach

The vector autoregression approach (VAR) provides a convenient way to treat issues related to dynamics between variables. Inflation, money growth, and exchange rate changes are assumed to be endogeneous, each one depending on its lagged values and on the lagged values of the other two variables. This approach allows a determination of how much of a change in a variable (e.g., inflation) is due to inflation and how much is due to shocks to other variables (money and exchange rate changes—variance decomposition—and also to help us determine and trace over time the effect of a one-time shock on current and future values of the endogeneous variables. Building on this VAR, a Vector Error Correction Model (VECM) is set up with the three variables to study the short-run adjustment dynamics and the gradual correction over the long term.

Due to the fact that all three variables (inflation, base money, and exchange rate) are integrated in the same order, the short-run and long-run effects were captured. Therefore, a VECM was used since it combines short-run information with long-run (static) information to provide a long-term relationship and the short-term dynamics between the CPI inflation, the base money, and the exchange rate. Through this model, the basic hypothesis will be verified: the CPI inflation depends on the base money (asymmetric shocks from the monetary policy and fiscal dominance) and the nominal exchange rate movements (relative prices).

Data and Variables Description

Quarterly data from 1998:4 to 2018:3 was used. Three significant events mark this period: (a) the end of the embargo which lasted from 1991 to 1994 followed by an IMF/World Bank funded program; (b) the formal adoption of a floating/flexible exchange rate regime; and (c) the introduction of an indirect monetary policy instrument bearing market interest rates. This central bank security called BRH Bond is issued in 7, 28, and 91 days to manage liquidity in the banking system.

The price level (*cpinfl*) is represented by the Consumer Price Index compiled and provided by IHSI. Also, the foreign exchange rate[15] (*txchfp*) is measured as the US dollar price in Gourdes (the local currency at end of period) as published by BRH (Banque de la République d'Haiti). In Haiti, there has been a dual currency circulation since 1919 that began 4 years after the beginning of the American occupation of the country. This is how the country started with the fixed exchange rate regime (Dubois, 2006). The base money—or high-powered money—(*bms*) directly controlled by the central bank is the sum of local currency in circulation and commercial banks gourde deposits at BRH, although US dollar deposits are also allowed since September 1990 in the banking system. The base money variable provides an indication of the level of liquidity in domestic currency in the economy. Changes in base money are the result of monetary financing or monetary policy measures through the use of bank mandatory reserve ratio, interest rate, BRH bonds, and forex interventions. Thus, considering the base money as a variable in the model should reflect the impact of monetary policy.

All the series have been log-linearized for the model estimation's purposes. Exchange rate and base money data are from the central bank.

[15] Indirect quotation.

Table 7.3 Augmented Dickey-Fuller (ADF) test

	Level			*First difference*		
	LCPINFL	*LBMS*	*LTXCHFP*	*DLCPINFL*	*DLBMS*	*DLTXCHFP*
Observations	85	85	85	84	84	84
Lags	5	5	5	5	5	5
Critical value 1%	−3.5093	−3.5093	−3.5093	−3.5093	−3.5093	−3.5093
Critical value 5%	−2.8959	−2.8959	−2.8959	−2.8959	−2.8959	−2.8959
Critical value 10%	−2.5852	−2.5852	−2.5852	−2.5852	−2.5852	−2.5852
Value	−1,123	−1,023	−1,137	−11,742*	−10,787*	−7,303*
Stationarity	No	No	No	Yes	Yes	Yes

Data Stationarity

Results of the Augmented Dickey-Fuller stationarity test made on the three variables are shown in Table 7.3. They indicate that all the log-linearized series were found to be non-stationary in level. Table 7.3 shows that stationarity was obtained for all of them (CPI inflation, base money, and the exchange rate) in first differences at the 5% threshold. As for the optimal lag choice, the test, based on the Schwartz Information Criteria (SIC), has suggested an optimal number of 5 quarters.

VAR Model

Specifications. To estimate the VAR model, 1 was found as the number of lags to include all the three variables; CPI inflation, exchange rate, and base money are stationary in the first difference using the Schwartz information criteria (SIC whose results are presented in Table 7.6). The Granger causality test results in Table 7.5 show that CPI inflation is the most endogenous variable, than the exchange rate. Such results indicate a strong link between theoretical and empirical evidence.

Results

The variance decomposition from an unrestricted estimated VAR is presented in Table 7.8. It shows that more than 80% of the variance in the forecast error of CPI inflation is explained by a shock to CPI inflation over a period of 10 quarters. A shock to the exchange rate impacts the (variance of the) forecast error of CPI inflation. It starts from the second quarter (0.52%) and goes up until it reaches 13% in the tenth quarter. Indeed, 13% of the variance in the forecast error of CPI inflation seems to be explained by shocks in exchange rate. Moreover, a shock to the money supply rate explains more than 16% of the (variance of the) forecast error of the exchange rate after 10 quarters while it counts only for 7.5% of the (variance of the) forecast error of CPI inflation. As shown in the Granger test, the variance decomposition indicates that monetary policy effects on inflation through money supply is twice less than the ones on foreign exchange rate. Strong evidence of cointegration was found between the three variables; so a vector error correction (VEC) model was estimated.

Vector Error Correction Model (VECM)

Specifications. To perform the trace test, a determination of the number of lags was needed. One (1) was found as the number of lags while using the Schwartz information criteria (SIC). Applying the Johansen procedure, there is one vector of cointegration between the three variables and an intercept in the equation. Furthermore, the adjustment coefficients are all negative, ensuring that the VEC estimation is correct, and the model converges to the steady-state equilibrium (Fig. 7.6).

Long-Run Equilibrium

The vector's coefficients are normalized in the coefficient of CPI inflation, a variable which is considered as the endogenous one in the model. Theoretically, the signs of the estimated coefficients of base money and exchange rate are correct, and they are statistically significant according to the *t-statistics*. The normalization of the cointegration vector in the coefficient of CPI inflation leads to the cointegration equation below:

$$\text{lcpinfl}_t = -2.779763 + 0.366134 * \underset{(-2.17417)}{\text{lbms}_t} + 1,069020 * \underset{(-3.39085)}{\text{ltxchfp}_t} \quad (7.1)$$

Short-Run Dynamics

In the short run, the results indicate that all the adjustment coefficients are negative but only the CPI Inflation's one is statistically significant as shown in Table 7.4.

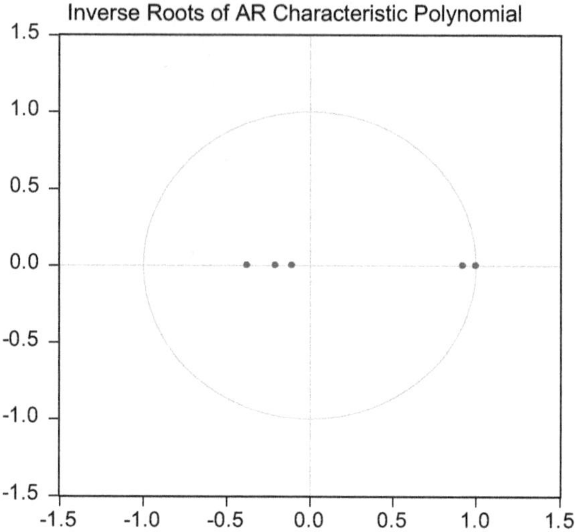

Fig. 7.6 Stability of the VECM

Table 7.4 Short run dynamics

Error correction	*D(LCPINFL)*	*D(LBMS)*	*D(LTXCHFP)*
CointEq1	−0.114872	−0.007911	−0.006753
	(0.02964)	(0.04062)	(0.04751)
	[−3.87505]	[−0.19476]	[−0.14213]
D(LCPINFL(−1))	−0.335673	−0.053324	−0.022661
	(0.10710)	(0.14676)	(0.17165)
	[−3.13422]	[−0.36336]	[−0.13202]
D(LBMS(−1))	−0.059860	−0.191684	0.062155
	(0.08528)	(0.11686)	(0.13669)
	[−0.70191]	[−1.64029]	[0.45473]
D(LTXCHFP(−1))	0.060759	0.056137	−0.139166
	(0.07854)	(0.10762)	(0.12588)
	[0.77363]	[0.52163]	[−1.10559]
C	0.038843	0.040433	0.018403
	(0.00634)	(0.00869)	(0.01017)
	[6.12406]	[4.65215]	[1.81033]
DUMMY	0.009478	−0.029655	0.007962
	(0.02236)	(0.03065)	(0.03584)
	[0.42381]	[−0.96768]	[0.22214]

Note Standard errors are reported in (.) and t-statistics in [.]

Model Diagnostic Tests

Diagnostic tests of the estimated VECM indicate that the residuals are free of serial correlation (LM) and heteroscedasticity. Nevertheless, a lack of normality was found in the residuals. For this reason, a binary variable (dummy) was introduced to take into account the structural breaks that could help resolve the problem. Stability tests were also performed to assess the stability of the estimated VECM. The inverse roots of the characteristic AR polynomial are equal to unity, indicating that all the coefficients in the VECM are stable.

Results

The cointegration Eq. (7.1) above describes the dynamics and the adjustment path of CPI inflation, base money, and exchange rate toward the long-term equilibrium. As for the results, money supply (base money) and exchange rate are the foremost determinants of CPI inflation in Haiti in the long run (over 40 quarters). This result is consistent with the predictions for Haiti, a small open economy where foreign exchange rate movements while strongly dependent on money supply (in domestic currency), which determines the price level and exert significant influence on the CPI inflation. A one-percent depreciation of the Gourde causes a jump of 1.069% in CPI inflation, as expected by conventional theory. This result suggests a strong role in Haiti for the direct exchange channel rate for the transmission of monetary policy to inflation.

Regarding the impact of money supply, it was found that a 1% increase in the base money will lead to a 0.366% change in CPI inflation. As is expected from the economic theory, money supply directly affects the inflation movements in the long run—the usual aggregate demand and expectation channels, weaker in Haiti because of the openness of the economy, cannot be ruled out as transmission mechanism.

The return to equilibrium is achieved only through CPI inflation, which reflects inflation inertia, as shown by the analysis of the short-run dynamics and adjustment to the long-term equation. The speed of adjustment is, however, slow (0.1148). A short-term disequilibrium in the dynamic of the variables will be corrected by 11.48% in the long run. Moreover, short-run dynamics in CPI inflation depend only on changes in past CPI inflation whose coefficient (0.335673) is statistically significant. This sluggishness can be explained by the persistence of inflation in Haiti, which could be derived from many factors, including the weak capacity of policymakers to achieve their goal in maintaining low inflation and stable foreign exchange through the current monetary policy framework. Against this background, the confidence of Haitian economic agents is affected and as a result, leads to expectations of higher inflation. A vicious circle that seems to be perpetuating, owing to the use of monetary financing as a primary means of financing government budget deficit.

Monetary Policy Power

Empirical evidence and results from the model show that the direct exchange channel is the main channel for the transmission of monetary policy impulse to inflation in Haiti. This finding gives us some understanding of the reason why for more than a decade, the central bank of Haiti (BRH) has been modulating its monetary policy in order to contain foreign exchange rate fluctuations and thus limit their impact on inflation. As a matter of fact, forex interventions have been one of the instruments mostly used by the central bank despite a limited cushion of external reserves. With regard to actions of BRH related to the movements in the foreign exchange markets, the exchange rate can be considered as the "de facto" anchor or intermediate target of the monetary policy. This also reflects an implicit fear of floating that features the monetary policy framework of the central bank of Haiti. This action is understandable because foreign exchange rate has become an economic indicator with high political sensitivity over time. However, it is impossible to have exchange rate stability, which is vital in the fight against inflation in a country like Haiti, while implementing budgetary measures that perpetuate the fiscal dominance.

Besides the openness of the economy, the weakness of the aggregate demand and expectations channels can be explained by the fact that Haiti is a remittance-recipient country (more than 25% GDP in 2018). Empirically, remittances have always been countercyclical to the macroeconomic outlook in Haiti. As a result, it increases with shocks that affect the Haitian economy. So even though it is viewed as conditional, remittances provide ability to help mitigate the impact of shocks to consumption (Barajas et al., 2016). This additional income seems to put the household in a situation where its demand is less affected by price shocks or it could provide the ability to be more effective in making necessary adjustments in time of rising prices. As a result, this part of the aggregate demand is apparently less sensitive to the monetary policy impulse through this channel. Furthermore, remittance funds have strengthened the banks' balance sheet over time, leading to ample liquidity in the banking system. Since the country has been dealing with a challenging and high-risk environment over the last 30 years, banks tend to give preference to investments in safe and liquid assets, including acquiring central bank securities (BRH bonds) and involving more and more in the foreign exchange market. That being the case, there is a disrupted link between their marginal cost of loanable funds and the movements in the policy rate. This disruption thus affects the financial intermediation and diminishes the ability of the credit channel to play its role in the fight against inflation through the possibility to slow down economic activity.

Effective liquidity management (in domestic currency) in the financial system by the BRH requires both effective monetary policy measures and fiscal consolidation associated with zero monetary financing. However, the central bank of Haiti only takes note of monetary financing because it has to pay the checks issued by the government, acting as its fiscal and banking agent in accordance with the law. In parallel, the monetization of budget deficit has continuously fed the deposits of the banking system as well as the liquidity. Thus, the central bank finds itself in a situation where it must always react afterward. This also creates an environment where the adverse effects of monetary financing on the exchange rate and prices can reach a level where it cannot be completely compensated by the reaction of the monetary policy. Accordingly, inflation has been mostly high and the government was obliged to adjust the minimum wage almost every year in order to help households keep up with the continuous rise in inflation. Furthermore, such a situation reduces the confidence of households and businesses in the ability of monetary authorities to achieve their goal in the process of fighting inflation. This generates uncertainty that is sometimes fed by the political situation which affects economic activity in a repetitive way.

Overall, it is surmised that the monetary policy framework has been effective in stabilizing inflation and foreign exchange rate in Haiti, mostly when there is a program that is being implemented under the supervision of the IMF and the World Bank and where fiscal consolidation is required. This has been observed during these sub-periods: 1995–1998, 2004–2009, and 2011–2015. The first period features a gradual drop of 17.4% while in the second period, there was a sharp decline of 24.5% in the inflation rate. The third and last sub-period shows a stable inflation rate averaging 6% over four years. Another feature is the fact that monetary financing, one of the main monetary policy constraints, was temporarily ruled out because of the compensation brought by external financing. Indeed, through those programs, Haiti has received external financing such as balance of payments support from the IMF and the World Bank. In addition, those programs usually play a catalytic role in mobilizing financial support from bilateral and multilateral partners, which provides more financial resources to the government to implement its development and poverty reduction plan.

Concluding Thoughts

The purpose of this chapter was to analyze empirically the exchange rate and inflation dynamics in Haiti, and the effectiveness of monetary policy as well as identifying its main impediments over the 1996–2018 period, in which inflation reached—and seems to stay at—new highs while growth remains sluggish. Evidence is presented that exchange rate fluctuations play a significant role in the inflation dynamics in Haiti, in aggravating the effects of an accommodating monetary policy, of downward price stickiness, and of inflation persistence. Given the strong exchange rate pass-through observed, the direct exchange rate transmission channel seems to be the most efficient way for monetary policy to stabilize CPI inflation, to anchor exchange rate expectations (under the current floating rate system), and to build up policy credibility. Having realized these occurrences, the central bank of Haiti has set its monetary framework while considering the foreign exchange rate as anchor and intermediate target, suggesting an implicit fear of floating.

Also noted is that inflation inertia remains a significant factor in explaining current inflation, a result that might come from the fact that Haitian economic agents have less confidence in the monetary policy to achieve its objectives of price stability owing to the bottlenecks that prevent the proper functioning of the monetary policy transmission channels. The results also indicate that the aggregate demand and expectation channels are somehow weaker in Haiti because of the openness of the economy and many other factors including the fact the country is a high remittance-recipient and the use of monetary financing as primary mean of government deficit. As an additional income, which increases with the socio-economic situation evolving in Haiti, remittances put households in a position where they can make better adjustments in time of rising prices. Thus, remittances seem to help them keep their demand less affected, which results in being less responsive to monetary policy actions. So, the demand channel is then not very effective in the search for stable inflation by the central bank. In parallel, it was found that remittances coupled with adverse shocks from social and political uncertainty, have pushed banks to focus mostly on investments in safe and liquid assets, including BRH bonds and foreign exchange transactions. As a result, financial intermediation has decreased, leading to less operable transmission of changes in the policy rate to the real economy and inflation.

By analyzing adverse effects of monetary financing, it is found that it becomes a significant impediment to the effectiveness of the monetary policy framework. The monetization of the government deficit, which has increased over time, expanding the domestic public debt level, which accounts for more than 29% GDP in 2018. As a result, the weight of debt service in public expenditure has increased, putting the government in a situation to rely more and more on monetary financing, especially in periods of underperformance in revenue mobilization. It is a vicious circle that needs to break for better results from the monetary authorities.

Finally, it is also interesting to note that a strong relationship exists between monetary policy effectiveness in fighting inflation and the IMF/World Bank-supported program implemented during the period under review. Three distinctive sub-periods, in which the country has been implementing an IMF/WB-supported program, have led disinflation and/or stable inflation. The main reason is because it is mandatory to implement fiscal consolidation to narrow government deficit and limit monetary financing. Furthermore, the fiscal policy under the program is designed to improve revenue mobilization and expenditure efficiency while ensuring adequate fiscal space for poverty-reducing and needed infrastructure spending. Additionally, budget deficit is mainly financed through external financing as a balance of payments support from IMF and World Bank and budget support from bilateral and multilateral partners.

Appendix

See Tables 7.5, 7.6, 7.7, 7.8, 7.9, 7.10, 7.11, 7.12, 7.13 and 7.14.

Table 7.5 Granger causality test

Null hypothesis	*Obs*	*F-Statistic*	*Prob*
LTXCHFP does not Granger Cause LCPINFL	85	8.46956	0.0005
LCPINFL does not Granger Cause LTXCHFP		0.06822	0.9341
LBMS does not Granger Cause LCPINFL	85	2.89291	0.0612
LCPINFL does not Granger Cause LBMS		0.29341	0.7465
LBMS does not Granger Cause LTXCHFP	85	1.51292	0.2265
LTXCHFP does not Granger Cause LBMS		0.03178	0.9687

Note This table presents the Pairwise Granger Causality Tests run with 2 lags on October 26th, 2018, to investigate causality between three variables of the model we estimate. We used a sample from December 1996 to June 2018

Table 7.6 Lags number determination

Lag	*LogL*	*LR*	*FPE*	*AIC*	*SC*	*HQ*
0	17.09919	NA	0.000140	−0.356942	−0.266963	−0.320893
1	356.7997	645.0010*	3.25e-08*	−8.729107*	−8.369191*	−8.584913*
2	365.2607	15.42250	3.30e-08	−8.715460	−8.085607	−8.463122
3	372.9869	13.49644	3.41e-08	−8.683213	−7.783422	−8.322729
4	376.5382	5.933797	3.94e-08	−8.545271	−7.375543	−8.076642

Note This table presents the VAR lag order selection criteria test run on October 23, 2018, that helped us determine the optimal lag for the VAR model we estimate with three variables: LCPINFL LBMS LTXCHFP. We used a sample of 79 observations from December 1998 to June 2018

*Indicates lag order selected by the criterion

LR: sequential modified LR test statistic (each test at 5% level)

FPE: Final prediction error

AIC: Akaike information criterion

SC: Schwarz information criterion

Table 7.7 Unrestricted VAR results

	DLCPINFL	*DLTXCHFP*	*DLBMS*
DLCPINFL(−1)	−0.231334	−0.057305	−0.011422
	(0.09480)	(0.22040)	(0.06398)
	[−2.44011]	[−0.26001]	[−0.17853]
DLTXCHFP(−1)	0.134134	−0.165880	0.018405
	(0.05122)	(0.11908)	(0.03457)
	[2.61861]	[−1.39299]	[0.53242]
DLBMS(−1)	−0.207887	0.238121	−0.196487
	(0.17559)	(0.40820)	(0.11850)
	[−1.18395]	[0.58335]	[−1.65813]
C	0.004978	0.004610	0.003529
	(0.00127)	(0.00296)	(0.00086)
	[3.90604]	[1.55570]	[4.10263]
DUMMY	0.015366	0.006741	0.001620
	(0.00258)	(0.00600)	(0.00174)
	[5.94939]	[1.12260]	[0.92951]
R-squared	0.394829	0.048337	0.044349
Adj. *R*-squared	0.362117	−0.003104	−0.007307
Sum sq. resids	0.005523	0.029848	0.002515
S.E. equation	0.008639	0.020084	0.005830
F-statistic	12.06989	0.939653	0.858541
Log likelihood	265.8522	199.2066	296.9179
Akaike AIC	−6.603853	−4.916623	−7.390327
Schwarz SC	−6.453888	−4.766658	−7.240361
Mean dependent	0.006330	0.005340	0.003207
S.D. dependent	0.010817	0.020053	0.005809
Determinant resid covariance (dof adj.)		8.95E-13	
Determinant resid covariance		7.36E-13	
Log likelihood		767.2667	
Akaike information criterion		−19.04473	
Schwarz criterion		−18.59483	

Note This table presents the Vector Autoregression (VAR) Estimates run on October 26, 2018, for the three variables: LCPINFL LBMS LTXCHFP. We used a sample of 79 observations from December 1998 to June 2018. Standard errors in () & t-statistics in []

Table 7.8 Variance Decomposition

Period	*S.E*	*DLCPINFL*	*DLTXCHFP*	*DLBMS*
Variance Decomposition of DLCPINFL				
1	0.040509	100.0000	0.000000	0.000000
2	0.056380	99.38444	0.519561	0.096000
3	0.068160	98.07313	1.572143	0.354722
4	0.077893	96.20064	2.995298	0.804057
5	0.086386	93.89530	4.646547	1.458156
6	0.094054	91.27446	6.407373	2.318167
7	0.101137	88.44169	8.184139	3.374173
8	0.107789	85.48540	9.906816	4.607780
9	0.114106	82.47880	11.52636	5.994840
10	0.120157	79.48059	13.01141	7.508004
Variance Decomposition of DLTXCHFP				
1	0.065380	3.234620	96.76538	0.000000
2	0.088318	2.766280	96.72776	0.505965
3	0.103727	2.387242	96.02838	1.584378
4	0.115266	2.085723	94.79328	3.121001
5	0.124414	1.848983	93.15192	4.999102
6	0.131939	1.664539	91.22699	7.108468
7	0.138294	1.521028	89.12748	9.351487
8	0.143763	1.408723	86.94491	11.64637
9	0.148537	1.319731	84.75226	13.92801
10	0.152748	1.247973	82.60479	16.14724
Variance Decomposition of DLBMS				
1	0.059493	3.102504	2.597507	94.29999
2	0.082310	3.639176	2.662563	93.69826
3	0.098750	4.200357	2.750588	93.04905
4	0.111838	4.778177	2.859784	92.36204
5	0.122788	5.365100	2.988622	91.64628
6	0.132239	5.954133	3.135689	90.91018
7	0.140579	6.538965	3.299578	90.16146
8	0.148064	7.114070	3.478826	89.40710
9	0.154873	7.674755	3.671881	88.65336
10	0.161137	8.217163	3.877097	87.90574

Cholesky Ordering: LCPINFL LTXCHFP LBMS

Table 7.9 Johansen Cointegration Test

Unrestricted Cointegration Rank Test (Trace)

Hypothesized No. of CE(s)	Eigenvalue	Trace Statistic	0.05 Critical Value	Prob.**
None*	0.445128	62.32596	35.19275	0.0000
At most 1	0.115810	15.79358	20.26184	0.1843
At most 2	0.073958	6.070020	9.164546	0.1854

Trace test indicates 1 cointegrating end(s) at the 0.05 level
*Denotes rejection of the hypothesis at the 0.05 level
**MacKinnon-Haug-Michelis (1999) p-values

Unrestricted Cointegration Rank Test (Maximum Eigenvalue)

Hypothesized No. of CE(s)	Eigenvalue	Max-Eigen Statistic	0.05 Critical Value	Prob.**
None*	0.445128	46.53239	22.29962	0.0000
At most 1	0.115810	9.723557	15.89210	0.3602
At most 2	0.073958	6.070020	9.164546	0.1854

Note This table presents the Johansen Cointegration test with no deterministic trend, run on October 23, 2018. It helped us determine whether there's a cointegration equation between three variables: LCPINFL LBMS LTXCHFP using the Trace and Maximum Eigenvalue. We used a sample of 79 observations from December 1998 to June 2018
Max-eigenvalue test indicates 1 cointegrating eqn(s) at the 0.05 level
*Denotes rejection of the hypothesis at the 0.05 level
**MacKinnon-Haug-Michelis (1999) *p*-values

Table 7.10 Vector Error Correction Estimates

Cointegrating Eq	*CointEq1*		
LCPINFL(−1)	1.000000		
LBMS(−1)	−0.366134		
	(0.16840)		
	[−2.17417]		
LTXCHFP(−1)	−1.069020		
	(0.31527)		
	[−3.39085]		
C	2.779763		
Error Correction	D(LCPINFL)	D(LBMS)	D(LTXCHFP)
CointEq1	−0.114872	−0.007911	−0.006753
	(0.02964)	(0.04062)	(0.04751)
	[−3.87505]	[−0.19476]	[−0.14213]
D(LCPINFL(−1))	−0.335673	−0.053324	−0.022661
	(0.10710)	(0.14676)	(0.17165)
	[−3.13422]	[−0.36336]	[−0.13202]
D(LBMS(−1))	−0.059860	−0.191684	0.062155
	(0.08528)	(0.11686)	(0.13669)
	[−0.70191]	[−1.64029]	[0.45473]
D(LTXCHFP(−1))	0.060759	0.056137	−0.139166
	(0.07854)	(0.10762)	(0.12588)
	[0.77363]	[0.52163]	[−1.10559]
C	0.038843	0.040433	0.018403
	(0.00634)	(0.00869)	(0.01017)
	[6.12406]	[4.65215]	[1.81033]
DUMMY	0.009478	−0.029655	0.007962
	(0.02236)	(0.03065)	(0.03584)
	[0.42381]	[−0.96768]	[0.22214]
R-squared	0.259636	0.050566	0.019948
Adj. R-squared	0.208926	−0.014464	−0.047179
Sum sq. resids	0.135515	0.254447	0.348105
S.E. equation	0.043086	0.059039	0.069055
F-statistic	5.120030	0.777583	0.297162
Log likelihood	139.4447	114.5592	102.1795
Akaike AIC	−3.378347	−2.748334	−2.434924
Schwarz SC	−3.198389	−2.568376	−2.254966
Mean dependent	0.029114	0.032235	0.017722
S.D. dependent	0.048442	0.058616	0.067481
Determinant resid covariance (dof adj.)		2.75E-08	

(continued)

Table 7.10 (continued)

Cointegrating Eq	*CointEq1*
Log likelihood	360.7192
Akaike information criterion	−8.600487
Schwarz criterion	−7.970634

Note This table presents the Vector Error Corrector (VEC) Estimates run on October 23, 2018. It shows the cointegration (long-run) equation between the three variables: LCPINFL LBMS LTXCHFP. We used a sample of 79 observations from December 1998 to June 2018. Standard errors in () & *t*-statistics in []

Table 7.11 VEC Residual Serial correlation

Lags	*LM-Stat*	*Prob*
1	9.664562	0.3783
2	8.460894	0.4884
3	7.873299	0.5470

Note This table presents the VEC Residual Serial Correlation LM test with Null Hypothesis: no serial correlation at lag order h. It was run on October 23, 2018 with a sample of 79 observations from December 1998 to June 2018
Probabilities from chi-square with 9 df

Table 7.12 VEC Residual Normality Test

Component	*Skewness*	*Chi-sq*	*df*	*Prob*
1	0.580899	3.443012	1	0.0550
2	0.260830	0.895760	1	0.3439
3	0.888074	5.038424	1	0.0513
Joint		5.72301	3	0.0553
Component	Kurtosis	Chi-sq	df	Prob
1	2.226233	1.970771	1	0.1604
2	3.500680	0.825156	1	0.3637
3	5.632757	2.815880	1	0.0812
Joint		1.90181	3	0.15572
Component	Jarque–Bera	df	Prob	
1	5.013783	2	0.0517	
2	1.720916	2	0.4230	
3	4.968121	2	0.0519	
Joint	5.011482	6	0.0506	

Note This table presents the VEC Residual Normality test with Null Hypothesis: residuals are multivariate normal. It was run on October 23, 2018 with a sample of 79 observations from December 1998 to June 2018

Table 7.13 VEC Residual Heteroskedasticity test

Joint test					
Chi-sq	*df*	*Prob*			
59.60333	54	0.2792			
Individual components					
Dependent	*R*-squared	F(9,69)	Prob	Chi-sq(9)	Prob
res1*res1	0.318148	3.577217	0.0011	25.13368	0.0028
res2*res2	0.047510	0.382415	0.9397	3.753321	0.9269
res3*res3	0.130730	1.152993	0.3388	10.32766	0.3246
res2*res1	0.144483	1.294780	0.2557	11.41418	0.2484
res3*res1	0.213075	2.075893	0.0436	16.83290	0.0514
res3*res2	0.019744	0.154420	0.9975	1.559783	0.9967

Note This table presents the VEC Residual Heteroskedasticity Test with no cross terms (only levels and squares). It was run on October 23, 2018 with a sample of 79 observations from December 1998 to June 2018

Table 7.14 AR roots of characteristic polynomial

Root	*Modulus*
1.000000 − 9.79e-17i	1.000000
1.000000 + 9.79e-17i	1.000000
0.921246	0.921246
−0.378572	0.378572
−0.206804	0.206804
−0.107149	0.107149

Note This table presents the AR roots of the characteristic polynomial of the process and its roots determine when the process is stationary or not. It was run on October 24, 2018 with three endogenous variables: LCPINFL LBMS LTXCHFPand a Dummy as exogenous variable
VEC specification imposes 2 unit root(s)

References

Agénor, P.-R. (2002). Monetary policy under flexible exchange rates: An introduction to inflation targeting, central banking, analysis, and economic policies book series, In N. Loayza, R. Soto, & K. Schmidt-Hebbel (Eds.), *Inflation targeting: Design, performance, challenges*, (1st ed., pp. 79–170). Central Bank of Chile.

Ahmad, E., & Saima, A. A. (1999). Exchange rate and inflation dynamics. *The Pakistan Development Review, 38*(3), 235–251.

Alexander, W. E., Balino, T. J. T. & Enoch. (1995). The adoption of indirect instruments of monetary policy (IMF Occasional Paper 126). International Monetary Fund. https://doi.org/10.5089/9781557754899.084.

Andrle, M., Berg, A., Morales, A. R., Portillo, R., & Vleck, J. (2013, March). *Forecasting and monetary policy in low-income countries: Food and non-food inflation in Kenya* (IMF WP/13/61). International Monetary Fund. https://www.imf.org/external/pubs/ft/wp/2013/wp1361.pdf.

Augustin, D. & Lebelon, D. (2007). Impact des fluctuations du taux de change sur l'inflation: Une estimation du coefficient pass-through du taux de change sur les prix en Haïti. Période octobre 1990-septembre 2005" [Mémoire de sortie, Centre de Techniques et d'Économie Applique-CTPEA]. https://www.memoireonline.com/07/09/2224/.html.

Augustin, T. E. (2009). *Taux de change et Inflation : Une analyse en modèle VAR du coefficient de Pass-Through* [Unpublished Working Paper]. Banque de la République d'Haiti/MAE.

Balino, T. J. T., Bennett, A. & Borensztein, E. (1999). Monetary policy in dollarized economies. *IMF Occasional Paper* 171. International Monetary Fund.

Ball, L. (1993). What causes inflation ?. *Federal Reserve Bank of Philadelphia Business Review, 77*(1), 3–12. https://fraser.stlouisfed.org/title/5580/item/557669/toc/523738.

Banque de la République d'Haïti. (2003). *Mécanisme de répercussion d'une fluctuation du taux de change à l'inflation : Cas d'Haïti*. Banque de République d'Haiti.

Barajas A., Chami R., Christian H. E. & Oeking A. (2016). *What's different about monetary policy transmission in remittance-dependent countries* (IMF WP 16/44). International Monetary Fund. https://www.imf.org/external/pubs/ft/wp/2016/wp1644.pdf.

Buss, T. F. (2009). *Haiti in the balance: Why foreign aid has failed and what we can do about it*. Brookings Institution Press.

Buteau, L. (2008). Evaluation empirique de l'impact de l'inflation sur le taux de change. *Cahier de Recherche de la BRH, 1*, 4–37. Banque de la République d'Haïti.

Cayemitte, J.-M. & Georges J. (2010). L'inflation sous-jacente en Haïti: Une approche structurelle de la modélisation VAR. *Cahier de Recherche de la BRH*, *2*, 48–63. Banque de la République d'Haïti.

Clairmond, J. M. J. (2007). *Estimation du pass-through. Septembre 1992-juillet 2007* (Unpublished Working Paper). Banque de la République d'Haiti/MAE.

Descieux, D. & Divers, C. J. (2017). Effets de seuil dans la realtion entre l'inflation et la croissance economique en Haiti. *Cahier de Recherche de la BRH*, *3*, 53–66. Banque de la République d'Haïti.

Dubois, H. R. (1999). *Contribution à une anatomie de l'Inflation en Haïti* (Unpublished Working Paper). Ministère de l'Economie et des Finances/DEE.

Dubois, H. R. (2003). *Evaluation du degré de report de la variation du taux de change sur l'inflation: Implications pour l'autorité monétaire* (Unpublished Working Paper). Banque de la République d'Haiti/MAE.

Dubois, H. R. (2006). *In a search of monetary policy rule in Haiti from 1996 to 2005* (Unpublished Working Paper). Banque de la République d'Haiti/MAE.

Friedman M. (1974, June 24). Perspective on inflation. *Newsweek*, *83*(25), 73.

Guerson, A. (2015, December). *Inflation dynamics and monetary policy in Bolivia* (IMF WP/15/266). International Monetary Fund. https://www.imf.org/-/media/Websites/IMF/imported-full-text-pdf/external/pubs/ft/wp/2015/_wp15266.ashx.

Guinigundo, D. C. (2005, June). *An official core inflation measure for the Philippines. Philippine Review of Economics*, *42*(1), 37–53.

Humpage, O. F. (2008). Rising relative prices or inflation: Why knowing the difference matters. *Economic Commentary*, Federal Reserve Bank of Cleveland. https://www.clevelandfed.org/en/newsroom-and-events/publications/economic-commentary/economic-commentary-archives/2008-economic-commentaries/ec-20080601-rising-relative-prices-or-inflation-why-knowing-the-difference-matters.aspx.

Humphrey, T. M. (1986). *Essays on inflation* (5th ed., pp. 80–90). Federal Reserve Bank of Richmond.

Jean-Baptiste, A. E. (2008). Prix relatifs, taux de change et prix en Haïti. *Cahier de Recherche de la BRH*, *1*, 52–68. Banque de la République d'Haïti.

Jean-Baptiste, J. M. & Augustin D. (2010). Calcul de l'Inflation sous-jacente dans le Cas d'Haïti". *Cahier de Recherche de la BRH, 2*, 32–47. Banque de la République d'Haïti.

Jean-Baptiste, J. M., Janvier, C. H., & Georges, J. (2017). Estimation de l'impact du financement monétaire du déficit budgétaire sur l'inflation en Haïti". *Cahier de Recherche de la BRH*, *3*, 69–99. Banque de la République d'Haïti.

Justinville, C. (2008). Les déterminants de la rigidité des prix à la consommation en Haïti : Une analyse empirique de 1996 à 2006. *Cahier de Recherche de la BRH*, *1*, 69–104. Banque de la République d'Haïti.

Kandil, M. (2000, November 1). *The asymetric effects of exchange rate fluctuations: Theory and evidence from developing countries* (IMF WP/00/184). International Monetary Fund. https://www.imf.org/-/media/Websites/IMF/imported-full-text-pdf/external/pubs/ft/wp/2000/_wp00184.ashx.

Kavila, W., & le Roux, P. (2016). Inflation dynamics in a dollarized economy: The case of Zimbabwe. *Southern Africa Business Review, 20*(1), 94–117.

Khan, M. S. (1980). Monetary shocks and the dynamics of inflation. *IMF Staff Papers, 27*(2), 250–284. https://doi.org/10.5089/9781451946864.024

Loungani, P. & Swagel P. (2001, December). *Sources of inflation in developing countries* (IMF WP/01/198). International Monetary Fund. https://www.imf.org/-/media/Websites/IMF/imported-full-text-pdf/external/pubs/ft/wp/2001/_wp01198.ashx.

Luciéné, M. & Jean-Baptiste A. E. (2006). *Le coefficient pass-through du taux de change en Haïti pour la période d'octobre 1998 à septembre 2005* (Unpublished Working Paper). Banque de la République d'Haiti/MAE.

Ministère de l'Économie et des Finances (2005). IHSI: *L'indice des prix à la consommation. Base 100 en Août 2004.* Ministère de l'Économie et des Finances.

Parkin, M. (2008). Inflation. In S. N. Durlauf, S. & L. E. Blume (Eds.), *The new Palgrave dictionary of economics* (pp. 293–302). Palgrave Macmillan.

Redifer, L. & Hartelius, K. (2007). Monetary policy in Haiti: Improving effectiveness. *IMF Selected Issues Paper*, 20–38.

Roger, S. (1994). An illustrated guide to the role of underlying inflation in monetary policy. *Reserve Bank of New Zealand Bulletin, 57*(3), 234–243.

Roger, S. (2000, March). *Relative prices, inflation and core inflation* (IMF WP/00/58). https://www.elibrary.imf.org/view/journals/001/2000/058/001.2000.issue-058-en.xml.

Taylor, J. B. (1996, August 29–31). How should monetary policy respond to shocks while maintaining price stability? *Conceptual issues. Achieving price stability.* A symposium sponsored by the Federal Reserve Bank of Kansas City. Jackson Hole.

CHAPTER 8

The Impact of Remittances on the Real Exchange Rate: Evidence from Haiti

Carl-Henri Prophète and Dudley Augustin

Introduction

Remittances have become a major financial flow on the global stage, reaching the record level of $646.2 billion in 2020 while overtaking foreign direct investment as the largest inflow of foreign capital to developing countries. The importance of these flows can be particularly observed in Haiti, where the economy has been increasingly reliant on migrants' transfers over the past 30 years. Indeed, remittances to Haiti have increased almost tenfold to $3.1 billion between 1998 and 2018, while their ratio to GDP went from 8.8 to 32.5% over the same period (see Fig. 8.1).

C.-H. Prophète (✉) · D. Augustin
Macroeconomic Analysis Department, Central Bank of Haiti (BRH), Port-au-Prince, Haiti
e-mail: carl-henri.prophete@brh.ht

D. Augustin
e-mail: dudley.augustin@brh.ht

C. Cannonier and M. Galloway Burke (eds.),
Contemporary Issues Within Caribbean Economies,
https://doi.org/10.1007/978-3-030-98865-4_8

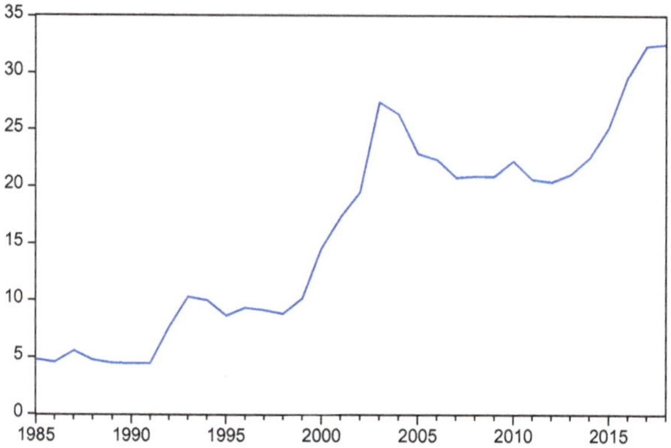

Fig. 8.1 Evolution of Haiti's remittances as a percentage of GDP

While their importance has been growing, migrants' transfers have been increasingly praised for their positive impact on household consumption and human development outcomes. More precisely, in the case of Haiti, they have been credited as one of the reasons behind the decline of the extreme poverty rate from 31% of the population in 2000 to 24% in 2012 (see Singh & Barton-Dock, 2015). Moreover, migrants' transfers often help pays for school fees and have helped in increasing the primary school enrollment rate from 80% in 2001 to over 90% currently. Anecdotal evidence also points to their substantial use in paying for medical expenses as the health system in Haiti is mostly private. However, there are also concerns about their potential macroeconomic unintended effects. Indeed, as a major financial flow, it is to be expected that remittances have major impacts on quantities and prices in an economy.

Among these various potential negative effects, a major concern has been the possibility of remittances induced "Dutch Disease" in the receiving countries. The "Dutch Disease" term was coined by "The Economist" in 1977 to describe the problems faced by the Dutch economy at that time. Large gas reserves had been discovered in the Netherlands in 1959, leading to a major growth in exports and a corresponding influx of foreign exchange. Ultimately, this inflow made other Dutch-made goods more expensive in international markets, amounting to a loss of external competitiveness of the country's tradable sector. The

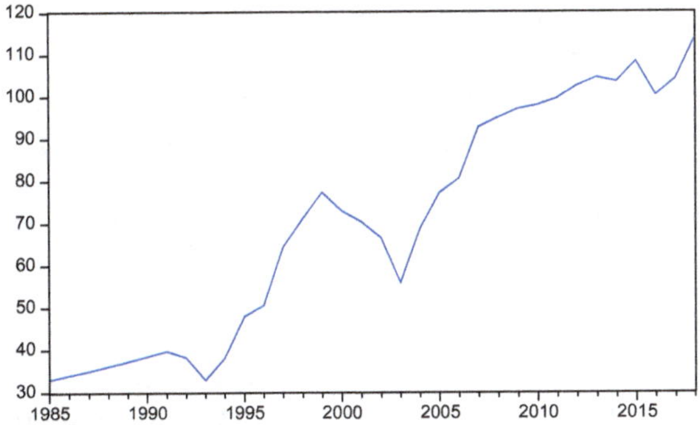

Fig. 8.2 Evolution of Haiti's real effective exchange rate

observations from "The Economist" were later analyzed more systematically in an economic model by Corden and Neary (1982). The authors found that the boom in a foreign exchange generating sector (natural gas in the Dutch case) led to severe loss of competitiveness in the tradable sectors of the economy such as manufacturing. Since then, various papers (e.g., Amuedo-Dorantes & Pozo, 2004; Chami et al., 2008; Lopez et al., 2007) have pointed to the potential adverse impacts of remittances regarding the export and import competing sectors.

As the flow of remittances to Haiti is becoming increasingly large, it is therefore important that we understand its impact beyond the household level and investigate its relationship with various macroeconomic indicators. One place to start is to look at the effect of these transfers on the external competitiveness of the country, a concept that is often approximated by the real exchange rate (RER). This chapter will therefore look at the link between the RER and a set of potential determinants including the remittances received by the Haitian economy. In other words, it would look at whether remittances sent to Haiti could possibly lead to some form of Dutch disease phenomenon (see Fig. 8.2).

The Haitian Economy

From Small Scale Farming to Remittances Dependency

For nearly two centuries, the Haitian economy was mainly organized around small scale subsistence farming. Additionally, peasants also produced a few cash crops such as coffee and cocoa, which provided foreign exchange as exports. By the 1970s, however, agriculture's share in output started to decline as the service sector's importance relatively grew and the country developed a small assembly manufacturing sector. Indeed, as noted by Lundahl (1979), while agriculture accounted for more than 50% of GDP in the 1950s and 1960s, it already fell to around 45% by the first half of the 1970s. At the same time, agriculture's share in employment went from around 85.3% in 1950 to a little over 70% by 1980 (Joachim, 1979).

This fall in the relative importance of agriculture was accompanied by increasing migration pressures as both agricultural productivity and incomes declined. While Haitians emigrated in greater number to various countries, especially in the Caribbean (Dominican Republic and the Bahamas for instance), a significant fraction ended up in the United States where they started sending back monetary transfers to close ones staying in Haiti. With increasing emigration abroad, and particularly to the United States, these remittances emerged as a major source of foreign exchange amounting to almost 10% of GDP by the end of the 1990s.

Since then, remittances to Haiti have increased almost tenfold to $3.1 billion between 1998 and 2018, while their share of GDP went from 8.8 to 32.5% over the same period. As a result, Haiti ranked as the fifth most remittances-dependent economy and the first most dependent among low-income countries. By large, these flows have become the country's biggest source of foreign exchange. For instance, in 2018, they amounted to 3.6 times of exports value, 10 times the flow of foreign aid, and 37 times the amount of foreign direct investment.

The Implications of Remittances' Dependency at a Low Level of Income Per Capita

The implications of the transformation of Haiti into a remittance-dependent country, at such a low level of income per capita, are numerous and have attracted relatively little attention. For instance, as remittances have been mainly used to finance household expenses on basic goods and services, they helped Haiti maintain a high level of consumption to GDP ratio, especially when compared with other low-income countries. As an example, in 2019, the country had the third-highest consumption to GDP ratio in the world at 101.2%, while the majority of low-income countries had ratios of less than 75%.

It is also worth noting that the high ratio of consumption to GDP means an increasing availability of private goods relative to a lower ability of the state to provide public goods in the form of public safety, basic infrastructure, education, health, and sanitation. This feature of the Haitian economy is related to the specific nature of remittances. Indeed, in contrast to flows of foreign exchange coming from the export of natural resources, remittances mostly bypass the state and go directly into the hands of households. Thus, they tend to increase the expenses on private goods while leaving the state with relatively less capacity to provide public goods. This occurrence can be observed through Haiti's very low government revenue to GDP ratio, which is barely above 6% while other low-income countries typically collect government revenues representing between 10 and 20% of GDP (Besley & Persson, 2014). This outcome is the opposite of what happens in a country that exports natural resources and where a significant share of the revenue coming from these resources go directly to the state coffers. One way to prevent such a situation would have been for the state to tax private consumption more heavily, whether through domestic taxes such as a value-added tax or higher import duties. However, such decisions are likely to be unpopular as they tend to increase the price of basic goods. Furthermore, import duties in Haiti are already the lowest in the Caribbean, a fact that limits the possibility for state revenues to indirectly benefit from the flow of remittances.

With remittances also came an increasing ability to acquire goods and services from abroad, which put the official ratio of imports to GDP at 32.3% in 2020. In reality, this ratio is likely to be higher as a significant share of Haiti's imports from the Dominican Republic is informal. Indeed, while it is estimated that around 25% of recorded imports come from the Dominican Republic, the informal trade between the two countries is estimated at around half the official data (IMF, 2020). Even though the country has adopted a very open trade regime with average import duties at 3%, it has to be highlighted that import duties have more or less remained the same since 1995, while the imports to GDP ratio has essentially doubled. In fact, the ratio went from 18.3% in 2000 to 36.3% in 2019. Meanwhile, imports have often moved in tandem with remittances especially during periods where they accounted for the most part of foreign exchange inflows. Therefore, while the growing import to GDP ratio of the Haitian economy has been often attributed to the trade liberalization policies of the 1980s and 1990s, it seems to be better explained by the increased import capacity that comes with a larger flow of remittances. It could be argued that the lower trade tariffs, even if they remained mostly constant since 1995, created a dynamic of lower competitiveness of domestically produced goods, which progressively translates into a higher import to GDP ratio. However, the previous round of trade liberalization in the late 1980s did not seem to lead to similar increases in trade to GDP ratio. Furthermore, given the size of the increase (a doubling over less than 20 years), it seems difficult that it could be explained by tariffs rates alone, which as we stressed have remained mostly unchanged for 25 years.

At the same time, the growing access to remittances allowed the country to avoid a larger depreciation of its nominal exchange rate. This situation is even starker when you consider the many episodes of macroeconomic instability that Haiti had to go through over the last decades. Indeed, a comparison of the nominal depreciation of the Haitian domestic currency (the Gourde) against the US dollar between 1988 and 2020 and the respective nominal depreciation in neighboring Dominican Republic and Jamaica highlights the relative moderation in the decrease in the value of the Gourde against the US dollar. Figure 8.2 shows that Haiti's nearby peers, such as the Dominican Republic and Jamaica, have seen their nominal exchange rates multiplied by a factor of 56 and 80 respectively, while Haiti's exchange rate was multiplied by 15. While these comparisons of nominal depreciation are by no means a definitive proof that Haitian currency nominal depreciation was moderate, they help to highlight the magnitude by which Haiti has seen significantly less depreciation than many Caribbean countries (Fig. 8.3).

Premature Tertiarization Induced by Remittances

The growing importance of remittances must also be put in relationship with the *premature tertiarization* of the Haitian economy, with the tertiary sector/services occupying an ever-increasing share of economic activity (Paul et al., 2010). It is well documented that countries that experience resource-driven appreciation of their currency should witness an excessive growth in their non-tradable (mainly services) sector at the expense of the tradable part of the economy. In the case of a low-income remittances' dependent country, such as Haiti, this development can be seen as a form of the "premature deindustrialization" hypothesis put forth by Dasgupta and Singh (2006) and Rodrik (2016).

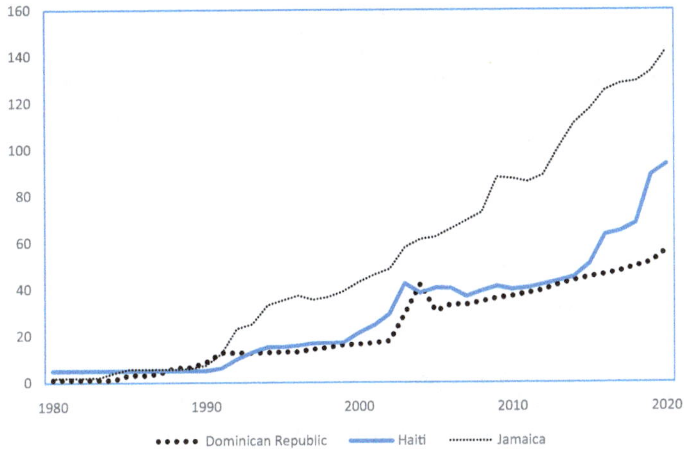

Fig. 8.3 Annual average exchange rate for Haiti, the Dominican Republic and Jamaica (domestic currency per USD)

According to this hypothesis, low- and middle-income countries, with some exceptions in East Asia, have seen a pattern of deindustrialization at lower levels of GDP per capita than advanced economies. Manufacturing has seen its share of output and employment decline and countries affected by this phenomenon have, most of the time, turned themselves into low value-added service economies. They did this without going through an industrialization phase as their richer counterparts did decades ago. This is a rather troubling trend as manufacturing offers a high potential for productivity growth relative to other sectors. Therefore, deindustrialization removes one of the main avenues for rapid GDP growth that has been historically available for poorer countries.

By hurting the growth of the tradable sector in general, remittances could be a significant factor behind premature deindustrialization, or more broadly "premature tertiarization," in a transfer-dependent country such as Haiti. This relationship would be similar to the results that Nguimkeu and Zeufack (2019) find for sub-Saharan African countries, namely that higher personal remittances are associated with a lower share of manufacturing in GDP. As mentioned, in the Haitian case, we would expect that remittances affect manufacturing and other tradables alike (agriculture, tradable services such as tourism, etc.), leading to a broader process that could be understood as "premature tertiarization." Haiti has been experiencing this trend over the last 40 years, going from a largely small farm-based economy to a mainly low added value service economy where services account for 53.2% of output in 2020 and more than 60% of employment (Institut Haïtien de Statistique et Informatique, 2013).

Literature Review

The discussion regarding the macroeconomic impacts of large capital flows can be traced back to the "transfer problem" debate between Keynes (1929) and Ohlin (1929) in the interwar period. One aspect of that discussion between the two renowned economists was whether the reparation transfers that Germany had to pay after World War I would have a negative impact on the competitiveness of the industries in the transfer receiving countries.

More recently, studies of the impact of remittances in developing countries have found that they are associated with a wide range of macroeconomic effects. For instance, Fajnzylber and Lopez (2006) found that remittances are associated with lower poverty levels and higher growth rates. Remittances are also found to be associated with lower output volatility in receiving countries as they are countercyclical (Ratha, 2006). This was observed following the 2010 earthquake in Haiti, as transfers from Haitians abroad rose by more than 7%, against 0.42% a year earlier, in order to ease the financial hardships faced by family and friends. Furthermore, Abdih et al. (2012) found that such inflows of foreign exchange increase aggregate private demand through higher private consumption, while having not much effect on investment. At the same time, they help expand the tax base, raise government revenue and more generally improve the fiscal space. In matters related to public debt, Abdih et al. (2009) have pointed to how these transfers help reduce country risk and improve the sustainability of government debt. Moreover, large flows of remittances increase bank liquid assets and are associated with weaker monetary policy transmission as highlighted by Barajas et al. (2016). Furthermore, the real appreciation of the domestic currency induced by remittances leads to rising employment in the non-traded goods sector at the expense of traded goods activities such as agriculture and manufacturing (Chami et al., 2008). This may be one of the factors behind the premature deindustrialization trend (Rodrik, 2016) observed in many developing countries.

In a broader political economy sense, remittances have been found to be a potential source of moral hazard as they weaken the incentives for government policy reforms in receiving countries (Chami et al., 2008). As a source of income largely independent from government initiatives and a cushion in the face of economic shocks, remittances reduce the incentive for citizens to lobby and pressure their government toward policies that could be beneficial to them. Thus, they decrease the sense of urgency that could have accelerated the pace of structural change.

As a financial inflow, migrants' transfers are similar to other foreign exchange flows in an economy and can therefore be analyzed through the dynamics of the Dutch disease phenomenon mentioned earlier. This relationship is often studied through two main models, the Fundamental Equilibrium Real Exchange Rate (FEER) and the Behavioral Equilibrium Real Exchange Rate (BEER). FEER models generally point to a necessary path for the RER in order for the economy to achieve internal and external balance. In order to do this, they usually express the RER as determined by the optimal level of domestic output and sustained capital flows. In contrast, BEER models shed light on major macroeconomic fundamentals (terms of trade, capital flows, openness to trade, etc.) in their relationship to the RER. This approach pioneered by Clark and Mc Donald (1999) uses a single equation expressing the behavior of the RER in terms of variables susceptible to affect the relative prices of traded and non-traded goods in the economy.

Among notable empirical studies of the determinants of the RER using the BEER approach, one could cite Edwards (1989). In this paper, Edwards develops a dynamic model of real exchange rate behavior in developing economies and highlights the role of devaluations and balance of payments crises using data from 12 countries. He also argues that only real variables are susceptible to affect the long-run equilibrium RER while an excessively loose monetary policy can lead to RER appreciation.

Using a similar BEER framework, Lopez et al. (2007) investigate the impact of transfers in the Latin American context and find that remittances contribute to significant real exchange rate appreciation. They also provide a succinct review of the mechanisms through which remittances may affect the external competitiveness. To do so, they consider the case of a small open economy model where an increase in remittances translates into a permanent increase in households' incomes. As the small economies are price takers in international markets, the increase in demand does not raise the price they face for tradables while the domestically determined price of non-tradables increases. Besides this "spending effect," there is a "resource movement effect." Indeed, the change in relative price makes the non-tradable sector more profitable, which will fuel the demand for factors of production that are widely used in these sectors. The greater demand for inputs by the most dynamic sectors will be met by factors leaving other sectors (resource movement effect) and will likely result ultimately in higher returns for that factor. The change in price and the movement of resources in favor of non-tradables will affect negatively the competitiveness of export-oriented and import-competing sectors. The real appreciation of the domestic currency will ultimately translate into increased imports and lower exports.

Among other empirical papers that have investigated the relationship between remittances and the real exchange rate, Amuedo-Dorantes and Pozo (2004) look at the data of 13 Latin American economies and found that a doubling of migrants' transfers induces a 22% overvaluation of the exchange rate on average. However, Rajan and Subramanian (2008) conclude that unlike other financial flows such as foreign aid, remittances do not lead to an adverse effect on external competitiveness. More recently, Tuuli (2015), studying the impact of remittances on the real exchange rate in Ghana with an error correction model, finds that they cause real appreciation in the long run. Similar results are found for Tunisia by Chnaina and Makhlouf (2015).

Following their line of work, our investigation will rely on the BEER approach taking advantage of its relatively easier applicability to empirical investigations and its wide use in the literature. More specifically, we will follow the general approach adopted by studies such as Ahmed (2009), Tuuli (2015) as well as Chnaina and Makhlouf (2015) given that they fit well with our available data.

Furthermore, Bussolo and Medvedev (2007) found that a negative relationship exists between the labor supply and remittances in Jamaica. Using a general equilibrium model, they concluded that diaspora transfers reduce labor force participation by pushing up the reservation wages of the recipients. The same model shows that the higher reserve wages lead to an appreciation of the real exchange rate, which as we know is detrimental to tradable goods in general and exports more particularly. In the same vein, Kim (2007), using cross-sectional data from Jamaica, finds that remittances have a negative impact on the labor supply by reducing labor force participation rates.

Moreover, as cited earlier, among the latest work related to the topic, Nguimkeu and Zeufack (2019) highlight some of the key themes of our chapter. In their work on manufacturing and structural change in Africa, they find a positive relationship not only between remittances and deindustrialization but also between the real exchange rate and manufacturing shares of output. They conclude their investigation by calling, among other things, for a better understanding of the Dutch disease phenomenon in relation to the place of manufacturing in low-income countries in Africa.

Beyond the relationship between inflows of foreign exchange and macroeconomic variables, some authors have looked at the relationship between the real exchange rate and economic growth. For instance, Rodrik (2008) finds that a relatively high real exchange rate is beneficial to GDP growth. More fundamentally, the author argues that tradable economic activities are "special" in the sense that they suffer disproportionately from institutional and market failures that are so pervasive in developing countries. Therefore, a high real exchange rate counteracts this negative effect by increasing the profitability of tradable activities relative to non-tradables. In other ways, according to this hypothesis, a high real exchange rate accelerates the process of structural change in the economy.

Along the same lines, Guzman et al. (2018) find that a stable and competitive real exchange rate policy help overcome the constraints to the development of sectors with a larger contribution to inclusive economic growth. They also stress that RER policies should be associated with traditional industrial policies that make aggregate output more responsive to changes in the real exchange rate. However, they acknowledge that a more "undervalued" RER will translate into higher prices of tradables in terms of domestic currency. Another recent work on the subject is by Seraj et al. (2020). Using a machine learning approach, they find that in an economy with a high rate of trade openness such as Slovakia, the real exchange rate takes precedence over all other determinants of economic growth.

Data and Methodology

This study uses annual data in order to estimate the long-run and short-run relationships between Haiti's Real Effective Exchange Rate (REER), remittances as a share of GDP (REM) as well as a set of macroeconomic fundamental variables from 1985 and 2018. This set of variables includes other capital inflows as a share of GDP (CAP), an index of the openness of the economy (LIB), government expenditure as a percentage of GDP (GOV) as well as the country's terms of trade (TOT).

Theoretically, the real exchange rate is supposed to reflect the relative price of tradable to non-tradable goods. Among its many approximations, we choose the Real Effective Exchange Rate (REER) computed by the IMF for Haiti. It is obtained using the number of foreign currency units per domestic currency unit (E), adjusted for the relative price differences between Haiti and its main trading partners. This difference is calculated by dividing the domestic CPI (P_d) by an average CPI index for the country's trading partners(P_f). Thus, the REER can be expressed as follows.

$$\text{REER} = \text{E}\left(\frac{P_d}{P_f}\right)$$

It follows that an increase in the ratio illustrates an appreciation of the real exchange rate. The main relationship we will be looking at will be the one between the REER and Remittances as a percentage of GDP (REM). That variable is obtained from the World Development Indicators database.

The other main capital inflows to Haiti during the study period have been foreign aid as measured by Official Development Assistance (ODA) as well as Foreign Direct Investment (FDI). Therefore, we add these two flows to create the Capital Flow (CAP) variable and use it in the model, given that all major flow of foreign exchange is expected to lead to real exchange rate appreciation. These data are taken from the Balance of Payments compiled by the Central Bank of Haiti (BRH).

We also use a measure of the openness or liberalization of the economy (LIB). This is usually approximated by a ratio of imports plus exports to GDP. Generally, it is expected that a more open economy is able to reap the benefits of global competitiveness in the form of technology transfers and turn into lower non-tradable price and ultimately to RER depreciation. Conversely, a more closed economy, through higher tariffs or quotas, is expected to be more susceptible to price pressures for imports and tradable goods. Ultimately, low openness of the economy should translate into an appreciation of the RER. The openness variable is taken from the World Development Indicators database.

Government expenditures (GOV) are included in the model as a more expansive fiscal policy is usually associated with inflationary pressures in developing economies. Indeed, given that non-tradables represent a major share of these expenditures (salaries for services provided by civil servants for instance), they particularly fuel non-tradable inflation and are expected to lead ultimately to RER appreciation. The government expenditures data are taken from data compiled by the Central Bank of Haiti.

Finally, we also include a Term of Trade (TOT) variable. As the relative price of exports to imports, this variable reflects the impact of foreign demand and supply on the export and import-competing sectors of an economy. However, its impact on the RER is ambiguous given its substitution and income effects. Through the income effect, an improvement in the terms of trade leaves more money to be spent on tradable and non-tradable goods. The latter sector is being constrained by domestic supply, its prices are expected to rise, leading to RER appreciation. Through the substitution effect, that TOT improvement, will lead to increased consumption of imports and a decrease in the demand for tradable goods as well as their price. The two effects will therefore translate into opposite impacts on the RER. The TOT variable is obtained from the World Development Indicators database.

Empirical Results

Using the above variables, we test the relationship between Haiti's Real Effective Exchange Rate (REER) and remittances as a share of GDP, with the following equation.

$$REER_t = f(REM_t, CAP_t, LIB_t, GOV_t, TOT_t)$$

In order to address the possibility of non-linear relationships, all variables will be taken in logarithm form except for CAP, which took negative values during the early 1990s.[1] An Augmented Dickey-Fuller test shows that the variable is not stationary in levels, excluding the possibility that ordinary least squares be used (see Table 8.1).

Since all the variables were integrated of order one, we proceeded to test for cointegration using the Johansen cointegration test. The values of

[1] Haiti was under an economic and financial embargo at that time and suffered from significant capital outflows.

Table 8.1 Unit root test with break

Variables	*Breaks*	*Augmented Dickey-Fuller test statistic*	*Test critical values*	*Conclusion*
CAP		−4.13	−3.61	I(1)
LLIB	2009	−7.80	−4.44	I(1)
LREM	2003	−4.73	−4.44	I(1)
LREER	1997	−4.92	−4.44	I(1)
LTOT	2008	−5.51	−4.44	I(1)
LGOV	1997	−7.24	−4.44	I(1)

the Trace Statistic indicate one cointegration equation at a 5% level (see Table 8.2).

We will therefore resort to an error correction model approach by estimating the following equation.

$$\Delta REER_t = \theta(REER_{t-1} + \beta_1 REM_{t-1} + \beta_2 X_{t-1}) + \delta_0 + \delta_1 \Delta REM_t + \delta_2 \Delta X_t + \varepsilon_t$$

where X is a set of macroeconomic fundamentals that include the following: other capital inflows as a share of GDP (CAP), the index of the openness of the economy (LIB), government expenditure as a percentage of GDP (GOV), as well as the country's terms of trade (TOT). This method will allow us to test the long-run relationship between the variables as well as the possibility of short-term disequilibrium among them. Table 8.3 reports the results of the long-run equation while Table 8.4 presents the results for the short run.

Table 8.2 Johansen cointegration results

H_0	H_1	*Trace statistic*	*5% critical value*	*Prob.***
$r = 0$	$r > 0$	139.7791*	117.7082	0.001
$r \leq 1$	$r > 1$	76.78522	88.8038	0.2677
$r \leq 2$	$r > 2$	44.32994	63.8761	0.6777
$r \leq 3$	$r > 3$	25.53894	42.91525	0.7621
$r \leq 4$	$r > 4$	9.52797	25.87211	0.9435
$r \leq 5$	$r > 5$	2.361411	12.51798	0.9422

Notes Trace test indicates 1 cointegrating equation(s) at the 0.05 level
*denotes rejection of the hypothesis at the 0.05 level
**MacKinnon-Haug-Michelis (1999) *p*-values

Table 8.3 Long run equation

Dependent variable: D(LREER)			
Variable	*Coefficient*	*Std. error*	*t-statistic*
LREM	0.4488	0.1116	4.0203
LLIB	2.1922	0.3662	5.9870
LGOV	−0.2494	0.1147	−2.1736
LTOT	0.0430	0.1251	0.3434
CAP	0.0263	0.0055	4.7831
Trend	−0.0941	0.0097	−9.7257
C	−10.8765		

The results in Table 8.3 are for the long-run relationship. Judging from t-statistic values, we conclude that all the variables significantly affect the real exchange rate, except for the term of trade variable. In the case of the remittances as a percentage of GDP, the long-run equation implies that an increase is related to an appreciation of the REER and at 0.45, the coefficient is important relatively to other variables in the model except for the trade openness variable. As expected, other capital flows (CAP) are also positively related to the REER in the long run. However, at 0.03, their coefficient is small relative to the other variables.

Contrary to the expectations of our analysis, an increase in trade openness is not positively associated with greater external competitiveness. Indeed, the coefficient on this variable is both positive and large, meaning that greater trade openness is associated with increasing real appreciation of the domestic currency in the long run. One possibility might be the presence of a reverse causation issue where real appreciation would lead to increased imports (as the variable is mostly driven by imports instead of exports) and a larger openness index. This observation should be the subject of further investigation given the magnitude and significance of the coefficient. The final result regarding this is its dynamics would also have significant policy implications in terms of external trade policy in the Haitian context.

Another result that goes against our previous analysis is the coefficient of the Government Expenditures as a share of GDP. With a negative sign, it shows that a more expansionary fiscal policy is associated with increased real depreciation in the long run. One explanation here could be that even if a large share of the government budget is seemingly spent on non-tradable goods such as labor and services; these amounts are ultimately spent by employees and contractors on tradable goods, mostly imports. This increased demand for imports may lead to a nominal depreciation of the domestic currency that doesn't translate fully into greater domestic inflation (see Table 8.4).

The results in Table 8.4 are for the short-run relationship. Short-run relationships may be different from the long-run ones as transitory factors can push variables away from their long-run equilibrium values. The results in this case show that in the short term, remittances have a positive but not significant relationship with the REER. The same can be said about the other capital flows variable. The term of trade variable remains significant and positive. As this variable is mainly driven by the price of imports in the Haitian case, its coefficient could be understood as evidence that import prices are quickly reflected into the inflation rate, leading therefore to short-run real appreciation of the currency. Also, the Government Expenditure maintains its sign although it loses in terms of significance in the short term. Furthermore, the trade openness remains significant while maintaining a relatively strong positive relationship with the REER. As discussed earlier, the sign exhibited by this coefficient warrants further investigation, especially in terms of a possible reverse causation issue. Finally, dummies for the years 1992, 1993, and 2003 are included in the model. They correspond to periods of major shocks in

Table 8.4 Short run equation

Dependent variable: D(LREER)			
Variable	*Coefficient*	*Std. error*	*t-statistic*
CointEq1	−0.3106	0.0723	−4.2962
C	0.0385	0.017	2.2694
D(LRER(−1))	0.0932	0.1847	0.5048
D(LREM(−1))	0.0977	0.1127	0.8665
D(LLIB(−1))	0.4606	0.1605	2.8701
D(LGOV(−1))	−0.1342	0.0817	−1.643
D(LTOT(−1))	0.213	0.1018	2.0929
D(CAP(−1))	0.0042	0.0031	1.3537
DUM92-93	−0.2065	0.0574	−3.5957
DUM2003	−0.1845	0.0737	−2.502
R-squared	0.6591		
Adj. R-squared	0.5197		
Residual serial correlation LM tests:		Prob = 58.75	

terms of nominal depreciation of the currency and domestic inflation due to an economic and financial embargo (1992 and 1993) as well as political instability (2003). Overall, 66% of the short-run movement in the REER can be explained by the specified model and the REER corrects itself toward the long-run equilibrium path by 31% in the first period.

Discussion of the Results and Other Considerations

Is There a Common Factor behind Remittances and Real Exchange Rate Appreciation?

While estimation results point to a strong positive and significant relationship between remittances, a share of Haiti's GDP, and its real exchange rate, various questions can be raised about whether the relationship is causal. This brings us, for instance, to the issue of endogeneity, or whether one could find factors that drive remittances as well as the real exchange rate. For example, it can be safely said that Haiti's remittances over the last 40 years are primarily fueled by increasing Haitian migration abroad. Therefore, could it be that some of the factors that are deteriorating the country's external competitiveness are at the same time leading more Haitians to emigrate? These factors could be as diverse as political instability, macroeconomic mismanagement leading to inflation, loss of purchasing power, and so on. However, it is worth noting that most countries in the Caribbean have witnessed a large increase in outmigration as well as in the absolute amount of remittances they received from their migrants, irrespectively of their economic performance. Case in point, if we consider the Dominican Republic, we notice that despite income per capita having almost tripled between 1990 and 2019,[2] the number of Dominicans living abroad has more than tripled between 1990 and 2015 (United Nations Department of Economic & Social Affairs, 2019), while remittances have been multiplied by 25. Therefore, even if Haiti had managed to have a better record in terms of economic performance or political stability, the number of Haitian migrants and the amount of remittances they send back would not have been lower. One can even make the prediction that these numbers would have been

[2] Using GDP per capita at Purchasing Power Parity and constant 2017 international dollars.

higher. In fact, various works such as Clemens (2014) have pointed out that economic growth in migrants-sending countries is not a deterrent to greater emigration while it can even serve as a catalyst. According to the aforementioned study, it is only after a country goes beyond the upper-middle-income status that the emigration pressures tend to decrease. Therefore, we cannot say that the deterioration of economic conditions in Haiti could be the reason behind increasing emigration and remittances as well as the appreciation of the real exchange rate.

Could the Real Exchange Rate Affect Remittances?

Nevertheless, other questions regarding causality could be raised. Among them, could there be a form of reverse causation where lower external competitiveness would lead to increasing out migration, which ultimately leads to more remittances? As an example, the loss of competitiveness in the agricultural sector could have a negative impact on rural incomes, leading to increased migration abroad of labor formerly occupied in the primary sector. To such an argument, one can provide a similar answer to the one provided in the paragraph above. Countries that had a better performance than Haiti in terms of external competitiveness experienced greater migration and received increased amount of remittances. Therefore, it is difficult to argue that the loss of external competitiveness, as measured by the real exchange rate, could be a major factor leading to the increase of the remittances to GDP ratio. Nevertheless, it can still be argued that an appreciating real exchange rate hurts GDP growth, which leads to a higher remittance to GDP ratio. However, in the case of foreign exchange inflows that come from natural resources exports, the GDP increases while the literature usually finds the appreciating effect on the RER. Therefore, a question would be why wouldn't remittances lead to the same effect?

Another hypothesis could be that increased remittances to Haiti and the real appreciation of the national currency are mostly independent phenomena that have tended to happen over the same period. Under that hypothesis, both trends would be simultaneous without much causal relationship between the two. Nevertheless, in such a case, one could ask how was Haiti's currency able to maintain a relatively moderate level of nominal depreciation over the last 40 years,[3] especially when you compare it to other currencies in the Caribbean or in other low-income countries. It seems that could not be achieved without the country receiving large inflows of foreign exchange at the same time. As most of these flows have been coming in the form of remittances, it can be argued that they indeed help limit nominal depreciation, which ultimately allowed the currency to appreciate in real terms.

Concluding and Implications for Policymakers

This chapter attempts to investigate the relationship between remittances and the real exchange rate in the case of Haiti. To do this, we look at whether remittances have induced a Dutch disease phenomenon in the form of a real appreciation of Haiti's currency. Using annual data and controlling for other macroeconomic factors that might affect the country's external competitiveness, our results point to a positive long-run relationship between the remittances as a share of GDP and the Real Effective Exchange Rate (REER). Therefore, it can be said that the available evidence leads us to think that migrant transfers to Haiti do induce some form of Dutch Disease.

While the relationship between the REER and some other variables such as trade openness requires further investigation, the results raise the issue of what policymakers could and should do to mitigate the negative impacts of migrants' transfers inflows. Some authors have pointed to the possible use of sterilization operations but also warn against their cost and sustainability (Lopez et al., 2007). However, one possible avenue for government intervention remains microeconomic policies that could address specific issues in export and import competing sectors while trying to insulate them from the challenge created by the resulting real appreciation of the Haitian currency.

Haiti's Central Bank already operates a number of loan incentive programs to a few priority sectors. With the exception of housing construction, these sectors could be mostly characterized as tradable goods and services and include tourism, agriculture, and exports. Under,

[3] This is not to say that the national currency has not witnessed significant absolute nominal depreciation during that period, in particular during the last six years. However, when the rate of nominal depreciation is compared with a group of peer countries, it is far from being the most severe.

these programs, financial institutions that provide loans to the priority sectors can benefit from exemptions in the amount of required reserves they must maintain at the Central Bank or access the Central Bank liquidity window at preferred interest rates. Such programs may not be perfect or, more than that, financing may not be the main constraint facing the tradable sectors in Haiti. However, these initiatives point to how a more microeconomic approach could be used to counter the negative effects of remittances on external competitiveness.

Another avenue for thinking about the possible policy responses to the real appreciation of the domestic currency is related to the use of foreign exchange deposits in the Haitian banking system. The question of how remittances could be used to finance investments has been often at the center of many public debates. This goal is inherently difficult given that remittances are by far mostly used to finance consumption. However, over the years, part of the remittances has been fueling the growth in foreign exchange deposits in the Haitian banking system. Thus, part of these deposits represents a share of the remittances that have been saved by the Haitian economy, and it will be welcomed if they could be directed to productive investments, preferably in the tradable sector. Currently, the Central Bank of Haiti has been very cautious in the use of this dollar-denominated deposit base to help finance credit to the private sector. This caution is understandable given that many beneficiaries of such loans would have revenues in domestic currency and foreign exchange loans will make them subject to significant exchange rate risk. Therefore, the BRH has limited loans in US dollars to clients that have revenues in foreign currency and additionally, it has put in place strict limits on the foreign exchange credit to deposits ratio while at the same time maintaining a relatively high reserve requirement on foreign exchange deposits.

While all these precautions are understandable and absolutely necessary, it might be useful to look at whether there is any possibility that these foreign exchange deposits could be better channeled to improve the financing conditions for the tradable sectors. However, such a proposition requires additional research and there is no specific recommendation in that area that could be implied directly from this chapter. Nevertheless, if we want more remittances to finance investment and if we agree that part of the dollar deposits in the Haitian banking system represent a share of remittances that have been saved, it might be worthwhile to investigate this issue.

References

Abdih, Y., Chami, R., Gapen, M., & Mati, A. (2009). *Fiscal sustainability in remittance dependent economies* (IMF Working Paper No. 09/190). https://www.imf.org/-/media/Websites/IMF/imported-full-text-pdf/external/pubs/ft/wp/2009/_wp09190.ashx.

Abdih, Y., Barajas A., Chami, R., & Ebeke, C. (2012). *Remittances channel and fiscal impact in the Middle East, North Africa and Central Asia* (IMF Working Paper No. 12/104). https://www.imf.org/external/pubs/ft/wp/2012/wp12104.pdf.

Ahmed, H. (2009). Capital flows and real exchange rate overvaluations—A chronic ailment: Evidence from Pakistan. *Lahore Journal of Economics, 14*, 51–81.

Amuedo-Dorantes, C., & Pozo, S. (2004). Workers' remittances and the real exchange rate: A paradox of gifts. *World Development, 32*, 1407–1417.

Barajas, A., Chami, R., Ebeke, C., & Oeking A. (2016). *What's different about monetary policy transmission in remittance-dependent countries?* (IMF Working Paper No. 16/44). https://www.imf.org/external/pubs/ft/wp/2016/wp1644.pdf.

Besley, T., & Persson, T. (2014). Why do developing countries tax so little? *Journal of Economic Perspectives, 28*(4), 99–120.

Bussolo, M., & Medvedev, D. (2007). *Do remittances have a flip side? A general equilibrium analysis of remittances, labor supply responses, and policy options for Jamaica* (World Bank Policy Research Working Paper No. 4143). World Bank. http://hdl.handle.net/10986/7159.

Chami, R., Barajas, A., Cosimano T. F., & Fullenkamp C. (2008). *Macroeconomic consequences of remittances*. (IMF Occasional Papers. 1–84). https://www.imf.org/external/pubs/ft/op/259/op259.pdf.

Chami, R., Ernst, E., Fullenkamp C., & Oeking A. (2018). *Are remittances good for labor markets in LICs, MICs and fragile states? Evidence from cross-country data*. (IMF Working Paper No. 18/102). International Monetary Fund. https://doi.org/10.5089/9781484353615.001.

Chnaina, K., & Makhlouf, F. (2015). Impact des transferts de fonds sur le taux de change réel effectif en Tunisie. *African Development Review, 27*, 145–160.

Clark, P., & MacDonald, R. (1999). Exchange rates and economic fundamentals: A methodological comparison of BEERs and FEERs. In J. Stein & R. MacDonald (Eds.), *Equilibrium exchange rates* (pp. 285–322). Kluwer.

Clemens, M. A. (2014). Does development reduce migration? In R. E. B. Lucas (Ed.), *International handbook on migration and economic development* (pp. 152–185). Edward Elgar Publishing.

Corden, W. M., & Neary, J. P. (1982). Booming sector and de-industrialisation in a small open economy. *Economic Journal, 92*(December), 825–848.

Dasgupta, S., & Singh, A. (2006). *Manufacturing, services and premature deindustrialization in developing countries: A Kaldorian analysis.* (UNU-WIDER, United Nations University Research Paper No. 2006/49). https://www.wider.unu.edu/sites/default/files/rp2006-49.pdf.

Edwards, S. (1988). Real and monetary determinants of real exchange rate behavior. Theory and evidence from developing countries. *Journal of Development Economics, 29* (November), 311–341.

Edwards, S. (1989). *Real exchange rate, devaluation and adjustment: Exchange rate policy in developing countries*. MIT Press.

Fajnzylber, P. & Lopez J. H. (2006). *Close to home: The development impact of remittances in Latin America* (World Bank Working Paper No. 48911). https://documents1.worldbank.org/curated/en/869061468266372115/pdf/489110WP0Close1Biox338933B01PUBLIC1.pdf.

Guzman, M., Ocampo, J. A., & Stiglitz, J. E. (2018). Real exchange rate policies for economic development. *World Development, 110*, 51–62.

Institut Haïtien de Statistique et Informatique. (2013). *Enquête sur les conditions de vie des ménages après le séisme*. https://www.haiti-now.org/wp-content/uploads/2017/05/2012-13-ENQUETE-SUR-LES-CONDITIONS-DE-VIE.pdf.

International Monetary Fund. (2020). *Haiti: Selected issues* (IMF Staff Country Report No 122). https://doi.org/10.5089/9781513541501.002.

Joachim, B. (1979). *Les Racines du sous-développement en Haïti*. H. Deschamps.

Keynes, J. M. (1929). The German transfer problem. *Economic Journal, 39*, 1–7.

Kim, N. (2007). *The impact of remittances on labor supply: The case of Jamaica* (World Bank Policy Research Working Paper No. 4120). World Bank. http://hdl.handle.net/10986/7152.

Lopez, H., Bussolo, M., & Molina, L. (2007). *Remittances and the real exchange rate* (World Bank Policy Research Paper No. 4213). World Bank Group. https://openknowledge.worldbank.org/handle/10986/7069.

Lundahl, M., (1979). *Peasants and poverty: A study of Haiti.* Croom Helm.

Nguimkeu, P., & Zeufack, A. G. (2019). *Manufacturing in structural change in Africa* (World Bank Policy Research Working Paper No. 8992). World Bank. http://hdl.handle.net/10986/32317.

Ohlin, B. (1929). The reparation problem: A discussion. *Economic Journal, 39*(172–178), 400–404.

Paul, B., Daméus, P., & Garrabe, M. (2010). Le processus de tertiarisation de l'économie haïtienne. *Études caribéennes, 16*. https://doi.org/10.4000/etudescaribeennes.18227

Rajan, R., & Subramanian, A. (2008). Aid and growth: What does the cross-country evidence really show? *The Review of Economics and Statistics, 90*, 643–665.

Ratha, D. (2006). Leveraging remittances for development. *Federal Reserve Bank of Dallas Proceedings* (pp. 73–185). https://www.dallasfed.org/-/media/Documents/research/pubs/migration/ratha.pdf?la=en http://dallasfed.org/assets/documents/research/pubs/migration/ratha.pdf.

Rodrik, D. (2008, Fall). The real exchange rate and economic growth. *Brookings Papers on Economic Activity. No. 2*. Brookings Institution Press.

Rodrik, D. (2016). Premature deindustrialization. *Journal of Economic Growth, 21*(1), 1–33.

Seraj, M., Alhassan, A., Bahramian, P., & Shahabad, R. D. (2020) The validity of Rodrik's conclusion on real exchange rate and economic growth: Factor priority evidence from feature selection approach. *Palgrave Communications, 6* (Article No. 76). https://doi.org/10.1057/s41599-020-0465-9.

Singh, R. J., & Barton-Dock, M. (2015). *Haiti: Toward a new narrative. Systematic country diagnostic*. World Bank. http://hdl.handle.net/10986/22580.

Tuuli, M. (2015). The impact of remittances on the real exchange rate: Empirical evidence from Ghana. *Journal of Economic Cooperation and Development, 36*(3), 43–66.

United Nations Department of Economic and Social Affairs. (2019). *International migration stock: The 2019 revision* [database]. https://www.un.org/en/development/desa/population/migration/data/estimates2/estimates19.asp.

CHAPTER 9

Remittances and Financial Development in Caribbean Countries

Colin Cannonier and Marcus Bansah

Introduction

This chapter examines the impact of remittances on financial development in the Caribbean. Remittances to the Caribbean have witnessed unprecedented growth over the past two and half decades—a phenomenon that is consistent with global trends. The significance of remittances to the region is most evident in the relative contribution to the economies. For example, World Bank estimates show that the Caribbean received about $3.1 billion in 2013, compared to $70 billion that went to India, which received the most remittances over this period (World Bank, 2019b). In terms of contribution to the economy, remittances over this period

C. Cannonier (✉)
Jack C. Massey College of Business, Belmont University, Nashville, TN, USA
e-mail: colin.cannonier@belmont.edu

M. Bansah
Department of Economics, St. Olaf College, Northfield, MN, USA
e-mail: bansah1@stolaf.edu

C. Cannonier and M. Galloway Burke (eds.),
Contemporary Issues Within Caribbean Economies,
https://doi.org/10.1007/978-3-030-98865-4_9

accounted for 4.9% of Gross Domestic Product (GDP) for the Caribbean, compared to 3.8% of GDP for India (World Bank, 2019b). Remittances are more important to Caribbean economies than other regions of the world (see Fig. 9.1). To date, there is not a comprehensive analysis in the Caribbean examining the impact of remittances on financial development which is crucial to addressing issues such as poverty, household consumption smoothing, education, and business in the Caribbean.

There is a voluminous literature on the importance of remittances. However, the existing empirical evidence on the impact of remittances as a facilitator of financial development is inconclusive. Some studies suggest that remittances serve as complementing the developments in the financial system of the recipient country. This scenario is possible if remittance recipients transmit remittances through the banking system and use these funds as leverage to make credit (Aggarwal et. al., 2011; Kakhkharov & Rohde, 2020). Similar findings were obtained from Fromentin's (2018) research on the remittances-financial development nexus in Latin America

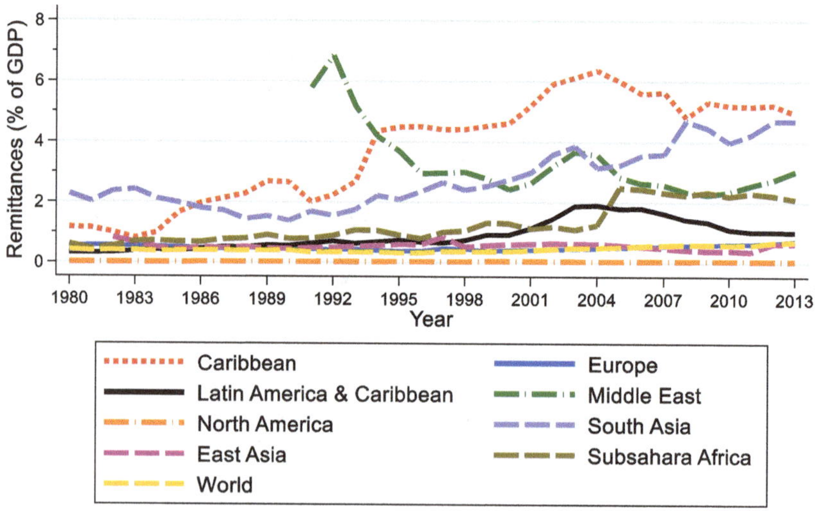

Source: World Development Indicators, World Bank
(Caribbean comprise Antigua and Barbuda, Bahamas, Barbados, Belize, Dominica, Grenada, Guyana, Jamaica, St. Kitts and Nevis, St. Lucia,
St. Vincent and the Grenadines, Suriname, Trinidad and Tobago).

Fig. 9.1 Remittances as a percentage of GDP by region, 1980–2013 (*Source* Authors' Calculations)

and Caribbean countries. The findings of this chapter, which contradicts those of Fromentin (2018), may be explained by the fact that this chapter focuses solely on Caribbean countries which are culturally different to those of Latin America. Other studies emphasize that remittances behave as substitutes because remittances recipients have a preference to avoid the use of bank channels due to higher costs and there is a general lack of trust in authorities monitoring these transactions or regulations that makes it increasingly prohibitive to open bank accounts in which to keep these remittances (Brown et al., 2013; Giuliano & Ruiz-Arranz, 2009; Sobiech, 2019). The finding that remittances are substitutes to financial development is consistent with results of this chapter.

The chapter adds to the growing list of literature linking remittances and financial development in two distinctly significant ways: limited scope and causal identification. First, while there is growing list of studies on the relationship between remittances and financial development, this chapter is the first to present systematic robust evidence on the effect of remittances on financial development across a comprehensive set of Caribbean economies. Second, this chapter utilizes multiple identification strategies to estimate the effect of remittances on financial development outcomes. Specifically, fixed effects are used with a rich set of control variables on a sample of countries over an extended time period. Another strategy is based on two dynamic panel data models to obtain estimates using the Generalized Method of Moments (GMM) technique. In this method, an appropriate number of lags of predetermined variables and endogenous variables are used as instruments in order to mitigate spurious correlations between these variables and the error term. The final strategy involves the traditional instrumental variables approach to control for reverse causality. This strategy uses external instruments based on unemployment rates in the major remittance-sending countries. The identifying assumption is that unemployment rates in the source countries provide exogenous variation in remittances but do not otherwise affect the financial development in the Caribbean.

This is perhaps the first study to document a negative causal effect of remittances on financial development in the Caribbean. Using the most conservative estimates, on average, a one percent increase in remittances is associated with a reduction in financial development in the range of 0.1 to 0.5%. The analysis also reveals that the negative effect of remittances on financial development is evident among the mostly lower-income, larger, higher-remittance-receiving countries that are not part of a common currency area. Overall, the results are valid across a variety of empirical specifications and functional forms. The evidence confirms that the relationship between remittances and financial development is one of substitutes and not complements. Since remittances constitute a growing proportion of economic activity, efforts to better facilitate these flows within the banking system could help to improve financial development.

Remittances and the Financial Systems in Caribbean Countries

The effect of remittances on financial development is mixed. The literature on remittances and financial development reveals that remittances can promote financial development by fostering financial literacy among the remittance-receiving communities, thereby increasing households' demand for and use of banking services. Remittance inflows can also increase financial depth by increasing the supply of loanable funds to the financial sector (Brown et al., 2013). On the other hand, remittances can serve as a substitute to bank credit (Chami et al., 2003).

Data from the World Bank shows that there has been a steady increase in remittance inflows to the Caribbean region between 1980 and 2013. The median share of remittances to GDP for the Caribbean countries included in this study is 4.79%, with a mean of 3.84% (see Table 9.1). While the average share of remittances to GDP declines to 3.37% for the period 1990–1989, from 3.89% for the period 1980–1989, it rises to 5.95% and 6.29% for the period 2000–2009 and 2010–2013, respectively (Table 9.2). The data in Tables 9.1 and 9.2 show the increasing importance of remittances to the economies of Caribbean countries. How does the rise in remittances inflow compare with financial development indicators over the period? To answer this question, three measures of financial development are the focus of this chapter—private sector credit to GDP ratio, bank credit to deposits ratio, and bank deposits to GDP ratio. The average share of private sector credit to GDP increases from 29.89% for the 1980–1989 period to 37.32% and 47% for the periods 1990–1999 and 2000–2009, respectively. The average share of private sector credit to GDP for the most recent period (2010–2013) is 53.35% while the average for the entire period (1980–2013) is 40.78%. The bank deposit to GDP ratio measure of financial development follows a similar pattern. The average share of bank deposits to GDP rises throughout the period from 38.30% for the period 1980–1989 to 45.11%, 59.94%, and 68.66%

Table 9.1 Descriptive statistics in levels

Variable	*Median*	*Mean*	*Standard deviation*	*Minimum*	*Maximum*	*Number of observations*
Private sector credit/GDP (%)	37.21	40.78	18.53	9.19	100.03	168
Bank credit/deposits (%)	75.87	74.35	19.21	34.71	129.63	168
Bank deposits/GDP (%)	47.68	51.53	22.78	12.69	138.86	168
FinDev Index	11.77	11.77	0.99	9.10	13.83	168
Remittances/GDP (%)	3.84	4.79	4.85	0.02	22.61	143
RGDP per capita (constant 2005 US $000s)	4.45	6.57	5.62	0.03	23.89	167
FDI/GDP (%)	5.67	5.99	6.69	−23.63	25.09	167
Trade/GDP (%)	105.57	109.93	39.6	25.49	299.47	166
Inflation (%)	4.17	9.07	20.64	−2.41	211.23	168
Investment/GDP (%)	24.07	25.11	7.67	9.27	53.24	168
Government Consumption/GDP (%)	14.85	14.79	4.58	2.07	36.97	168

Note Summary statistics (unweighted) are based on 3-year averaged data for the period 1980 to 2013
Source Authors' computations based on data from the various sources as shown in Table 9.18

Table 9.2 Period averages—remittances and financial development indicators

Variables (%)	*1980–1989*	*1990–1999*	*2000–2009*	*2010–2013*
Domestic Credit/GDP	29.89	37.32	47.00	53.35
Bank Credit/Deposits	74.56	75.37	72.38	75.46
Bank Deposit/GDP	38.30	45.11	59.94	68.66
Remittances/GDP	3.89	3.37	5.95	6.29

Source Authors' computations based on data from the various sources as shown in Table 9.18

for the periods 1990–1999, 2000–2009, and 2010–2013, respectively. Unlike the two other measures of financial development, the bank credit to deposit ratio remains relatively stable throughout the period. Apart from the 2000–2009 period where the share of bank credit to deposit is

72.38%, which is below the average for the entire period (74.35%), the average bank credit to deposit ratio for periods 1980–1989, 1990–1989, and 2010–2013 does not deviate much from the entire period average value. The analysis based on data shown in Tables 9.1 and 9.2 suggests that two of the financial development indicators—the average private sector credit to GDP ratio and bank deposits to GDP ratio—increased consistently overtime while the bank credit to GDP financial development indicator remains relatively stable during the period. Also, average remittances to GDP ratio falls initially between the first two decades but rises continually afterward (Tables 9.1 and 9.2).

The significance of remittances for the individual countries is in stark contrast to the rankings of the countries based on the various financial development indicators. For instance, Table 9.3 shows that Haiti, Jamaica, and Guyana have the top three highest share of remittances to GDP, while Antigua and Barbuda, Trinidad and Tobago, and Suriname are the three lowest ranked countries. Although Haiti ranks the highest in terms of the share of remittances to GDP, it ranks the lowest for two of the three indicators of financial development (i.e., private sector credit to GDP and bank deposits to GDP) and ranks the second lowest in the other measure of financial development—bank credit to deposits. The data in Table 9.3 also reveal that while Jamaica and Guyana, respectively, rank second and third in terms of the share of remittances to GDP, both countries have lower rankings in terms of their levels of financial development. Guyana is ranked 10th for each of the three financial development measures while Jamaica is ranked 11th, 8th, and 13th in private sector credit to GDP, bank credit to deposits, and bank deposits to GDP, respectively. Only two countries, Suriname and Trinidad and Tobago, have low rankings in both remittances and financial development measures. The third lowest ranked country in terms of remittances, Antigua and Barbuda, ranked fairly well in two out of the three financial development indicators. The ranking of other countries, such as St Kitts and Nevis and St. Lucia, reveals some interesting dynamics about how remittance inflows are related to the financial development indicators across these countries. For instance, while St. Kitts and Nevis ranks fourth in terms of remittance to GDP ratio, the twin-island federation ranks 7th, 14th, and 1st for the three measures of financial indicators, respectively. On the other hand, St. Lucia which ranks 10th in terms of remittances to GDP ratio, ranks 1st for the first two financial development indicators and 6th for the bank deposit GDP ratio indicator.

Table 9.3 Country rank on remittances and financial development indicators, 2013

Country	*Remittances/GDP (%)*	*Remittances/GDP*	*Private sector credit/GDP*	*Bank credit/Deposits*	*Bank deposits/GDP*
Haiti	20.99	1	14	13	14
Jamaica	15.23	2	11	8	13
Guyana	10.98	3	10	10	10
St. Kitts and Nevis	6.14	4	7	14	1
Dominica	4.73	5	8	9	4
Belize	4.71	6	6	5	7
St. Vincent	4.38	7	9	6	8
Grenada	3.52	8	3	3	5
Barbados	2.32	9	2	4	2
St. Lucia	2.03	10	1	1	6
Antigua	1.79	11	4	7	3
Trinidad and Tobago	0.53	12	12	12	11
Suriname	0.14	13	13	11	12
Bahamas	N.A	N.A	5	2	9

Notes All ranking are based on data for 2013. N.A. means not available
Source Authors' computations based on data from the various sources as shown in Table 9.18

Literature Review

Remittances from international migrants to their home countries, mostly developing countries, have been on a rising trend. Estimates show that remittance flows to low and middle-income countries in 2019 amounted to $550 billion, exceeding official development assistance and were projected to overtake foreign direct investment within the next two years (World Bank, 2019a). This growing importance of remittances to the economy of developing countries has ignited research interest on how migrant remittances affect key economic and financial variables including poverty, educational outcomes, entrepreneurship, and financial development.

Aggarwal et al. (2011) employed a panel of 109 developing countries spanning 1975–2007 to investigate whether remittances contribute to financial development. They find that worker remittances have a positive impact on the level of deposit and bank credit—two proxies for financial development. While remittance inflows may lead to financial development, a well-developed financial system can facilitate remittance inflows by lowering transaction costs. Accounting for endogeneity concerns and using different estimation techniques does not have any fundamental change on the results. Aggarwal et al.'s (2011) study, though influential, is not the first to explore how remittances affect financial development. Giuliano and Ruiz-Arranz (2009) employ a new data set of 100 developing countries to show that remittance inflows stimulate growth particularly in countries with low levels of financial development. While the impact of migrant remittances on financial development has been investigated extensively, there is lack of consensus on whether remittances have positive effect on financial development and the channels through which it may affect the sector. This lack of consensus is due to the different empirical methodologies used and the diversity of countries and regions involved in these studies (Fromentin, 2018).

One of the earlier studies that investigated the link between migrant remittances and financial development is Mundaca's (2009). Mundaca (2009) develops a theoretical model to analyze the effect of migrant remittances and financial development on growth. Remittance data were used on Latin America and Caribbean (LAC) countries to test the theoretical model. Results show that financial intermediation tends to increase the responsiveness of growth to remittances. Unlike Aggrawal et al. (2011), which used a panel data of developing countries, Mundaca (2009) focuses on how remittances impact financial development depending on whether there is a heterogeneous group with starkly different cultural practices or a homogenous group with similar cultural practices. This chapter adopts an approach similar to Mundaca (2009), focusing on Caribbean countries, a much more homogenous group in terms of culture and historical background. This strategy is important because while nations in Latin America and Caribbean reside in the same geographical region, they differ significantly in terms of culture and historical background. Culture can affect financial development by shaping attitudes toward owning a bank account and saving habits.

Fromentin (2017) explores how a country's level of development may impact the relationship between remittances and financial development.

The author employs a Pool Mean Group approach and accounted for differences in income levels. The results from the study show that remittances have a positive effect on financial development in both the short run and the long run for a panel of middle-income developing countries. No short-run effect of remittances on financial development was found among low-income countries. The author argued that this finding may be due to the fact that remittances received in low-income countries are primarily used for consumption in the short run. In a recent study, Fromentin (2018) employs a panel data of 32 Latin American and Caribbean countries to explore the relationship between migrant remittances and financial development. The author uses a dynamic Generalized Method of Moments (GMM) technique to account for the potential endogeneity between remittances and financial development. The author confirms a positive relationship between remittances and financial development. Additionally, the author finds a bidirectional relationship between remittances and financial development.

Arezki and Brückner (2012) use annual variation in rainfall as a proxy for a shock to agricultural activity to examine whether remittance inflow to Africa is motivated by the desire to restore shortfalls in transitory income. Accounting for the level of financial development, they find no relationship between remittance inflows and rainfall-induced transitory shocks to income. However, they find that rainfall-induced transitory shocks have significant effect on the share of domestic credit to the private sector. Other studies that analyze the relationship between remittances and financial development in Africa include Gupta et al. (2009) and Coulibaly (2015). Coulibaly (2015) employs bank liabilities as a proxy for financial development and finds that remittances have a positive effect on financial development in some African countries (i.e., Niger, Senegal, Sierra Leone, and Sudan). The author finds no evidence of a bidirectional relationship between remittance and financial development in those countries. Besides, the study finds evidence that financial development positively affects remittances in Gambia. The findings from these studies explain the lack of consensus on the true relationship between remittances and financial development. While there is enough evidence to show that remittances impact positively on financial development, the results vary depending on the methodology used and the country or region studied. Although there have been some studies (Demirguc-Kunt et al., 2011; Ramirez, 2013; Ramirez & Sharma, 2009) on the relationship between remittances and financial development for Latin America and

Caribbean (LAC) countries, none of the studies have focused exclusively on Caribbean countries. By focusing on Caribbean countries instead of the greater LAC group, this chapter explores the mediating role of culture in shaping the relationship between remittances and financial development. Independent Caribbean countries are more culturally homogenous than the greater LAC group.

Data Sources and Main Variables

The focus of this chapter is on testing the overall relationship running from remittances to financial development. Data for the main sample covers information for 13 countries over the period 1980 to 2013. Similar to most empirical studies using cross-sectional data, this research utilizes panel data that was transformed to 11 non-overlapping 3-year period averages for each country, with the last period (i.e., 2013) consisting of one year. This means a maximum of 12 observations is available for each country or the equivalent maximum of 168 country-period observations. Due to missing observations, mainly arising from the unavailability of some data, the total observation count is lower in the analyses. The justification for the 3-year averaging is to help smooth out business cycles present in the data. In the appendix section, Table 9.17 lists the countries, while Table 9.18 provides the definitions and sources for each of the variables used in the analyses.

Financial Development Variables

Three different financial development variables are used. The first is bank credit to the private sector as a percent of GDP (Private sector credit/GDP). This comprises domestic credit (in the form of loans, purchases of nonequity securities, trade credits, and other receivable accounts) to the private sector divided by GDP. It is a measure of the depth of financial institutions in the provision of credit to the economy. The second is financial resources provided by banks to the private sector divided by the summation of demand, time, and savings deposits (Bank credit/Deposits). It measures the stability of financial institutions and markets in addressing volatility in the financial system. Third, is the sum of demand, time, and saving deposits at commercial banks and other deposit-taking financial institutions relative to GDP

(Bank deposits/GDP). Similar to the first indicator of financial development, this measures the size or depth of financial institutions and markets.

The study also considers a fourth measure, which combines information from the three measures of financial development to construct an index of financial development (FinDev Index). To construct the index, the summation of the log modulus transformation of the data for each of the financial development measures was undertaken as follows: $\text{FinDev} = \sum_{i=1}^{3} \text{lm}(x_i) = \sum_{i=1}^{3} \text{sign}(x_i) \times \ln(\text{abs}(x_i) + 1)$, where x_i is the ith measure of financial development, such that x_1 represents Private sector credit/GDP measure, x_2 indicates Bank credit/Deposits, and x_3 is Bank deposits/GDP.

One benefit of this index is that it improves the normality of the distribution and thereby, improves the efficiency in the estimation. The use of the index, instead of a single financial development measure, helps to reduce any concerns of significant collinearity among the financial development variables. Later in the chapter, it is shown that the correlations between these measures fall below the traditional thresholds for multicollinearity.

Remittances Variable

The key independent variable is based on remittances, which is a summation of personal transfers and compensation of employees as defined in the sixth edition of the *Balance of Payments and International Investment Position Manual* (IMF, 2009). In this chapter, the independent variable of interest is the ratio of remittances expressed to Gross Domestic Product (GDP), which is readily obtained from the World Development Indicators (World Bank, 2019b).

Control Variables

To improve the model estimation, the study includes various indicators that may be relevant in influencing financial development. The following variables were included as controls: real GDP per capita, foreign direct investments (FDI) as a percent of GDP, trade openness (sum of exports and imports to GDP ratio), inflation, investment (gross fixed capital formation as a percentage of GDP), and government consumption to

GDP ratio. The inclusion of these variables is consistent with the extant literature. For example, GDP per capita, which captures the level of economic development, has been shown to have a negative relationship to financial development, especially in small-island or lower-income economies (Gregorio & Guidotti, 1995; Khan & Senhadji, 2003). FDI is important in enhancing financial development (Alfaro et al., 2009) with non-linear effects (Dutta & Roy, 2011). Trade openness is important in facilitating financial development and may be associated with increased (e.g., Chin & Ito, 2006) or decreased (e.g., Baltagi et al., 2009) financial flows. Empirical research documents that inflation rate, which is a proxy for price instability, contributes to a shallower and less active financial sector (Aggarwal et al., 2011). Accordingly, the estimated impact is expected to be negative. The literature points to a positive relationship between investments and financial development (Benhabib & Spiegel, 2000). Government spending is a proxy for macroeconomic stability, which is conducive to financial development. The data are obtained from three main sources, namely, the International Monetary Fund, the World Development Indicators, and the United Nations National Accounts database. Also, the models control for the equivalent country and period fixed effects to mitigate the effects of unobserved geographical, political, cultural, and temporal heterogeneity.

Descriptive Analysis

Table 9.1 shows the summary statistics of the main variables after transforming the data into non-overlapping 3-year period averages. Key variables—remittances and financial development—display wide variations in the studied sample. The average ratio of remittances to GDP is 4.8%; however, the standard deviation of 4.9 is indicative of significant heterogeneity across the Caribbean countries. With respect to the three measures of financial development: Private sector credit percent share of GDP ranges from 9.2 to 100; Bank credit to deposits ranges from 34.7 to 129.6 % while Bank deposits as a percentage share of GDP range from 12.7 to 138.9%. Remittances relative to GDP range from 0.02% (Trinidad and Tobago) to 22.6% (Haiti), indicating its greater importance to lower-income economies.

Figures 9.2, 9.3, 9.4, and 9.5 summarize the unconditional relationship between remittances and the three measures of financial development as well as the constructed financial development index. The lines represent

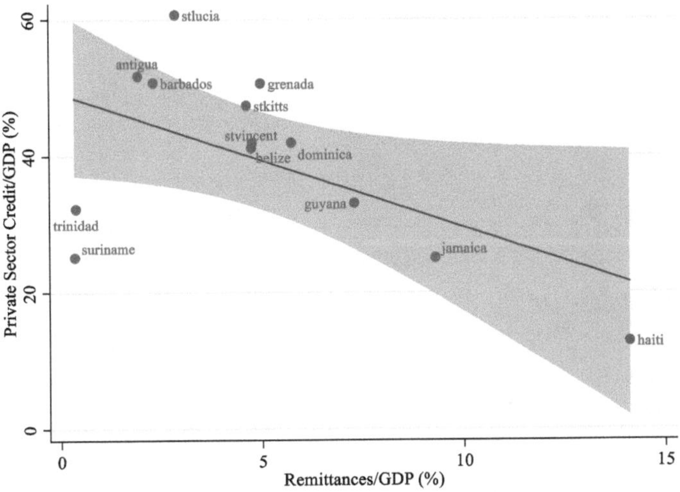

Fig. 9.2 Relationship between Remittances and Private Sector Credit to GDP (Based on 3-year non-overlapping period for the years 1980 to 2013 from 13 countries) (*Source* Authors' Calculations)

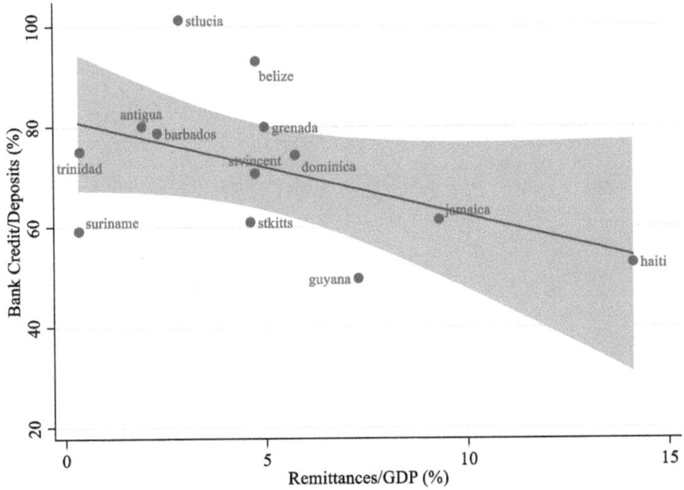

Fig. 9.3 Relationship between Remittances and Bank Credit to Deposits (Based on 3-year non-overlapping period for the years 1980 to 2013 from 13 countries) (*Source* Authors' Calculations)

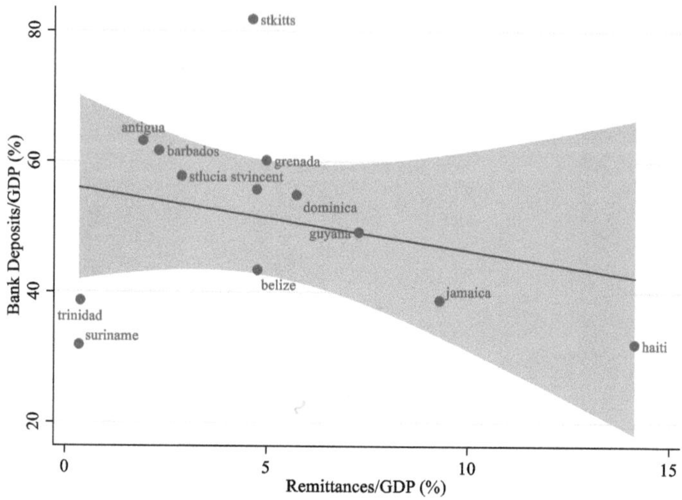

Fig. 9.4 Relationship between Remittances and Bank Deposits to GDP (Based on 3-year non-overlapping period for the years 1980 to 2013 from 13 countries) (*Source* Authors' Calculations)

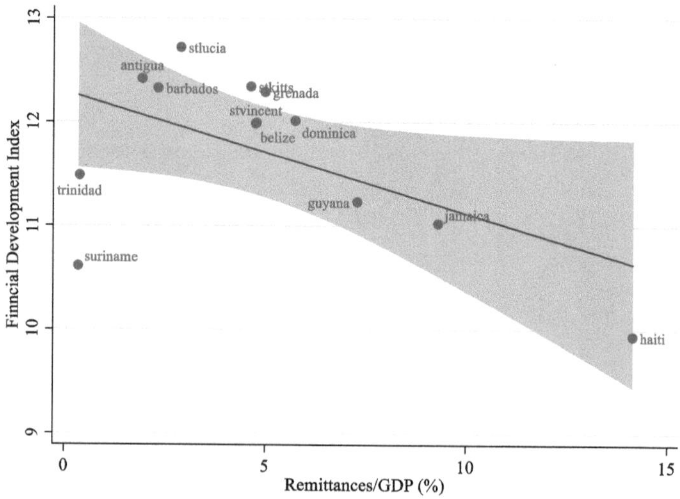

Fig. 9.5 Relationship between Remittances and Financial Development Index (Based on 3-year non-overlapping period for the years 1980 to 2013 from 13 countries) (*Source* Authors' Calculations)

the linear fit and the shaded area represents the 95% confidence intervals. Each variable is based on a computation of the average of the non-overlapping 3-year period data. Private sector credit to GDP, Bank credit to deposits, and Bank deposits to GDP are on the Y axis in Figs. 9.2–9.5, respectively, and remittances as a percent of GDP, are measured on the X axis. The regression fit lines for remittances are downward sloping, indicating remittances are negatively correlated with financial development. In other words, higher remittances-receiving countries are associated with lower levels of financial development. These patterns are strongly suggestive that financial development is a negative function of remittances. However, this relationship may be driven by factors unrelated to remittances. The patterns exhibited in the figures may be reflective of the extent of globalization, economic policies, and other factors originating in the remittance-receiving countries. Although the observed patterns provide some cross-country (i.e., cross-sectional) evidence, further investigation that exploits within-country variation is warranted in order to determine any causal impact of remittances on financial development.

Pairwise correlations are calculated and presented in Table 9.4 for the main variables used in the analysis. Focusing on the correlation between the main independent variables, remittances as a percentage of GDP, this table helps to highlight the relationship between financial development and remittances. As seen in row 4 of Table 9.4, there is a negative relationship between remittances and all three measures of financial development. These relationships are statistically significant and indicate that an increase in remittances is associated with a decrease in the following proxy measures of financial development: Private sector credit/GDP, Bank credit/deposits, and Bank deposits/GDP. This consistent negative relationship between remittances and the financial development variables aligns with the main findings of the chapter; that is, remittances and financial development are substitutes for each other.

The results from the table also show a positive relationship among most of the financial development variables. These results, as well as the correlation coefficients among the other variables, also provide some evidence that multicollinearity is of less concern as the correlation values are all below the typically acceptable level of 0.80.

The next section discusses the empirical methodology that allows the model to control for other factors to establish the remittances-financial development nexus.

Table 9.4 Pairwise correlation among variables

	Variables	*1*	*2*	*3*	*4*	*5*	*6*	*7*	*8*	*9*	*10*	*11*
1	Private sector credit/GDP	1.00										
2	Bank credit/deposits	0.55***	1.00									
3	Bank deposits/GDP	0.76***	−0.02	1.00								
4	FinDev	0.95***	0.55***	0.77***	1.00							
5	Remittances/GDP	−0.30***	−0.34***	−0.14*	−0.30***	1.00						
6	FDI/GDP	0.47***	0.16**	0.50***	0.51***	0.00	1.00					
7	RGDP per capita	0.39***	0.45***	0.18**	0.39***	−0.44***	0.11	1.00				
8	Trade/GDP	0.04	0.08	−0.12	0.05	−0.13	0.11	−0.04	1.00			
9	Inflation	−0.31***	−0.31***	−0.27***	−0.42***	−0.04	−0.34***	−0.20**	0.34***	1.00		
10	Investment/GDP	−0.03	−0.13*	0.04	−0.06	0.05	0.25***	−0.03	−0.10	0.04	1.00	
11	Government Consumption/GDP	0.16**	0.05	0.16**	0.21***	−0.36***	−0.11	−0.10	0.17**	0.02	−0.13*	1.00

Notes Statistical levels of significance are: * indicates $p < 0.10$, ** indicates $p < 0.05$, *** indicates $p < 0.01$. Correlations are unweighted and are based on 3-year averaged data for the period 1980 to 2013

Source Authors' computations based on data from the various sources as shown in Table 9.18

Empirical Methodology

Estimation Model

The main purpose of this study is to capture the relationship between remittances and financial development. To do so, the study utilizes panel dataset of Caribbean countries consisting of a sample period ranging from 1980 to 2013 and split into non-overlapping 3-year periods, except for the last year. The following baseline dynamic panel econometric model is used to estimate the impact of remittances on financial development:

$$\mathrm{FD}_{it} = \alpha_0 + \alpha_1 \mathrm{FD}_{i,t-1} + \alpha_2 \mathrm{Rem}_{i,t-1} + \boldsymbol{X}_{it}\Omega + \gamma_i + \delta_t + \varepsilon_{it} \quad (9.1)$$

where subscripts denote country i in period t. The outcome variable FD_{it} represents the different measures of financial development, $\mathrm{Rem}_{i,t-1}$ denotes lagged remittances as a percent of GDP, and X_{it} is the matrix of control variables including the real GDP per capita, trade openness, inflation, gross fixed capital formation, and government spending. A composite error term comprises unobserved country fixed effects γ_i, time specific effects δ_t, and a random disturbance term ε_{it}. The inclusion of a lagged value of the outcome variable, $\mathrm{FD}_{i,t-1}$, is to account for dynamics in financial development overtime and to serve as a proxy for omitted variables. For the empirical analyses, the variables are log transformed prior to the commencement of any econometric estimation. All regression estimates are weighted by population, and clustering of the standard errors is done at the country level.

The model utilizes fixed effects to account for unobserved heterogeneity. For example, Caribbean countries such as Jamaica and Haiti that experience high levels of remittances are fundamentally different to relatively lower-remittance-receiving economies. Furthermore, the Hausman (1978) test was performed prior to estimations to determine whether fixed effects models or random effects models were more appropriate. The results of this test consistently point to a fixed effects model. Therefore, the study will focus on the outcomes of the fixed effects model estimation.

One way to eliminate the unobserved heterogeneity associated with fixed effects is to generate a differenced model of the form shown:

$$\Delta \mathrm{Y}_{it} = \alpha_0 + \alpha_1 \Delta \mathrm{Y}_{i,t-1} + \alpha_2 \Delta \mathrm{Rem}_{i,t-1} + \Delta \boldsymbol{X}_{it}\Omega + \Delta\delta_t + \Delta\varepsilon_{it} \quad (9.2)$$

where Δ is the difference operator and all variables are as earlier described. The elimination of the time-constant unobserved effect is useful in obtaining causal effects (Wooldridge, 2013). The first difference model is also easy to apply. For example, the log transformations allow for a straightforward interpretation of the estimated coefficients as elasticities. Despite the ease of application and its potential to infer causality, there are downsides to this model (and fixed effects models in general). Fixed effects models suffer from a loss of degrees of freedom when the number of cross-sectional units (i.e., countries), compared to the time period, is significant—the incidental parameters problem. First differencing—which reduces variation in the variables with the differenced error—has no practical value for any key explanatory variables that show no variation over time. Finally, first differencing estimators perform poorly in cases where one or more of the explanatory variables have measurement error, which is prevalent in macroeconomic data. Differencing a poorly measured key explanatory variable can lead to large biases that overestimate/underestimate the true effect of the regressor—this is the classical error-in-variables problem (Wooldridge, 2010).

Identification Strategy

Generalized Method of Moments (GMM)

The drawbacks associated with the estimation of fixed effects models almost guarantee that the resulting estimates will be affected by endogeneity problems. From a theoretical perspective, it is plausible for growth in remittances to lead to an increase in financial development in the remittance-receiving country. However, this relationship can also be explained the other way around—reverse causality—whereby the level of financial development in a country is a driving force behind the flow of remittances. In the Caribbean, most emigrants rely on established financial institutions, mainly commercials banks, as well as official money transfer operators (e.g., Western Union) to dispatch remittances. A higher number of formal remittances channels that lower the costs of sending remittances and greater advances in technology to facilitate financial transactions are likely to increase the flow of remittances. Indeed, the opposite of these factors can also prohibit the flow of remittances. Remittances may also be endogenous if unobserved factors that influence the decision to remit money are correlated with unobserved financial development confounders.

One way to address the above simultaneity problems is to employ Generalized Method of Moments (GMM) estimation techniques that incorporate instrumental variables with the GMM estimator. More specifically, this chapter considers the difference GMM (DGMM), proposed by Arellano and Bond (1991), and the system GMM (SGMM), à la Arellano and Bover (1995). In the DGMM method, lagged levels of endogenous variables are used as instruments in a first-differenced model as shown in Eq. (9.2). This method performs poorly in producing biased and imprecise estimates when the instruments are weak. Arellano and Bover (1995) and Blundell and Bond (1998) showed that more plausible and accurate estimates can be achieved through a system of two equations: the original one and a levels equation, Eq. (9.1), which uses the lagged differences of the endogenous variables as instruments. As a result, the SGMM method is superior to the DGMM in that it produces efficient and consistent parameter estimates and addresses the problems of endogeneity.

Several diagnostics to test the validity of the instruments were used. To check the over-identifying restrictions, we use the Sargan test which is considered more appropriate in small sample setting. GMM methods, in particular SGMM, yield inconsistent estimates in the presence of autocorrelation. Therefore, we use the Arellano and Bond (1991) tests for first order (AR1) and second order (AR2) autocorrelation to determine the validity and suitability of the instruments.

Instrumental Variables (IV)
Despite the appropriateness of GMM to address simultaneity bias in the remittances-financial development relationship, other endogeneity issues related to measurement error and omitted variables may produce biased estimates from these models. For example, it is well documented that data on remittances is measured with error (Aggarwal et al., 2011). Unrecorded remittances are estimated to be as large as three times the officially recorded amounts (Freund & Spatafora, 2008). This chasm in recorded and actual estimates is partly due to changes in the way remittances are measured over time as well as misreporting. Omitted variable bias may also occur since it is impossible to control for all factors that affect remittances and financial development.

Another strategy to address these endogeneity issues is to use an instrumental variable (IV) approach that identifies at least one external instrument for remittances. Under this approach, the study uses the unemployment rates of the major remittance-sending countries, namely, the United States, Canada, and the United Kingdom (Beaton et al., 2020). For the instrument to be valid, it must affect financial development only through remittances exposure and lastly, conditional on the explanatory variables, there are no unobserved factors that are correlated with the instruments. The underlying idea is that remittances are influenced by prevailing macroeconomic conditions, such as the unemployment rate in the countries from which migrants are sending remittances. Migrants' ability to send remittances will be influenced by their employment situation: high employment (low unemployment) means more income from which to send remittances and vice versa. At the same time, there is no reason to believe a direct link exists between the unemployment rates of the migrants' countries of residence and the level of financial development in the countries being analyzed after controlling for global transactions and international business cycle conditions as proxied by trade openness and foreign investment.

To test the relative strength of the instruments, the Kliebergen-Paap F-statistic is used. An F-statistic in the region of 10 or greater indicates that the instruments are sufficiently strong predictors of remittances. The related Kleibergen-Paap LM statistic is also utilized to test whether the instruments are under-identified.

Results

This section of the chapter presents results of fixed effects, DGMM, SGMM, and instrumental variables (IV) estimations. For each of the methods, estimations are reported for four outcomes: three measures of financial development and an index which was constructed from these measures. The three variables referring to financial development are Private sector credit/GDP, Bank credit/Deposits, and Bank deposits/GDP. The goal of this section is to quantify the effects of remittances on financial development in the Caribbean. In all regressions, the standard errors are robust to heteroskedasticity and are clustered within country.

Benchmark Results: Fixed Effects

The baseline panel fixed effects data results are reported in Table 9.5 which shows the estimates of the effect of remittances on each of Private sector credit/GDP (column 1), Bank credit/Deposits (column 2), and Bank deposits/GDP (column 3) as well as an overall financial development index (column 4) constructed from these individual measures.

Table 9.5 The impact of remittances on financial development—fixed-effects regression

Variables	*(1)*	*(2)*	*(3)*	*(4)*
	Private sector credit /GDP	*Bank credit/Deposits*	*Bank deposits/GDP*	*FinDev Index*
Lagged Remittances/GDP	−0.201***	−0.161	−0.228**	−0.016***
	(0.055)	(0.092)	(0.104)	(0.003)
Lagged Dependent Variable	0.943***	1.010***	0.918***	0.890***
	(0.025)	(0.034)	(0.036)	(0.035)
Log Real GDP per capita	−1.622***	−1.966***	−0.740	−0.114***
	(0.193)	(0.530)	(0.498)	(0.025)
FDI/GDP	0.106**	0.126	−0.073	0.005
	(0.044)	(0.119)	(0.106)	(0.005)
Trade/GDP	0.008	0.025*	−0.010	0.001
	(0.005)	(0.013)	(0.008)	(0.001)
Inflation	−0.050**	0.010	−0.071**	−0.004**
	(0.021)	(0.038)	(0.025)	(0.002)
Investment/GDP	0.056	0.241**	−0.075	0.002
	(0.055)	(0.091)	(0.068)	(0.005)
Government Consumption/GDP	0.241***	0.480***	0.062	0.019***
	(0.132)	(0.072)	(0.126)	(0.024)
Country dummies	Yes	Yes	Yes	Yes
Time dummies	Yes	Yes	Yes	Yes
Mean of outcome	40.78	74.35	51.53	11.77
Observations	135	135	135	135
R-square	0.992	0.976	0.980	0.990

Notes Dependent variable is shown is at the top of each column of results. Heteroskedastic and autocorrelation robust standard errors are shown in parentheses are clustered at the country level. Statistical significance at the 10%, 5%, and 1% confidence levels are denoted by *, **, and ***, respectively. Regressions are weighted by country population and are based on 11 non-overlapping 3-year periods. Variables are defined in Table 9.18

The coefficients on remittances are negative and statistically significant, except for the results in column (2). In other words, controlling for a range of other variables, including unobservable country and period effects, countries experiencing an increase in remittances have seen significant reductions in private sector credit as a percentage of GDP, bank credit relative to deposits, bank deposits as a ratio to GDP, and overall financial development. The estimated effects are relatively small. Evaluated at the mean across all specifications, a one percentage point increase in remittances relative to GDP is associated with 0.20, 0.16, 0.23, and 0.02 percentage point reductions in the respective outcomes moving from columns 1 to 4. These changes translate to equivalent reductions of approximately 0.5, 0.2, 0.4, and 0.1%.

Looking at the coefficients on the other explanatory variables in Table 9.3, the coefficients on the lagged values of the dependent variable are close to one, indicating that these variables are highly persistent. This result is often a justification for the use of dynamic GMM, in particular SGMM, which dramatically improves the accuracy of the estimates (Blundell & Bond, 2000). The coefficients on the log of real GDP per capita are negative. These findings are consistent with research highlighting a possible negative relationship between growth and financial development, especially in weakly regulated and supervised financial systems (Demetriades & Rousseau, 2016). As expected, FDI inflows relative to GDP (a measure of the degree of the movement of capital), trade (a measure of globalization), investment, and government spending (important for regulations) are associated with improved financial development and are consistent with the prior expectations discussed earlier. On the other hand, inflation has been shown to be detrimental to financial sector performance (Boyd et al., 2001).

In summary, the fixed effects estimates yield statistically significant support to an initial negative relationship between remittances and financial development. There is adequate theoretical or empirical evidence that point to this—the possibility that shallow and inefficient financial systems may discourage individuals from transacting with these institutions and may instead turn to remittances. Therefore, in the remainder of this section as well as the section on robustness analysis, the chapter provides estimates of GMM and instrumental variables (IV) models to obtain some exogenous variation in remittances and so insulate the estimates from concerns related to endogeneity such as in the form of reverse causality, omitted variables, and measurement error.

GMM Results

Fixed effects estimates are likely to be biased downwards when lagged dependent variables are present in the models (Bond, 2002). To address this endogeneity, Blundell and Bond (1998) suggest using the DGMM estimation where the data are transformed, and lagged values of the explanatory variables are used as instruments. As discussed earlier, DGMM models are likely to produce biased estimates arising from weak instruments and high persistence in the dependent variable. Blundell and Bond (1998) show that SGMM models represent an improvement over DGMM by using both lagged levels and lagged differences of the dependent and explanatory variables as instruments.

Tables 9.6 and 9.7 present the results from the difference GMM and system GMM estimation, respectively. Identification is based on the lags of remittances in addition to the lags of other predetermined variables. More specifically, for the DGMM model, two and three lags of the dependent variable and all the control variables are used as instruments. For system GMM, one and two period lagged levels of remittances and the other predetermined variables are used as instruments in both the levels and difference equations. Table 9.6 presents the results of the DGMM estimation. Across each of the financial development variables, the coefficient on remittances is negative but only significant for bank credit to deposits. The relationship between remittances and the overall financial development index is negative and statistically significant. Table 9.7 reports the estimates of the preferred model, SGMM. These results are more precisely estimated with all but one of the coefficients on the main explanatory variable, remittances, being negative and statistically significant. A one percentage point increase in remittances is associated with decreases of 0.25 percentage points (0.6%) in private sector deposits to GDP and 0.24 percentage points (0.5%) in bank credit to deposits. Overall financial development declined by about 0.02 percentage points (0.2%).

With respect to the control variables, the estimated coefficient of log of real per capita GDP is negative and mostly statistically significant for each of the outcomes as shown in Tables 9.6 and 9.7. These results are qualitatively similar to those obtained in the fixed effects regressions. Inflation is the only other control that is constantly negative and significant across all financial development outcomes except one. Few of the other control variables have a strong and significant effect on the financial development measures. One likely explanation is that financial markets in the Caribbean have tended to be highly sticky. Another factor for the lack of statistical significance in most of the control variables is that the empirical model controls for the lagged dependent variable.

Table 9.6 The impact of remittances on financial development—Difference GMM (DGMM) Regression

Variables	*(1)*	*(2)*	*(3)*	*(4)*
	Private sector credit /GDP	*Bank credit/Deposits*	*Bank deposits/GDP*	*FinDev Index*
Lagged Remittances/GDP	−0.197	−0.232**	−0.070	−0.016**
	(0.128)	(0.086)	(0.172)	(0.007)
Lagged Dependent Variable	0.940***	1.000***	0.927***	0.867***
	(0.046)	(0.056)	(0.029)	(0.081)
Log Real GDP per capita	−1.734	−4.592***	1.676	−0.128
	(1.146)	(0.441)	(1.930)	(0.074)
FDI/GDP	0.085	0.038	−0.069	−0.000
	(0.050)	(0.129)	(0.134)	(0.002)
Trade/GDP	0.012	0.033	0.013	0.001
	(0.012)	(0.026)	(0.011)	(0.001)
Inflation	−0.054**	−0.008	−0.105***	−0.005**
	(0.019)	(0.029)	(0.027)	(0.002)
Investment/GDP	0.052	0.183	−0.063	0.000
	(0.072)	(0.161)	(0.080)	(0.006)
Government Consumption/GDP	0.248***	0.537***	0.031	0.023***
	(0.053)	(0.168)	(0.114)	(0.007)
Country dummies	Yes	Yes	Yes	Yes
Time dummies	Yes	Yes	Yes	Yes
Observations	120	120	120	120
No. of countries	13	13	13	13
AR(1) test statistic	−1.613	−1.600	−2.316	−1.551
p-value of AR(1) test	0.107	0.110	0.021	0.121
AR(2) test statistic	1.218	−0.062	1.130	0.822
p-value of AR(2) test	0.223	0.950	0.259	0.411
p-value of Sargan test	0.303	0.421	0.141	0.543

Notes Dependent variable is shown is at the top of each column of results. Heteroskedastic and autocorrelation robust standard errors are shown in parentheses. Statistical significance at the 10%, 5%, and 1% confidence levels are denoted by *, **, and ***, respectively. Regressions are weighted by country population and are based on 11 non-overlapping 3-year periods. Variables are defined in Table 9.18

Table 9.7 The impact of remittances on financial development—system GMM (SGMM) regression

Variables	*(1)* *Private sector credit /GDP*	*(2)* *Bank credit/Deposits*	*(3)* *Bank deposits/GDP*	*(4)* *FinDev Index*
Lagged Remittances/GDP	−0.247**	−0.082	−0.236*	−0.018***
	(0.082)	(0.135)	(0.113)	(0.004)
Lagged Dependent Variable	0.936***	1.043***	0.920***	0.876***
	(0.031)	(0.055)	(0.034)	(0.065)
Log Real GDP per capita	−1.505***	−1.993**	−0.584	−0.112***
	(0.190)	(0.807)	(0.472)	(0.023)
FDI/GDP	0.061	0.174	−0.075	0.003
	(0.058)	(0.137)	(0.108)	(0.004)
Trade/GDP	0.010	0.032*	−0.011	0.000
	(0.006)	(0.016)	(0.010)	(0.001)
Inflation	−0.056***	−0.011	−0.064***	−0.004***
	(0.018)	(0.036)	(0.015)	(0.001)
Investment/GDP	0.092	0.241*	−0.062	0.003
	(0.061)	(0.123)	(0.078)	(0.005)
Government Consumption/GDP	0.241***	0.368***	0.040	0.018***
	(0.063)	(0.109)	(0.069)	(0.003)
Country dummies	Yes	Yes	Yes	Yes
Time dummies	Yes	Yes	Yes	Yes
Observations	135	135	135	135
No. of countries	13	13	13	13
AR(1) test statistic	−1.402	−1.640	−2.242	−1.509
p-value of AR(1) test	0.161	0.101	0.025	0.131
AR(2) test statistic	1.078	0.541	0.913	0.790
p-value of AR(2) test	0.281	0.588	0.361	0.430
p-value of Sargan test	0.400	0.624	0.258	0.698

Notes Dependent variable is shown is at the top of each column of results. Heteroskedastic and autocorrelation robust standard errors are shown in parentheses. Statistical significance at the 10%, 5%, and 1% confidence levels are denoted by *, **, and ***, respectively. Regressions are weighted by country population and are based on 11 non-overlapping 3-year periods. Variables are defined in Table 9.18

The validity of both the DGMM and SGMM estimators is dependent on the validity of the instruments. Several specification tests are employed to address this issue. For each estimation, test statistic and *p*-values of the Arellano-Bond tests for first order (AR1) and second order (AR2) serial correlation in the disturbances. The Arellano-Bond test for AR1 serial correlation rejects the null hypothesis that there is no first-order serial correlation but cannot reject the null hypothesis of no second-order serial correlation. Furthermore, the *p*-value of the Sargan test of over-identified restrictions is unable to reject the null hypothesis that all instruments are valid for all four outcome variables in both GMM models. These diagnostics offer support that the empirical results provided by the GMM models are unlikely to suffer from statistical biases.

The magnitude of the SGMM estimate of the effect of remittances in reducing financial development is higher than the fixed effects estimates. The increased magnitude of the GMM estimates relative to fixed effect estimate is consistent with the downward bias in the estimates of fixed effects models containing a lagged dependent variable. Importantly, the estimated coefficient associated with remittances remains remarkably comparable in magnitude to the benchmark fixed effects results in Table 9.5. The findings from this identification strategy confirm the validity of the previous findings. Despite the robustness of the results, the following section uses an alternative identification strategy, instrumental variables, to provide further evidence of the negative impact of remittances on financial development.

Instrumental Variables (IV) Results

Thus far, both fixed effects and GMM specifications have shown the estimated effect of remittances is negative and statistically different from zero in most cases. As discussed in the previous section, the results from fixed effects estimation might be biased given the potential reverse causality between financial development and remittances, and other endogeneity issues such as omitted variables and measurement error, which GMM estimations are less equipped to handle.

To deal with the endogeneity issue, Table 9.8 reports the instrumental variable (IV) estimates in which remittances are treated as endogenous to financial development. The study uses lagged values of the unemployment rates for the United States, Canada, and the United Kingdom as external instruments for remittances. The validity of this IV

Table 9.8 The impact of remittances on financial development—Instrumental Variables (IV) regression

Variables	*(1)* *log (Private sector credit /GDP)*	*(2)* *log (Bank credit/Deposits)*	*(3)* *log (Bank deposits/GDP)*	*(4)* *log (FinDev Index)*
Log (Remittances/GDP)	−0.155***	−0.190***	0.020	−0.028***
	(0.052)	(0.054)	(0.053)	(0.009)
Lagged Dependent Variable	0.615***	0.305*	0.650***	0.574***
	(0.093)	(0.185)	(0.095)	(0.114)
Lagged log (Real GDP per capita)	−0.144***	−0.068	0.105	−0.016*
	(0.045)	(0.054)	(0.071)	(0.010)
Lagged log (FDI/GDP)	0.100***	0.140***	−0.082**	0.014**
	(0.030)	(0.044)	(0.041)	(0.006)
Lagged log (Trade/GDP)	−0.211**	0.010	−0.143	−0.035*
	(0.100)	(0.119)	(0.131)	(0.019)
Lagged log (1+Inflation)	−0.161***	−0.070	−0.094**	−0.031***
	(0.050)	(0.056)	(0.038)	(0.010)
Lagged log (Investment/GDP)	0.188	0.078	−0.044	0.020
	(0.129)	(0.132)	(0.129)	(0.022)
Lagged log (Government Consumption/GDP)	0.031	0.201***	−0.205***	−0.002
	(0.057)	(0.075)	(0.073)	(0.012)
Country dummies	Yes	Yes	Yes	Yes
Time dummies	Yes	Yes	Yes	Yes
Observations	123	123	123	123
No. of countries	13	13	13	13
Kleibergen-Paap first stage *F*-stat	12.927	12.574	12.914	13.784
Kleibergen-Paap LM test stat	12.350	11.867	11.975	12.249
Kleibergen-Paap LM test (*p*-value)	0.006	0.008	0.007	0.007

Notes Dependent variable is shown is at the top of each column of results. Heteroskedastic and autocorrelation robust standard errors are shown in parentheses. Statistical significance at the 10%, 5%, and 1% confidence levels are denoted by *, **, and ***, respectively. The instruments for the IV estimation are lagged values of the unemployment rates for the United States, Canada, and the United Kingdom. Regressions are weighted by country population and are based on 11 non-overlapping 3-year periods. Variables are defined in Table 9.18

strategy is reliant on the standard IV assumptions, which may be satisfied through the following diagnostics. To test for whether the unemployment rates in these major remittance-sending countries are weak instruments, the Kleibergen-Paap F-statistic is used. The values of the F-statistics (ranging between 12.9 and 13.8) surpass the Stock et al. (2002) critical threshold value of 10 and thus rejects the null hypothesis that the instruments are weak. In other words, the high values of the F-statistics are evidence that the instruments for remittances are relevant. To test for the validity of the instrumental variable approach, the Kleibergen-Paap LM statistic and associated *p*-values strongly reject the null hypothesis of under-identification.

Turning to the results of the main variable of interest, the estimated coefficients of remittances are negative and statistically significant in all but one case. A 1% increase in remittances leads to a decrease of about 0.2% in each private sector credit and bank credit, while a smaller decrease of about 0.03% is observed for the overall financial development index. Overall, the results obtained using the IV technique are consistent and similar in magnitude with those obtained in the SGMM models (in Table 9.5). That is, the IV and GMM estimates provide a lower bound while the fixed effects estimates provide an upper bound. An advantage of GMM is that it produces consistent estimates (and is preferred to IV) when heteroskedasticity is present. The similarity in IV and SGMM estimates provides some assurance that arbitrary heteroskedasticity is absent.

To summarize the results reported in Table 9.8, remittances negatively impact financial development. In terms of the control variables, most are of the expected signs and in line with estimates shown in the benchmark fixed effects and GMM estimations. FDI, investment, and government spending are conducive to financial development, while GDP per capita, trade, and inflation are negatively correlated with the measures of financial development.

Robustness Analyses

Alternative Definitions of Remittances

The chapter begins by considering an alternative definition of remittances, remittances per 100,000 population. Data on remittances is typically measured as a percent of GDP rather than in per capita terms. Tables 9.9, 9.10, 9.11, 9.12 present the results for all four empirical methods: fixed

Table 9.9 The impact of remittances on financial development—fixed-effects regression (alternative measure of remittances)

Variables	*(1)*	*(2)*	*(3)*	*(4)*
	Private sector credit /GDP	*Bank credit/Deposits*	*Bank deposits/GDP*	*FinDev Index*
Lagged Remittances per capita	−0.481	−0.733**	−0.221	−0.036**
	(0.288)	(0.285)	(0.299)	(0.016)
Lagged Dependent Variable	0.963***	1.004***	0.945***	0.911***
	(0.027)	(0.038)	(0.035)	(0.037)
Log Real GDP per capita	−0.909***	−1.357*	0.222	−0.055**
	(0.271)	(0.757)	(0.383)	(0.020)
FDI/GDP	0.118***	0.133	−0.067	0.006
	(0.034)	(0.115)	(0.109)	(0.005)
Trade/GDP	0.005	0.023	−0.010*	0.000
	(0.005)	(0.014)	(0.005)	(0.001)
Inflation	−0.051**	0.013	−0.077**	−0.004**
	(0.023)	(0.038)	(0.027)	(0.002)
Investment/GDP	0.049	0.243**	−0.087	0.001
	(0.049)	(0.092)	(0.060)	(0.004)
Government Consumption/GDP	0.157***	0.446***	−0.055	0.013***
	(0.046)	(0.101)	(0.072)	(0.004)
Country dummies	Yes	Yes	Yes	Yes
Time dummies	Yes	Yes	Yes	Yes
Observations	135	135	135	135
R-square	0.991	0.976	0.979	0.989

Notes Dependent variable is shown is at the top of each column of results. Heteroskedastic and autocorrelation robust standard errors are shown in parentheses. Statistical significance at the 10%, 5%, and 1% confidence levels are denoted by *, **, and ***, respectively. Regressions are weighted by country population and are based on 11 non-overlapping 3-year periods. Variables are defined in Table 9.18

effects, DGMM, SGMM, and IV, respectively. The results are generally consistent with those found in the respective Tables 9.5–9.8 but with a few minor differences. With respect to the results shown in the preferred SGMM model (see Table 9.11), the diagnostic tests, specifically the Arellano-Bond test for second-order autocorrelation and the Sargan test for under-identification, support the validity of this approach. Similarly, the strength of the external instruments used in the IV strategy is

Table 9.10 The impact of remittances on financial development—difference GMM (DGMM) Regression (Alternative measure of remittances)

Variables	*(1)*	*(2)*	*(3)*	*(4)*
	Private sector credit /GDP	*Bank credit/Deposits*	*Bank deposits/GDP*	*FinDev Index*
Lagged Remittances per capita	−0.504	−0.788**	0.004	−0.037*
	(0.345)	(0.314)	(0.256)	(0.018)
Lagged Dependent Variable	0.959***	1.009***	0.937***	0.896***
	(0.034)	(0.054)	(0.027)	(0.074)
Log Real GDP per capita	−0.086	−2.734***	2.351***	0.014
	(0.576)	(0.678)	(0.612)	(0.033)
FDI/GDP	0.115***	0.077	−0.061	0.003
	(0.035)	(0.120)	(0.126)	(0.003)
Trade/GDP	0.016*	0.037	0.016	0.002**
	(0.009)	(0.022)	(0.010)	(0.001)
Inflation	−0.061***	−0.008	−0.113***	−0.006***
	(0.013)	(0.023)	(0.022)	(0.001)
Investment/GDP	0.060	0.198	−0.066	0.001
	(0.064)	(0.150)	(0.080)	(0.006)
Government Consumption/GDP	0.190***	0.478**	0.004	0.018***
	(0.041)	(0.177)	(0.120)	(0.005)
Country dummies	Yes	Yes	Yes	Yes
Time dummies	Yes	Yes	Yes	Yes
Observations	120	120	120	120
No. of countries	13	13	13	13
AR(1) test statistic	−1.583	−1.601	−2.297	−1.519
p-value of AR(1) test	0.113	0.109	0.022	0.129
AR(2) test statistic	1.264	0.344	1.076	0.939
p-value of AR(2) test	0.206	0.731	0.282	0.348
p-value of Sargan test	0.342	0.433	0.138	0.560

Notes Dependent variable is shown is at the top of each column of results. Heteroskedastic and autocorrelation robust standard errors are shown in parentheses. Statistical significance at the 10%, 5%, and 1% confidence levels are denoted by *, **, and ***, respectively. Regressions are weighted by country population and are based on 11 non-overlapping 3-year periods. Variables are defined in Table 9.18

Table 9.11 The impact of remittances on financial development—system GMM (SGMM) Regression (alternative measure of remittances)

Variables	*(1)*	*(2)*	*(3)*	*(4)*
	Private sector credit /GDP	*Bank credit/Deposits*	*Bank deposits/GDP*	*FinDev Index*
Lagged Remittances per capita	−0.652*	−0.637**	−0.312	−0.033*
	(0.352)	(0.291)	(0.361)	(0.015)
Lagged Dependent Variable	0.960***	1.035***	0.946***	0.904***
	(0.037)	(0.058)	(0.033)	(0.073)
Log Real GDP per capita	−0.678**	−1.607	0.410	−0.048***
	(0.227)	(1.198)	(0.397)	(0.015)
FDI/GDP	0.082	0.164	−0.071	0.005
	(0.047)	(0.127)	(0.113)	(0.003)
Trade/GDP	0.006	0.030	−0.011	0.000
	(0.006)	(0.017)	(0.007)	(0.001)
Inflation	−0.055***	−0.007	−0.070***	−0.005***
	(0.016)	(0.034)	(0.017)	(0.001)
Investment/GDP	0.084*	0.255**	−0.074	0.002
	(0.042)	(0.108)	(0.067)	(0.004)
Government Consumption/GDP	0.150***	0.363***	−0.079	0.011***
	(0.032)	(0.099)	(0.047)	(0.002)
Country dummies	Yes	Yes	Yes	Yes
Time dummies	Yes	Yes	Yes	Yes
Observations	135	135	135	135
No. of countries	13	13	13	13
AR(1) test statistic	−1.385	−1.604	−2.215	−1.473
p-value of AR(1) test	0.166	0.109	0.027	0.141
AR(2) test statistic	1.051	0.595	0.742	0.780
p-value of AR(2) test	0.293	0.552	0.458	0.435
p-value of Sargan test	0.353	0.605	0.204	0.529

Notes Dependent variable is shown is at the top of each column of results. Heteroskedastic and autocorrelation robust standard errors are shown in parentheses. Statistical significance at the 10%, 5%, and 1% confidence levels are denoted by *, **, and ***, respectively. Regressions are weighted by country population and are based on 11 non-overlapping 3-year periods. Variables are defined in Table 9.18

Table 9.12 The impact of remittances on financial development—Instrumental Variables (IV) regression (Alternative measure of remittances)

Variables	*(1)*	*(2)*	*(3)*	*(4)*
	log (Private sector credit /GDP)	*log (Bank credit/Deposits)*	*log (Bank deposits/GDP)*	*log (FinDev Index)*
Log (Remittances per capita)	−0.164***	−0.200***	0.021	−0.029***
	(0.057)	(0.059)	(0.056)	(0.010)
Lagged log (Dependent Variable)	0.605***	0.331*	0.653***	0.563***
	(0.091)	(0.182)	(0.093)	(0.112)
Lagged log (Real GDP per capita)	−0.135***	−0.058	0.105	−0.014
	(0.043)	(0.053)	(0.071)	(0.009)
Lagged log (FDI/GDP)	0.101***	0.140***	−0.082*	0.014**
	(0.029)	(0.044)	(0.042)	(0.006)
Lagged log (Trade/GDP)	−0.195*	0.030	−0.144	−0.032*
	(0.102)	(0.120)	(0.131)	(0.019)
Lagged log (1+Inflation)	−0.158***	−0.065	−0.095**	−0.030***
	(0.051)	(0.057)	(0.038)	(0.010)
Lagged log (Investment/GDP)	0.175	0.069	−0.042	0.018
	(0.130)	(0.135)	(0.129)	(0.022)
Lagged log (Government Consumption/GDP)	0.048	0.218***	−0.207***	0.001
	(0.056)	(0.074)	(0.077)	(0.012)
Country dummies	Yes	Yes	Yes	Yes
Time dummies	Yes	Yes	Yes	Yes
Observations	123	123	123	123
No. of countries	13	13	13	13
Kleibergen-Paap first stage *F*-stat	11.574	11.473	11.521	12.170
Kleibergen-Paap LM test stat	11.894	11.614	11.571	11.783
Kleibergen-Paap LM test (*p*-value)	0.008	0.009	0.009	0.008

Notes Dependent variable is shown is at the top of each column of results. Heteroskedastic and autocorrelation robust standard errors are shown in parentheses. Statistical significance at the 10%, 5%, and 1% confidence levels are denoted by *, **, and ***, respectively. The instruments for the IV estimation are lagged values of the unemployment rates for the United States, Canada, and the United Kingdom. Regressions are weighted by country population and are based on 11 non-overlapping 3-year periods. Variables are defined in Table 9.18

satisfied by first stage F-statistics above the threshold value of 10 (see Table 9.12).

Limited Information Maximum Likelihood (LIML) Estimation

To further consider the validity of the IV estimation approach, this section tests the sensitivity of the results using Limited Information Maximum Likelihood (LIML) estimation. LIML estimation is found to be more effective in small sample estimation and represents an improvement over traditional IV strategy when instruments are weak. In addition, the application of LIML within a dynamic panel setting can offer efficiency gains in which the LIML estimates may be preferred over GMM and standard IV in both theory (Baltagi, 2021) and application (Cannonier & Burke, 2017). After rerunning the regressions of Table 9.8 (Panel A), the results from the LIML estimates remain practically unaffected. Panel B also shows the regression results when the main explanatory variable is remittances per capita. Again, these estimates are remarkably similar to those found in Table 9.13. It is noteworthy that the LIML estimates produce higher first stage F-statistics, suggesting that the instruments are strongly correlated with remittances.

Alternative Specification: Fixed Effects Model (no Lagged Dependent Variable)

Table 9.14 conveys results from an alternative specification that excludes lagged remittances from the fixed effects model. Fixed effects estimators are thought to be inconsistent in the presence of the lagged dependent variable. Since previous financial development can influence current financial development as well as remittances, excluding the lagged dependent variable may result in attenuation bias due to omitted variables. This downward bias may be more severe if measurement error is an important component of this estimator. The estimated effects are qualitatively similar to the previous results (see Table 9.5) and are larger in magnitude. This finding suggests that fixed effects specification provides reliable estimates of the impact of remittances on financial development.

Table 9.13 The impact of remittances on financial development—Limited Information Maximum Likelihood (LIML) Instrumental Variables (IV) regression

Variables	*(1)*	*(2)*	*(3)*	*(4)*
Panel A				
	log (Private sector credit /GDP)	log (Bank credit/Deposits)	log (Bank deposits/GDP)	log (FinDev Index)
Log (Remittances/GDP)	−0.155***	−0.195***	0.020	−0.030***
	(0.043)	(0.042)	(0.045)	(0.008)
Control Variables	Yes	Yes	Yes	Yes
Country Dummies	Yes	Yes	Yes	Yes
Time dummies	Yes	Yes	Yes	Yes
Observations	123	123	123	123
No. of countries	13	13	13	13
Kleibergen-Paap first stage *F*-stat	14.968	16.404	15.137	15.345
Kleibergen-Paap LM test stat	38.116	40.568	38.412	38.774
Kleibergen-Paap LM test (*p*-value)	0.000	0.000	0.000	0.000
Panel B: alternative definition of remittances				
Log (Remittances per capita)	−0.164***	−0.208***	0.021	−0.032***
	(0.046)	(0.046)	(0.048)	(0.009)
Control Variables	Yes	Yes	Yes	Yes
Country Dummies	Yes	Yes	Yes	Yes
Time dummies	Yes	Yes	Yes	Yes
Observations	123	123	123	123
No. of countries	13	13	13	13
Kleibergen-Paap first stage *F*-stat	13.521	14.834	13.771	13.818
Kleibergen-Paap LM test stat	35.496	37.881	35.959	36.045
Kleibergen-Paap LM test (*p*-value)	0.000	0.000	0.000	0.000

Notes Dependent variable is shown is at the top of each column of results. Heteroskedastic and autocorrelation robust standard errors are shown in parentheses. Statistical significance at the 10%, 5%, and 1% confidence levels are denoted by *, **, and ***, respectively. Control variables are in logarithm and comprise the following: lagged dependent variables, real GDP per capita, FDI/GDP, Trade/GDP, inflation, investment/GDP, and government consumption/GDP. The instruments for the IV estimation are lagged values of the unemployment rates for the United States, Canada, and the United Kingdom. Regressions are weighted by country population and are based on 11 non-overlapping 3-year periods. Variables are defined in Table 9.18

Table 9.14 The impact of remittances on financial development—fixed-effects regression (No lagged dependent variable)

Variables	*(1)*	*(2)*	*(3)*	*(4)*
	Private sector credit /GDP	*Bank credit/Deposits*	*Bank deposits/GDP*	*FinDev Index*
Lagged Remittances/GDP	−1.264***	0.160	−1.341**	−0.051**
	(0.406)	(0.324)	(0.509)	(0.019)
Control variables	Yes	Yes	Yes	Yes
Country dummies	Yes	Yes	Yes	Yes
Time dummies	Yes	Yes	Yes	Yes
Mean of outcome	40.78	74.35	51.53	11.77
Observations	135	135	135	135
R-square	0.885	0.850	0.858	0.926

Notes Dependent variable is shown is at the top of each column of results. Heteroskedastic and autocorrelation robust standard errors are shown in parentheses are clustered at the country level. Statistical significance at the 10%, 5%, and 1% confidence levels are denoted by *, **, and ***, respectively. Control variables comprise the following: lagged dependent variables, real GDP per capita, FDI/GDP, Trade/GDP, inflation, investment/GDP, and government consumption/GDP. Regressions are weighted by country population and are based on 11 non-overlapping 3-year periods. Variables are defined in Table 9.18

Splitting Sample into Common Currency Region and Non-Common Currency Regions

To further explore some of the channels through which remittances might influence financial development, Table 9.15 (Panels A and B) shows the IV results of splitting the sample into two groups: countries that operate within the same currency union and those that have individual currencies. The following countries are part of the Eastern Caribbean Currency Union (ECCU): Antigua and Barbuda, Dominica, Grenada, St. Kitts and Nevis, St. Lucia, and St. Vincent and the Grenadines. Several studies suggest that countries having a common currency may better facilitate the flow of remittances (Ruiz & Vargas-Silva, 2014). The results in Panel A show that remittances have no significant impact on financial development in countries with a common currency. On the other hand, for those countries without a common currency, remittances continue to have a negative effect on most of the financial development measures (see Panel B).

Table 9.15 The impact of remittances on financial development—Instrumental Variables (IV) regression

Variables	*(1)*	*(2)*	*(3)*	*(4)*
Panel A: countries with a common currency				
	log (Private sector credit /GDP)	log (Bank credit/Deposits)	log (Bank deposits/GDP)	log (FinDev Index)
Log (Remittances/GDP)	0.044	−0.010	0.051	−0.001
	(0.076)	(0.069)	(0.046)	(0.012)
Control Variables	Yes	Yes	Yes	Yes
Country Dummies	Yes	Yes	Yes	Yes
Time dummies	Yes	Yes	Yes	Yes
Observations	62	62	62	62
No. of countries	6	6	6	6
Kleibergen-Paap first stage *F*-stat	5.794	6.131	6.172	5.881
Kleibergen-Paap LM test stat	12.213	11.103	11.469	12.327
Kleibergen-Paap LM test (*p*-value)	0.007	0.011	0.009	0.006
Panel B: other countries				
	log (Private sector credit /GDP)	log (Bank credit/Deposits)	log (Bank deposits/GDP)	log (FinDev Index)
Log (Remittances/GDP)	−0.155***	−0.188***	0.029	−0.026***
	(0.050)	(0.053)	(0.055)	(0.009)
Control Variables	Yes	Yes	Yes	Yes
Country Dummies	Yes	Yes	Yes	Yes
Time dummies	Yes	Yes	Yes	Yes
Observations	61	61	61	61
No. of countries	7	7	7	7
Kleibergen-Paap first stage *F*-stat	12.679	11.246	12.699	13.765
Kleibergen-Paap LM test stat	12.537	11.874	12.265	12.626
Kleibergen-Paap LM test (*p*-value)	0.006	0.008	0.007	0.006

Notes Dependent variable is shown is at the top of each column of results. Heteroskedastic and autocorrelation robust standard errors are shown in parentheses. Statistical significance at the 10%, 5%, and 1% confidence levels are denoted by *, **, and ***, respectively. Control variables are in logarithm and comprise the following: lagged dependent variables, real GDP per capita, FDI/GDP, Trade/GDP, inflation, investment/GDP, and government consumption/GDP. The instruments for the IV estimation are lagged values of the unemployment rates for the United States, Canada, and the United Kingdom. Regressions are weighted by country population and are based on 11 non-overlapping 3-year periods. Variables are defined in Table 9.18

Table 9.16 The impact of remittances on financial development—fixed-effects regression (5-year period averages)

Variables	*(1)*	*(2)*	*(3)*	*(4)*
	Private sector credit /GDP	*Bank credit/Deposits*	*Bank deposits/GDP*	*FinDev Index*
Lagged Remittances/GDP	−0.108**	−0.090	−0.179*	−0.013***
	(0.044)	(0.099)	(0.096)	(0.004)
Control variables	Yes	Yes	Yes	Yes
Country dummies	Yes	Yes	Yes	Yes
Time dummies	Yes	Yes	Yes	Yes
Observations	84	84	84	84
R-square	0.996	0.991	0.985	0.995

Notes Dependent variable is shown is at the top of each column of results. Heteroskedastic and autocorrelation robust standard errors are shown in parentheses are clustered at the country level. Statistical significance at the 10%, 5%, and 1% confidence levels are denoted by *, **, and ***, respectively. Control variables comprise the following: lagged dependent variables, real GDP per capita, FDI/GDP, Trade/GDP, inflation, investment/GDP, and government consumption/GDP. Regressions are weighted by country population and are based on 7 non-overlapping 5-year periods. Variables are defined in Table 9.18

Alternative Specification (Using 5-year Period Averages)

To explore the sensitivity of the results, the models were estimated with the sample split into 7 non-overlapping 5-year periods. Despite the reduction in the sample sizes, the longer time period helps to mitigate short-term simultaneity issues associated with business cycle fluctuations but also allows for an examination of long-term effects of remittances on financial development. As shown in Table 9.16, the coefficient on remittances is negative for each of the outcome variables and statistically significant in most cases.

Discussion and Conclusion

The chapter analyzes how remittances influence financial development using a rich panel of data from more than a dozen Caribbean countries over the period 1980–2013. To infer causality, the study utilizes the traditional IV and GMM methodologies that, respectively, make use of external and internal instruments for identification. The study finds that remittances have a negative impact on financial development in recipient Caribbean countries, suggesting that remittances and financial development are substitutes. There is suggestive evidence that this negative relationship is driven by countries that have relatively lower income, are larger, and are not part of a common currency area. The results hold for a rich set of covariates, alternative specifications, and different methodological techniques, which account for unobserved heterogeneity and time-invariant factors which may influence financial development.

This study comes with limitations. First, the estimated effect of remittances on financial development should be qualified because the remittances data are likely to suffer from underreporting. This occurrence is because the World Bank reports only remittances sent via formal channels. Consequently, the estimates may understate the true [beneficial] impact of effect remittances. Second, the study takes a cross-country approach to estimating the effect of remittances on financial development in line with the extant literature. Notwithstanding, the effect of remittances is identified using within-country changes in remittances and financial development over time, the estimated effect is nonetheless an average across a relatively small number of countries that are similar in many respects but also sufficiently unique in other ways. These cross-country estimates represent a first step in this line of analysis that ought to be complemented by country-specific case studies that explore the nature and causes of remittances within these relatively small, coastal, and mostly sovereign states. Finally, the evidence about the exact mechanisms through which remittances affect financial development is largely suggestive. A more rigorous investigation might consider the links relating costs of sending remittances and the technology facilitating its movement to a broader set of financial development measures.

Overall, the findings from this study offer some clear policy implications. If a goal is to increase the level of financial inclusion of households receiving remittances, then policymakers should consider pursuing policies that improve the mechanisms that offer easier channels for remittances to enter the domestic banking system. This policy modification will in turn increase competition among banks that will stimulate a greater flow of financial resources to the private sector and thus help to reduce the strain on the poor in accessing credit. The finding that remittances appear to serve as substitutes in the non-common currency regions, which are mostly the larger and lower-income countries, is discouraging from a macroeconomic perspective. Recent increases in the cost of remittances imply households are receiving less net income, ceteris paribus, and lower consumption smoothing with the resultant negative effects on poverty and inequality.

Future work assessing the mechanisms through which remittances impact financial development is essential. Further, estimating the spillover effects associated with the negative influences of remittances on financial development is a non-trivial exercise that is pertinent for effective policy making. Ultimately, the effectiveness of remittances in serving as complements (rather than substitutes) to the process of financial development hinges on a policy approach that is designed to foster a more diversified and fully integrated financial system.

Appendix

See Tables 9.17 and 9.18.

Table 9.17 Sample of countries

Country name
Antigua and Barbuda
Barbados
Belize
Dominica
Grenada
Guyana
Haiti
Jamaica
St. Kitts-Nevis
St. Lucia
St. Vincent and the Grenadines
Suriname
Trinidad and Tobago

Table 9.18 Description of variables and sources of data

Variables	*Definition*	*Sources*
Financial development		
Private sector credit/GDP	Bank credit to the private sector in percent of GDP	World Bank (2019b)
Bank credit/Deposits	Bank credit to deposits (in percent)	World Bank (2019b)
Bank deposits/GDP	Bank deposits as a percent of GDP	World Bank (2019b)
FinDev Index	Composite index of financial development	Derived
Remittances		
Remittances/GDP	Gross remittances as a percentage of GDP	World Bank (2019b)
Remittances per capita	Gross remittances per 100,000 population	Derived
Economic and Policy Variables		
RGDP	Real GDP in thousands of constant 2005 US dollars	World Bank (2019b), IMF (2019), and United Nations (2019)
RGDP per capita	Real GDP per capita in thousands of constant 2005 US dollars	World Bank (2019b), IMF (2019), and United Nations (2019)
FDI/GDP	FDI as a percentage of GDP	IMF (2019), UNCTADStat (2019), and World Bank (2019b)
Trade/GDP	Sum of exports and imports of goods and services as a percentage of GDP	World Bank (2019b)
Inflation	Percentage change in the annual GDP deflator	World Bank (2019b) and United Nations (2019)
Investment/GDP	Gross capital formation as a percentage of GDP	World Bank (2019b) and United Nations (2019)
Government Consumption/GDP	General Government Final Consumption as a percent of GDP	World Bank (2019b) and United Nations (2019)

Note GDP = Gross Domestic Product; FDI = Foreign Direct Investment

References

Aggarwal, R., Demirguc-Kunt, A., & Martínez Pería, M. S. (2011). Do remittances promote financial development? *Journal of Development Economics, 96*(2), 255–264. https://doi.org/10.1016/j.jdeveco.2010.10.005

Alfaro, L., Chanda, A., & Sayek, S. (2009). FDI, productivity and financial development. *World Economy, 32*(1), 111–135. https://doi.org/10.1111/j.1467-9701.2009.01159.x

Arellano, M., & Bond, S. R. (1991). Some tests of specification for panel data: Monte Carlo evidence and an application to employment equations. *Review of Economic Studies, 58*(2), 277–297. https://doi.org/10.2307/2297968

Arellano, M., & Bover, O. (1995). Another look at the instrumental variables estimation of error components models. *Journal of Econometrics, 68*(1), 29–51. https://doi.org/10.1016/0304-4076(94)01642-D

Arezki, R., & Brückner, M. (2012). Rainfall, financial development, and remittances: Evidence from Sub-Saharan Africa. *Journal of International Economics, 8*, 377–385. https://doi.org/10.1016/j.jinteco.2011.12.010

Baltagi B. H. (2021). *Econometric analysis of panel data* (6th ed.). Springer Texts in Business and Economics. https://doi.org/10.1007/978-3-030-539 53-5_8

Baltagi, B. H., Demetriades, P. O., & Law, S. H. (2009). Financial development and openness: Evidence from panel data. *Journal of Development Economics, 89*(2), 285–296. https://doi.org/10.1007/978-3-030-53953-5_8

Beaton, K., Cerovic, S., Galdamez, M., Hadzi-Vaskov, M., Loyola, F., Koczan, Z., Lissovolik, B., Martijn, J.K., Ustyugova, Y., & Wong, J. (2020). *Migration and remittances in Latin America and the Caribbean: Engines of growth and macroeconomic stabilizers?* (IMF Working Paper No. 17/144). International Monetary Fund. https://www.imf.org/-/media/Files/Publications/WP/2017/wp17144.ashx

Benhabib, J., & Spiegel, M. M. (2000). The role of financial development in growth and investment. *Journal of Economic Growth, 5*(4), 341–360. https://doi.org/10.1023/A:1026599402490

Blundell, R., & Bond, S. (1998). Initial conditions and moment restrictions in dynamic panel data models. *Journal of Econometrics, 87*(1), 115–143. https://doi.org/10.1016/S0304-4076(98)00009-8

Blundell, R., & Bond, S. (2000). GMM estimation with persistent panel data, an application to production functions. *Econometric Reviews, 19*(3), 321–340. https://doi.org/10.1080/07474930008800475

Bond, S. R. (2002). Dynamic data panel models: A guide to micro data methods and practice. *Portuguese Economic Journal, 1*, 141–162. https://doi.org/10.1007/s10258-002-0009-9

Boyd, J., Levine, R., & Smith, B. (2001). The impact of inflation on financial sector performance. *Journal of Monetary Economics, 47*(2), 221–248. https://doi.org/10.1016/S0304-3932(01)00049-6

Brown, R. P. C., Carmignani, F., & Fayad, G. (2013). Migrants' remittances and financial development: Macro- and micro-level evidence of a perverse relationship. *The World Economy, 36*(5), 636–660. https://doi.org/10.1111/twec.12016

Cannonier, C., & Burke, M. G. (2017). Tourism and financial development in small states: Evidence from Caribbean countries. *Tourism Economics, 23*(6), 1369–1377. https://doi.org/10.1177/1354816617689870

Chami, R., Fullenkamp, C., & Jahjah, S. (2003). *Are immigrant remittances flows a source of capital for development?* (IMF Working Paper No. 03/189). International Monetary Fund. https://www.imf.org/en/Publications/WP/Issues/2016/12/30/Are-Immigrant-Remittance-Flows-a-Source-of-Capital-for-Development-16801

Chin, M. D., & Ito, H. (2006). What matters for financial development? Capital controls, institutions, and interactions. *Journal of Development Economics, 81*(1), 163–192. https://doi.org/10.1016/j.jdeveco.2005.05.010

Coulibaly, D. (2015). Remittances and financial development in Sub-Saharan African countries: A system approach. *Economic Modelling, 45*, 249–258. https://doi.org/10.1016/j.econmod.2014.12.005

Demetriades, P. O., & Rousseau, P. L. (2016). The changing face of financial development. *Economics Letters, 141*(1), 87–90. https://doi.org/10.1016/j.econlet.2016.02.009

Demirguc-Kunt, A., Cordova, E. L., Martínez Pería, M. S., & Woodruff, C. (2011). Remittances and banking sector breadth and depth: Evidence from Mexico. *Journal of Development Economics, 95*(2), 229–241. https://doi.org/10.1016/j.jdeveco.2010.04.002

Dutta, N., & Roy, S. (2011). Foreign direct investment, financial development and political risks. *The Journal of Developing Areas, 44*(2), 303–327. https://doi.org/10.1353/jda.0.0106

Freund, C., & Spatafora, N. (2008). Remittances, transaction costs, and informality. *Journal of Development Economics, 86*(2), 356–366. https://doi.org/10.1016/j.jdeveco.2007.09.002

Fromentin, V. (2017). The long-run and short-run impacts of remittances on financial development in developing countries. *The Quarterly Review of Economics and Finance, 66*, 192–201. https://doi.org/10.1016/j.qref.2017.02.006

Fromentin, V. (2018). Remittances and financial development in Latin America and the Caribbean countries: A dynamic approach. *Review of Development Economics, 22*(2), 808–826. https://doi.org/10.1111/rode.12368

Giuliano, P., & Ruiz-Arranz, M. (2009). Remittances, financial development, and growth. *Journal of Development Economics, 90*(1), 144–152. https://doi.org/10.1016/j.jdeveco.2008.10.005

Gregorio, J. D., & Guidotti, P. E. (1995). Financial development and economic growth. *World Development, 23*(3), 433–448. https://doi.org/10.1016/0305-750X(94)00132-I

Gupta, S., Pattillo, C. A., & Wagh, S. (2009). Effect of remittances on poverty and financial development in Sub-Saharan Africa. *World Development, 37*(1), 104–115. https://doi.org/10.1016/j.worlddev.2008.05.007

Hausman, J. A. (1978). Specification tests in econometrics. *Econometrica, 46*(6), 1251–1271. https://doi.org/10.2307/1913827

International Monetary Fund (IMF). (2009). Appendix 5: Remittances. In *Balance of payments and international investment position manual* (6th ed., pp. 272–277). International Monetary Fund. https://www.imf.org/external/pubs/ft/bop/2007/pdf/appx5.pdf

International Monetary Fund (IMF). (2019). *IMF balance of payments statistics, 1948–2018* (97th ed.). UK Data Service [data collection]. https://doi.org/10.5257/imf/bops/2019a-02.

Kakhkharov, J., & Rohde, N. (2020). Remittances and financial development in transition economies. *Empirical Economics, 59*(1), 731–763. https://doi.org/10.1007/s00181-019-01642-3

Khan, M. S., & Senhadji, A. S. (2003). Financial development and economic growth: A review and new evidence. *Journal of African Economies, 12*(2), 89–110. https://doi.org/10.1093/jae/12.suppl_2.ii89

Mundaca, B. G. (2009). Remittances, financial market development, and economic growth: The case of Latin America and the Caribbean. *Review of Development Economics, 13*(2), 288–303. https://doi.org/10.1111/j.1467-9361.2008.00487.x

Ramirez, M. D. (2013). Do financial and institutional variables enhance the impact of remittances on economic growth in Latin America and the Caribbean? A panel cointegration analysis. *International Advances in Economic Research, 19*(3), 273–288. https://doi.org/10.1007/s11294-013-9407-2

Ramirez, M. D., & Sharma, H. (2009). Remittances and growth in Latin America: A panel unit root and panel cointegration analysis. *Estudios Economicos De Desarrollo Internacional, 9*(1), 1–33.

Ruiz, I., & Vargas-Silva, C. (2014). Remittances and the business cycle: A reliable relationship? *Journal of Ethnic and Migration Studies*, *40*(3), 456–474. https://doi.org/10.1080/1369183X.2013.787704

Sobiech, I. (2019). Remittances, finance and growth: Does financial development foster the impact of remittances on economic growth? *World Development, 113*(1), 44–59. https://doi.org/10.1016/j.worlddev.2018.08.016

Stock, J. H., Wright, J. H., & Yogo, M. (2002). A survey of weak instruments and weak identification in generalized method of moments. *Journal of Business and Economic Statistics, 20*(4), 518–529. https://doi.org/10.1198/073500102288618658

UNCTADStat. (2019). *Foreign direct investment: Inward and outward flows and stock, annual* [Online]. Retrieved October 17, 2019, from http://unctadstat.unctad.org/wds/ReportFolders/reportFolders.aspx?sCS_ChosenLang=en

United Nations. (2019). *National accounts main aggregates database*. Economics and Statistics Branch, United Nations Statistics Division. Retrieved October 30, 2019, from http://unstats.un.org/unsd/snaama/introduction.asp

Wooldridge, J. M. (2010). *Econometric analysis of cross section and panel data* (2nd ed.). MIT Press.

Wooldridge, J. M. (2013). *Introductory econometrics: A modern approach* (6th ed.). South-Western Cengage Learning.

World Bank. (2019a). *Leveraging economic migration for development: A briefing for the World Bank board*. World Bank.

World Bank. (2019b). *World development indicators* (WDI). http://data.worldbank.org/data-catalog/world-development-indicators

CHAPTER 10

Caribbean Tourism Development, Sustainability, and Impacts

David Mc. Arthur Baker

Introduction

Travel and tourism make up the largest service industry in the world and it continues to grow (Manzoor et al., 2019). Ohlan's (2017) analysis deduced that tourism and economic growth are intertwined in the short and long run, so tourism plays a great role in the development of a country. International tourism is one of the most important and certainly the fastest developing sector of the world's economy. In 2019 international tourist arrivals reached a total of 1.5 billion (UNWTO, 2019). The growth of tourism in recent years confirms that the sector is today one of the most powerful drivers of economic growth and development. Adrian (2017) stated that tourism has a close relationship with other branches of the economy because tourism increases the demand of the commodities

D. Mc. A. Baker (✉)
Hospitality & Tourism Management, College of Business,
Tennessee State University, Nashville, TN, USA
e-mail: dmbaker@tnstate.edu

C. Cannonier and M. Galloway Burke (eds.),
Contemporary Issues Within Caribbean Economies,
https://doi.org/10.1007/978-3-030-98865-4_10

through foreigner population which further push the industrial development in the country and solve the problem of unemployment. It is each destination's responsibility to manage it in a sustainable manner and translate this expansion into real benefits particularly to all local communities, creating opportunities for jobs and entrepreneurship. By creating employment opportunities, improving the infrastructure, generating financial flux, and contributing to diversification of the local and national economies, tourism represents one of the principal motors of socioeconomic progress of a modern society.

One of the core elements of sustainable tourism development is to encourage local communities' participation as it is central to the sustainability of the tourism industry (Choi & Sirakaya, 2006). The community approach to tourism development is an attempt to integrate the interests of all community stakeholders, including residents as a critically important group, in analyses and proposals for development (Murphy & Murphy, 2004). Local communities form an integral part of the tourism development agenda (Aref et al., 2010; Bushell & McCool, 2007; Jamal & Stronza, 2009; Tosun, 2006). Given the complex nature of most tourist destinations, there are also numerous stakeholders with varying interests and views. This stance provides good environment for resource use conflicts within and around tourist destinations (Haukeland, 2011; Jamal & Stronza, 2009; Tosun, 2006). The representation of interests of the local communities in the tourism development agenda is a complex issue that needs to be addressed carefully.

Sustainable tourism is described as environmentally responsible travel and visitation to natural areas to enjoy and appreciate nature (and any accompanying cultural features, both past and present) in a way that promotes conservation, which has a low visitor impact and provides for beneficially active socioeconomic involvement of local peoples (World Conservation Union, 1996). Sustainable tourism has three key components, sometimes referred to as the "triple bottom line" (International Ecotourism Society, 2004), which are (1) environmentally the activity has a low impact on natural resources, particularly in protected areas, minimizing damage to the environment (i.e., flora, fauna, habitats, water, living marine resources, energy use, contamination, etc.) and ideally tries to benefit the environment; (2) socially and culturally the activity does not harm the social structure or culture of the community where it is located; instead it respects local cultures and tradition and involves stakeholders (individuals, communities, tour operators, government institutions) in all phases of planning, development, and monitoring, and educates stakeholders about their roles; and (3) economically it contributes to the economic well-being of the community, generating sustainable and equitable income for local communities and as many other stakeholders as possible. It means that tourism can become a concrete tool of policymakers to stimulate sustainable development, but it has to be understood and well-managed, taking into full account both the positive and negative impacts.

Background

The Caribbean had a long history of idyllic paradise which induces consumption, luxury, and privilege (Sheller, 2004). Colonization of the Caribbean began with the first contact with Europeans in 1492 with Christopher Columbus. In the following centuries, numerous wars were fought among Europeans for political and economic control of these islands. After sugar cane plantations were introduced in the eighteenth century, the Caribbean islands became the most lucrative colonies of the European powers. The then indigenous people (i.e., Arawaks and Caribs) were worked to death to be replaced by slaves imported from West Africa, and when the slave trade was officially abolished in the mid-nineteenth century, indentured workers were subsequently imported from India to work on these sugar plantations. Present-day tourism reflects to a large extent of the legacy of past colonial practices.

Mass tourism in the Caribbean began in earnest in the 1980s when air travel became economically accessible to middle-class North Americans and Europeans. By the 1990s, large-scale sea cruises became commonplace for this class of tourists. During the past decade, tourism trade has been expanding steadily to capture the disposable income available to these middle-class citizens from abroad. Indeed, the economy of many Caribbean island states is now organized and re-configured to provide goods and services to the increasing middle class of North American and Europe tourists. The advent of mass tourism in the Caribbean has been accompanied by a redistribution of the tourism functions and flows within the Caribbean region. The significant growth in tourism, although essential to the economies of the Caribbean islands, has given rise to a number of issues, the first being the necessity to examine the multiplier effect from tourism revenue within these externally dependent economies.

Tourism is of significant importance to the Caribbean region and based on the World Travel & Tourism Council's (WTTC, 2019) statistical data, tourism in the Caribbean generated more than 2.76 million direct and indirect jobs (equivalent to 15.5% of the total labor force). Its impact on local economies is significant considering that the tourism demand generated around $62 billion dollars in tourism activities and travel and tourism in the Caribbean is responsible for over 20% of its exports and 13.5% of employment (WTTC, 2019). In 2019, the travel and tourism sector accounted for 15.2% of the gross domestic product (GDP) in the Caribbean, directly and indirectly. Nevertheless, the majority of Caribbean islands registered higher shares of tourism contribution to their GDPs that year. For instance, the travel and tourism sector directly represented around one-third of Aruba's GDP and accounted for nearly 74% of the island's GDP in total. The British and the U.S. Virgin Islands also registered shares of over 55% of total tourism contribution to GDP that year. The other island's GDP from the tourism sector were Cayman Islands at 25.5%; St. Kitts & Nevis at 28.2%; St. Vincent & the Grenadines at 28.6%; Barbados at 30.9%; Jamaica at 31.1%; Dominica at 36.9%; Anguilla at 37.1%; Grenada at 40.5%; St. Lucia at 40.7%; Antigua & Barbuda at 42.7%; Bahamas at 43.3%; Dominican Republic at 16.3%; and Bermuda at 18.7% with the remaining islands having 10% or less. Caribbean islands rely heavily on travel and tourism for employment—the industry accounted for 90.7% of jobs in Antigua and Barbuda in 2019; 51.3% in Anguilla; 52.2% in Bahamas; 59.1% in St. Kitts & Nevis; 66.4% in British Virgin Islands; 68.8% in US Virgin Islands; 78.1% in St. Lucia; and 84.3% in Aruba (WTTC, 2019). Travel and tourism is extremely important for the Caribbean as expanding the tourism industry leads to increased employment. From resorts and hotels to restaurants, clubs, bars, diving schools, and other adventure activities, Caribbean countries thrive on the jobs tourism creates because increasing jobs also increases tax revenue, which can go into services and facilities for the local people that can result in increased standards of living.

The adoption of the Tourism Satellite Account can be of great significance to the islands of the Caribbean. Additionally, there is both the question of access to resources and the closing of tourist sites in a context where local communities are focusing on coastlines to develop their own numerous tourism and recreational activities. These developments will inevitably require us to consider economic, sociocultural, and environmental issues as well as the sustainability of today's predominant tourism activities.

There have been thousands of sustainable tourism initiatives and projects carried out by national governments, international organizations, private stakeholders, and local communities in the Caribbean region in the last decade. These entities concern all different aspects of the development which, considering their sustainable goals, could be grouped as follows: (i) projects focused on the tourism stakeholders' development (e.g., certification process, minimal quality standard, marketing, brand strategies, etc.); (ii) projects focused on the preservation of the social, cultural, and environmental factors; and (iii) projects focused on poverty reduction through tourism—the Pro-Poor Tourism concept initiated by the United Nations. Skeptics argue that because tourism is often driven by foreign, private sector interests, it has limited potential to contribute much to poverty elimination in developing countries. It is noted for high levels of revenue "leakage" and of the revenue that is retained in the destination country, much is captured by rich or middle-income groups and not the poor. Tourism is also a volatile industry, being extremely susceptible to events which are difficult to control—i.e., political unrest, exchange rate fluctuations, natural disasters, and pandemics. Nevertheless, analysis of tourism data shows that in most countries with high levels of poverty, tourism is significant or growing (WTTC, 2019). Tourism is therefore a fact of life for many of the world's poor. A reduction in world poverty is an internationally agreed priority and targets have been set to halve poverty by the year 2015. Achieving poverty reduction requires actions on a variety of complementary fronts and scales. The tourism industry is clearly important in many poor countries, it takes good planning and development strategies to significantly reduce poverty.

The Caribbean region has developed various tourism products, with particular emphasis on its natural assets of "sun, sea and sand," and cruise tourism as the main tourism products supplied by the Caribbean region. Other products such as eco-tourism, cultural tourism, and health tourism have immense potential. The Caribbean region, over the last decade, has moved with affirmation in the arena of sustainable tourism development. The Policy Framework development process began with the hosting of two inter-sectoral policy planning workshops in 2005 (Barbados) and 2006 (St. Lucia). At these meetings, stakeholders met to discuss the concept and design of the Policy Framework. Six thematic areas were identified as being critical to the sustainability of Caribbean tourism: tourism management capacity, marketing, transportation, environment, linkages, and health, safety, and security issues. The Caribbean Tourism Organization (CTO) released the first draft in July 2007 that outlined the Policy Framework consisting of an overarching vision, ten guiding principles, and six integrated policies relating to the critical areas identified in the stakeholder consultations. Each policy is comprised of an overarching development goal and policy guidelines clustered into specific policy objectives. In 2020, The Caribbean Sustainable Tourism Policy and Development Framework (CSTPDF) was officially released. Specifically, the CSTPDF 2020 serves to enable the tourism sector to effectively contribute to not only the national development of member countries but also to the region's adoption of the global 2030 Agenda for Sustainable Development, and particularly to the attainment of the United Nations Sustainable Development Goals. The goals include:

- Goal 1—Destination Management Capacity Policy: Ensure adequate and appropriate national capacity to manage the sustainability of the tourism sector.
- Goal 2—Destination Access and Transportation Policy: Develop efficient and cost-effective transportation options to facilitate a sustainable level of destination accessibility.
- Goal 3—Destination Marketing, Public Relations and Product Development Policy: Continuously improve the sustainability of the marketing mix in light of emerging global market trends.
- Goal 4—Linkages and Value Chain Management Policy: Develop and strengthen the links between tourism and other economic sectors nationally and regionally.
- Goal 5—Resource use and Management Policy: Ensure the sustainable use of the natural environment and the cultural heritage for the benefit of all.
- Goal 6—Climate Smart Action: To reduce the vulnerability of Caribbean tourism to the potential impacts of climate variability and change.
- Goal 7—Risk Resilience Policy: Manage the health safety and security issues that impact the sustainability of tourism in a proactive manner.

Achieving sustainable and climate-responsive tourism is a continuous process requiring constant monitoring, measuring the results, and taking corrective actions. Given the very dynamic and diversified nature of tourism, sustainable tourism policies, practices, and approaches must, therefore, be continually reviewed for relevance and consistency with the changing needs of the sector. The CSTPDF 2020, therefore, includes a closing section on Monitoring and Evaluation (CSTPDF, 2020).

Economic, Sociocultural, and Environmental Impacts of Tourism in the Caribbean Region

The Caribbean is the most tourism-dependent region of the world (Chappell & Frank, 2020; UNWTO, 2001). The tourism sector, acknowledged as one of the major attributes for economic, cultural, and environmental development today, is perceived as a significant source of opportunity to the local communities (Baker & Unni, 2021; Croes & Vanegas, 2008; Ramesh, 2002). The growth of the tourism industry is crucial to the economic growth and related fields such as transportation, leisure services, and many other sectors (Adrain, 2017; Telfer, 2002). On the other side, tourism has also become the means of support for the local communities in the Caribbean, especially in changing the economic atmosphere. Tourism is vital for the success of Caribbean economies as it comes with several benefits—boosts the revenue of the economy, creates thousands of jobs, helps to develop the infrastructures of a country, and plants a sense of cultural exchange between foreigners and locals. The number of jobs created by tourism in many different areas is significant. These jobs are not only a part of the tourism sector but may also include the agricultural sector, communication sector, health sector, and the educational sector. Many tourists travel to experience the hosting destination's culture, different traditions, and gastronomy.

The tourism industry generates income and provides employment opportunities (Hanafiah et al., 2010). Increased tourism leads to increased employment. From resorts and hotels to restaurants, clubs, bars, diving schools, and other adventure activities, Caribbean countries thrive on the jobs tourists create. Even people you would not normally think work in tourism industry either directly or indirectly—e.g., fishermen and farmers who provide seafood and agricultural produce for cafes, restaurants, and hotels—are all a part of tourism. This relationship also shows linkages within the economy. Increasing jobs also increases tax revenue, which can go into services and facilities for the local people. Everything from infrastructure to health services (which accommodates health tourism travelers) needs to improve in order to cater to the tourists who come for these reasons. This benefit then passes down to the local population like a trickledown effect. Ultimately, local residents are the main stakeholders of tourism developments.

Currently, the number of studies on local community attitudes toward future tourism development is increasing due to the nexus between community support and future government development. However, there is only limited research on understanding the roles of personal benefit on residents' support toward future tourism development (Petkova et al., 2012).

Abdool's (2002) study addressed the issue of residents' perception of tourism and sought to compare resident's support for tourism between a mature destination of Barbados and a less developed destination of Tobago in the Caribbean. Abdool found that key variables that influence support for tourism were found to be personal and community benefits, socio-environmental impacts, and community attachment. The findings suggest that there was widespread support for tourism development in both communities despite their varying levels of tourism sophistication and residents' perceptions of negative consequences of tourism. This apparent paradox was explained by social exchange theory, a concept based on the notion that a relationship between two people is created through a process of cost–benefit analysis. In other words, it is a metric designed to determine the effort poured in by an individual in a person-to-person relationship (Homans, 1958).

Waterman (2009) discussed the negative social, environmental, and economic impacts of tourism development in Barbados and measured their preferences for environmental management changes using the island's lone marine reserve, the Folkestone Marine Reserve, as a case study. This research's outcomes demonstrated that environmental management within the context of tourism development in Barbados requires the balancing of public needs with the environmental and economic consequences of development. As such, the results reinforced some of the theoretical and empirical revelations in the field of tourism and environmental management and further cemented the assertion that environmental management becomes onerous because of the presence of a number of innately complex and interlinked inferences. The reasonings are preservation of an environment that satisfies the divergent needs of users incurs both social and economic costs; perceptions of tourism's impacts are not mutually exclusive, which makes the issue of support for tourism development complex; both the positive and negative impacts of tourism should be considered; prudent environmental management is arguably the sine qua non for a viable tourism product; and concerns remain as to whether the country can absorb the environmental and socioeconomic shocks associated with tourism development.

Jordan (2014) surveyed residents of Falmouth, Jamaica, where a new cruise port was being developed to serve some of the largest cruise ships in the world several days per week. Analysis showed 78% of surveyed Falmouth residents experienced stress from the development and operation of the new cruise port. Residents indicated unmet expectations, overtaxed infrastructure, crowding, increased cost of living, pollution, and police harassment were major causes of stress. Stressors were interrelated with each other and exacerbated daily hassles already faced by Falmouth residents. Research findings indicated stress and coping provide a suitable framework from which to examine how individuals respond to tourism development.

Greening (2014) highlighted community perceptions of ecotourism and the value held for sea turtles as well as explained the emergence of these perceptions within two villages on the Caribbean island of Saint Kitts. The field data indicated that community members did not perceive ecotourism to be widely beneficial but instead viewed the government, people who work in the tourism industry, and tourists themselves to benefit from ecotourism practices. Further, community members perceived ecotourism as negatively affecting poor people, people who do not work in the tourism industry, and the environment. These perceptions of who or what is affected by ecotourism development were traced back through centuries of political-ecological processes on Saint Kitts that have mediated local people's relationship with their land and resources as well as their relationships with each other. The results of this research suggest a focus on the role of ecotourism in amending the persistent marginalization of local people from their resources by applying a participatory development approach to ecotourism development through collaboration with existing community groups and social networks. Furthermore, results from Laville-Wilson's (2017) study of Saint Kitts and Nevis residents' perceptions of the economic, sociocultural, and environmental and community impacts of tourism development suggest that those working in the tourism sector had more favorable attitudes toward tourism development and favorable perceptions about benefits from the tourism sector.

MacNeill and Wozniak (2018) measured economic, social, cultural, and environmental factors before and after the opening of a new cruise ship port in a new Western Caribbean port in Trujillo, Honduras in 2014. This $20 million Banana Coast project included a 50,000-square-foot shopping facility and a transportation hub along a 10-acre beachfront. Through the measurement of multidimensional indicators before and after the opening of the cruise ship port, and using control groups, the authors were able to compare community impacts with greater detail and control than previous studies. One observed benefit to communities was a decrease in crime due to an increase in government expenditure on policing. Although theory and industry multiplier estimates predict gains in employment, income, and related measures, the study found surprisingly little evidence of improvement. In fact, results show that the local population's ability to provide for necessities and obtain sufficient food worsened, corruption increased, and there were substantial negative environmental impacts. Local populations also lost wealth and property due to tourism. The authors concluded that low taxation and little to no regulation of the environments, which are the norm for cruise ship destinations in developing countries, are partly to blame for the negative impacts. Most of the profits and benefits funnel through networks formed by the cruise ship port management, bypassing local workers and community members. MacNeill and Wozniak (2018) recommend major investments in community resources and positive environmental practices before introducing tourism to any given area.

Charles (2013) noted that the Caribbean region is highly dependent upon tourism; however, in order to continue to use tourism as a means of economic advancement, sustainable practices must be adopted. In this regard, Caribbean hotels and resorts are now adopting environmental management systems as a means of improving resource use efficiency, reducing operating costs, increasing staff involvement and guest awareness, and obtaining both regional and international recognition in the travel and tourism marketplace. Consequently, the Caribbean accommodations sector has adopted a number of environmental best practices to prolong the tourism's product life cycle. Charles (2013) study found that internal factors were the main factors for the accommodations sector adopting sustainable practices. The cost saving from energy conservation, water conservation, and solid waste management were the main motives for adopting sustainable practices. However, the actions of the accommodations sector are insufficient for environmental preservation and there is the need for government intervention for the coordination of action and policy measures.

Baker and Unni (2021) studied residents' perception of sustainable tourism development in St. Kitts and Nevis, two islands forming one nation in the Caribbean. Their paper examined differences in the perceived economic, sociocultural, and environmental impacts of tourism between residents of St. Kitts and residents of Nevis and the residents' attitudes about the pace and direction of tourism development. A self-administered household survey was used to assess perceptions of these impacts of tourism among residents. Residents of both islands shared similar perceptions being generally very satisfied about the pace and direction of tourism development in their islands. However, there were significant differences in their perceptions of the impacts of tourism. Nevis's residents, more so than St. Kitts' residents, had more favorable perceptions about the economic benefits of tourism and looked at land-based tourism more favorably than cruise tourism. Negative impacts on the environment were not salient and residents had favorable perceptions of a positive sociocultural impact from tourism. The results emphasize the importance of understanding and taking into account views of local community members for sustainable tourism development. Local community support for tourism is vital for effective tourism planning and management.

Peterson et al. (2017) stated that despite the growth of tourism in the Caribbean, sustainable tourism studies of island societies remain fragmented and inconsistent. The authors provided a critical inquiry into sustainability and resilience in small island tourism economies in the Caribbean from an emic perspective, contending that current models are incompatible with understanding sustainable tourism in small island economies, let alone guiding scholars and policymakers in pursuit of strengthening resilience. The authors question the scientific status quo emphasizing linear modeling and steady state economics and called for a critical reconsideration of adaptation and resilience within small island economies of the Caribbean.

Cannonier and Burke (2019) stated that tourism's contribution to economic output in the Caribbean exceeds that in other regions of the world. In their research, they used panel data over a period of three decades, focusing exclusively on Caribbean islands, to study the causal link between tourism and economic growth. The results show that tourism has a positive and statistically significant effect on real Gross Domestic Product growth. A 10% increase in tourism spending was found to increase economic growth from 0.3 to 1%, a finding that is consistent with similar studies. A simple back-of-the-envelope calculation suggested that the overall tourism multiplier is around 0.25, which is smaller than estimates from previous studies. These results have important implications for researchers, industry practitioners, and Caribbean policymakers.

The aforementioned studies provide an idea of how tourism impacts communities and its residents in the Caribbean. These impacts and the structure of the tourism sector determine the sectors economic impact on a country. Tourism growth, on its own, is not enough because poorly managed tourism can result in negative economic, environmental, and social and cultural impacts that undermine local communities. To possibly ensure that benefits are maximized and any negative externalities are minimized, a continuous process of planning and management that evolves and is measured over time should be incorporated.

Cruise Ships and Caribbean Sustainable Development

Cruise ship tourism is one of the fastest growing tourism sectors in the world. As the popularity and geographical reach of cruising has grown, so have its economic, social, and environmental impacts and there is growing interest and scrutiny from governments, investors, environmental pressure groups, and the media about the management of these impacts. Such interest is part of much wider concerns that the transition to more sustainable patterns of production and personal consumption is not optional (Deloitte, 2012). In a similar vein, Lubin and Esty (2010) have argued that customers in many countries are seeking out sustainable products and services or leaning on companies to improve the sustainability of traditional ones and that management can no longer ignore sustainability as a central factor in their companies' long-term competitiveness. Research has shown that with the growing popularity of cruising, the environmental and social impacts of the industry are growing in scale (Brida & Zapata, 2010; Sustainability Accounting Standards Board, 2014). Laville-Wilson's (2017) study found that the city of Basseterre's bayfront has suffered erosion as a result of building cruise ports in the capitol of St. Kitts and that erosion at Friars Bay has occurred because of tourism development projects. Environmentally, the impacts associated with large cruise ships in the ports include the emission of greenhouse gases that contributes to climate change and waste from ships that causes pollution and reduces the resilience of marine ecosystems, which cause damage to fragile coastal and marine environments. Conversely, the development of infrastructure combined with the short-term host–guest interaction could be influential in visitors' future decisions to return to the destinations for a longer land-based vacation (Baker & Unni, 2018). While it is important to recognize that all shipping traffic generates environmental impacts, cruise ships create disproportionate impacts because they carry thousands of passengers who produce their own personal waste streams.

In some ways, the social and economic impacts of cruising are interlinked. The increasing numbers of cruise ship tourists generate a range of economic benefits to host economies and communities, including port expenses and the purchase of fuel, water, food, and beverage supplies as well as passenger expenditure in cafes, restaurants, excursions, tours, and souvenirs. However, these economic benefits can be limited if there are no concerted efforts by the Caribbean region to convert cruise passengers to land-based tourists staying at destination hotels (Baker & Unni, 2018). In grappling with the issue of converting cruise passengers into return stayover vacationers, the Bahamas people-to-people program was set up more than 30 years ago, whereby visitors go into the local people's homes to meet the families, eat with them, talk with them, and share ideas and interests. The British Virgin Islands–Tortola and Cuba—have embarked on similar programs. These programs can greatly influence cruise ship passengers' intentions to return to the destination for land-based vacations. However, cruise ships can also contribute to changes in traditional value systems, lifestyles, and behaviors at destinations. Cruise ships can also be an important source of employment, both aboard ship and onshore, and while several cruising companies employ people from the destinations they visit, low pay, long hours, job insecurity, and exploitation are currently commonplace. That said, the environmental, social, and economic impacts of cruising and the development of sustainability strategies and programs within the cruising industry have received limited attention within the academic literature in large part because of the difficulties in collecting data.

Johnson (2002) stated that cruising's socioeconomic, cultural, and environmental considerations need to be continually analyzed as a contribution to achieving sustainable tourism. Johnson concluded that secondary evidence suggested that the cruise industry was taking some belated but positive steps to address their environmental impacts but suggested that decision makers in the cruise tourism destinations needed to work more closely with cruise operators to facilitate both integrated waste management and intergenerational and intra-societal equity rather than merely accept the prospect of short-term economic gain. More generally, Mansfield (2009) argued that conventional approaches to sustainability fail to recognize the political nature of the socioeconomic processes that produce environmental degradation poverty and injustice. In a similar vein, Castro (2004) has questioned the very possibility of sustainable development under capitalism and argued that economic growth relies upon the continuing and inevitable exploitation of both natural and social capital. Butt (2007) estimated that cruise ships are responsible for 25% of all waste generated by the world's merchant fleet and following his investigation of the impacts of this waste for ports, concluded that all cruise vessels should vigorously pursue a waste reduction strategy and that ports should provide adequate recycling, reduction, and re-use facilities. Brida and Zapata (2010) examined a range of the economic, environmental, social, and cultural effects of cruise tourism on destinations and by way of a conclusion, they suggested that ensuring the sustainable development of a cruise destination has a very high cost and questioned if the benefits of attracting cruises to a tourism destination are higher than the costs. More definitive research remains to be done.

Klein (2011) used case study examples to examine the impact of the growth of cruise tourism on coastal and marine environments, local economies, and on the sociocultural dynamics of port environments. Having reviewed a range of impacts including wastewater treatment, solid waste, air emissions from fuel, the distribution of benefits, sociocultural authenticity, and the homogenization of the port experience, Klein concluded that using the responsible tourism lens can be a useful exercise in that it helps focus the analysis of sustainability on the local community and stakeholders that are affected by cruise tourism. Some of the ocean cruising companies, including Carnival Cruises, MSC Cruises, Royal Caribbean Cruises, Norwegian Cruise Lines, Paul Gauguin Cruises, Holland America, Disney Cruises, and Virgin Cruises, either own or lease small islands, or areas of them, in the Bahamas and the Caribbean. On these islands, passengers are offered a range of service and leisure facilities including exclusive beach access, barbecue buffet lunches, water parks, parasailing, bars, and shops, and passengers can use their cruise card when purchasing goods and services on the islands; thus, effectively eliminating many benefits for local traders and reducing the economic benefits to the destination's economy.

COVID-19, Tourism, and Public Health

The academic literature on COVID-19's impact on tourism focuses on reversing economic loss. The goal seems singularly focused on assuaging traveler fears and protecting the traveler (ostensibly from local populations and environments) so they, in turn, can resuscitate the local destination economy through spending (Bakar & Rosbi, 2020; Mansfeld & Pizam, 2006; Osland et al., 2017; Rittichainuwat & Chakraborty, 2009; Wilks et al., 2013; Zheng et al., 2021). The presumed assumption is that the destination communities' health and well-being will benefit once the economic engine of tourism is resumed. The emphasis on the health of the tourist is exemplified in travel medicine, an important variable in the tourism and public health relationship. Travel medicine exists to protect the traveler. Treating and removing infectious disease threats in local communities are touted not for the health of the local community but as a means to increase the number of tourists who feel comfortable visiting (Rosselló et al., 2017). The health of locals is an afterthought, if considered at all. While recommencing tourism will bring essential financial resources into communities, it comes with many public health costs that must be considered if we are concerned about sustainable development. Tourism, while it has the possibility to benefit local populations, is often a threat to local public health in a myriad of ways (Richter, 2003).

Tourism expansion is associated with increased traffic accidents, including drunk driving (Bellos et al., 2020; Castillo-Manzano et al., 2020; Walker & Page, 2004), and increased crime (Mawby, 2017). Tourism also impacts the social determinants of health, including creating conditions of water scarcity (Becken, 2014; Cole, 2014; Gössling et al., 2012) and environmental hazards related to trash and solid waste management, to name a few (Darma et al., 2020; Ghadban et al., 2017; Kaseva & Moirana, 2010). These public health impacts are compounded by the more nefarious issues of widespread sexual harassment (Ram, 2021), sexual assault, sex tourism and trafficking (Lyneham & Facchini, 2019; Miller-Perrin & Wurtele, 2017; Ryan & Kinder, 1996) which occurs globally within the tourism industry. Tourism also impacts mental health. Evidence of mental and emotional illnesses caused by the increased stress of tourism on local populations is evident (Jordan & Vogt, 2017; Jordan et al., 2021). For example, studies have found escalating prevalence of eating disorders related to body image among indigenous populations (Anderson-Fye, 2004; Becker, 2004; Becker et al., 2010).

Tourism can stigmatize local populations when they are defined by global perceptions of health and safety threats (Cook et al., 2018; Hoppe, 2018; Person et al., 2004). For example, there is increased racism toward Asian people due to the perceived origins of COVID-19 (Cheng & Conca-Cheng, 2020; Li & Galea, 2020).

COVID-19 has highlighted the important relationship between infectious diseases and tourism. Traditionally, infectious diseases are treated as threats to tourists rather than to local destination populations (Albattat, 2017; Baker, 2015; Zheng et al., 2021). However, infectious diseases, including COVID-19, pose serious threats to local communities. Cruise ships that carry thousands of people in close proximity to each other can create an environment for the rapid spread of contagious diseases and outbreaks of gastroenteritis, Norovirus, and Legionnaires Disease (Baker, 2015; Brewster et al., 2020; Minooee & Rickman, 1999), and now COVID-19 can be a serious cause for concern. HIV has been a longstanding public health consequence of tourism with tourists promoting and engaging in behaviors that increase the risk of the introduction and spread of HIV and other sexually transmitted infections (Farmer, 2006; Harry-Hernández et al., 2019; Nofriya, 2018; Quevedo-Gómez et al., 2020). Tourists' role in the emergence and spread of infectious disease is not limited to HIV, as many pathogens have benefitted from the travel industry facilitating their spread through global populations (Findlater & Bogoch, 2018; Schwartz & Morris, 2018; Sönmez et al., 2019). Tourism can have deleterious consequences for destination communities' health at individual, social, structural, and environmental levels.

One of the few studies measuring local residents' views regarding inbound tourism and the pandemic (Qiu et al., 2020) found that the vast majority of respondents were "willing to pay" to reduce the risk associated with tourism-generated pandemic effects. The economic impact of the pandemic will widen the power disparity between local communities and tourists, particularly in survival tourism economies. The industry has benefited greatly from a dependency model—whereas overselling the economic benefits of tourism leads communities to economic reliance on the industry—where communities need tourism to survive (Britton, 1989; Hung & Wu, 2017). COVID-19 amplifies problems with this model. A shock such as COVID-19 can lead to economic collapse as communities that are dependent on tourism have no capacity to respond to the loss of their primary revenue source. Such shocks do not need to be at the level of a global pandemic. For local communities that are dependent upon tourism, even small regional challenges can have deep impacts. While sustainable tourism models focus on capacity building and development, the industry has failed in this regard (UNCTAD, 2020). Currently, communities are forced to risk their health to open up to tourism and the money it brings (Wallen, 2020). While the tourism industry ponders the question "how can we protect tourists?" we need to ask also "how can we protect the health of local populations from tourists and our industry?".

Current State of Affairs

Tourism-dependent economies, like those in the Caribbean region, are among those harmed the most by the pandemic and tourism-dependent countries will likely feel the negative impacts of the crisis for much longer than other economies. Before COVID-19, travel and tourism had become one of the most important sectors in the world economy, accounting for 10% of global GDP and more than 320 million jobs worldwide (WTTC, 2019). According to the United Nations World Tourism Organization (Behsudi, 2020), "the global pandemic, the first of its scale in a new era of globalization and interconnectedness, put millions of tourism jobs at risk, many in small and medium-sized enterprises that employ a high share of women, who represent 54 percent of the tourism workforce" (p. 37). Contact-intensive services, key to the tourism and travel sectors, are disproportionately affected by the pandemic and will continue to struggle until COVID-19 is under control and people feel safe to travel again.

Tourism-dependent countries are grappling with how to lure back visitors while avoiding new outbreaks of infection. The highly transmissible COVID-19 has variants (i.e., the delta and omicron variants) that cause concern. Highly dependent tourist destinations have been trying to come up with some solutions ranging from wooing the ultra-rich, who can quarantine on their yachts, to inviting people to stay in a beach bubble for periods of up to a year and work virtually while enjoying a tropical view. At this time, there is no telling when cruise ships would be back in the Caribbean Sea like pre-pandemic levels and tourism receipts worldwide are not expected to recover any time soon. It is too early to determine whether the crisis represents a permanent shock and how it will shape the tourism industry going forward.

In a study done for the Caribbean Hotel Association (2014), the greatest barriers to the sustainable development of tourism identified include a lack of information on funding opportunities and a lack of access to low-interest finance. Government engagement with sustainability is also a key issue. However, Caribbean hotels have been making progress as it relates to being more environmentally friendly businesses. Since 1997, the Caribbean Hotel Association formed the Caribbean Alliance for Sustainable Tourism (CAST) to undertake collaborative environmental activities in the hotel and tourism sector, to promote effective management of natural resources, to provide access to expertise on sustainable tourism, and to assist hotel and tourism operations in the Caribbean region to achieve the goals of Agenda 21 for Sustainable Tourism. Green Globe Certification (GGC) is a global recognized certification program developed specifically to recognize sustainable tourism.

An Environmental Management System (EMS) is a systematic framework for integrating environmental management into an organization's activities, products, and services. Hotels on each island of the Caribbean have been encouraged by their hotel associations to transfer their operation to one that is environmentally friendly and committed to adopt an EMS. USAID has extended its program to many small hotels in the Eastern Caribbean. Governments of several countries (e.g., Bahamas and Cayman Islands) have drawn up plans to sponsor their own EMS programs. For all intents and purposes, EMS has become a part of the Caribbean hoteliers' permanent vocabulary. A large number of hotels in the Caribbean have obtained Green Globe Certification and the number is increasing as many hotels and resorts see the benefits of a green labeled hotel/resort. Green globe requires that an environmental management system be in place, hotels meet minimum requirements, and be audited before an organization is certified (Bohdanowicz et al., 2004). Hotel training schools are now looking to "green" their curricula by integrating "best practices" into management and line staff training. Training courses for "certified" environmental officers have become available. There is a preliminary plan to establish a Green Hotel Fund that will extend financing for hotels to implement "best practices" associated with being a green labeled facility.

The Caribbean Hotel and Tourism Association has projected that as many as 60% of the 30,000 new hotel rooms that were in the planning or construction phase throughout the Caribbean region will not be completed as a result of the COVID-19 crisis. Still, the crisis is being viewed as an opportunity to improve the industry in the medium-

and long-term through greater digitalization and environmental sustainability. The United Nations World Tourism Organization (UNWTO) has encouraged support for worker training in order to build digital skills for harnessing the value of big data, data analytics, and artificial intelligence. Recovery should also be leveraged to improve the industry's efficient use of energy and water, waste management, and sustainable sourcing of food.

The crisis has crystallized the importance of tourism as a development pathway for many countries to decrease poverty and improve their economies. Smaller, tourism-dependent nations—like those of the Caribbean region—are in many ways locked into their economic destinies. Among small island nations, there are few, if any, alternative sectors to which they can shift labor and capital. Some countries might be able to benefit from increases in exports during the COVID-19 period, which can somewhat offset tourism losses, but any additional earnings will be a fraction of tourism receipts. Governments have paid a percentage of normal wages to displaced tourism-sector workers while offering opportunities for retraining. However, this practice can only be limited since the pandemic began in Spring 2019 with no end in sight at this time.

Conclusion

No other event, natural or human caused, has disrupted the travel and tourism sector as much as COVID-19. Perhaps no other topic has spurred as much tourism-related research and publications in such a short time. This focus is warranted as COVID-19-related reductions in tourism have devastated communities. Measured in economic terms, as of September 2020, 121 million jobs in the travel and tourism sector were lost and forecasts of up to 197 million and 5.5 USD trillion are expected (WTTC, 2020). Globally, "hundreds of thousands of small- to medium-sized enterprises worldwide were ordered to close; thirty to forty percent never to be revived, with similar effects cascading throughout supply chains" (Haywood, 2020, p. 600). Recognizing the COVID-19 pandemic as an opportunity for self-reflection, tourism-related research is putting forth calls for action to reimagine, reevaluate, and restructure travel and tourism to be more sustainable, balanced, and equitable (Chang et al., 2020; MacKenzie & Goodnow, 2020). Haywood (2020) noted that "urgent demands of the present necessitate an interrogation—a re-exploration and a re-envisioning of the future of tourism—of what has to change (and remain constant)" (p. 599). This design, Haywood emphasized, needs to allow the revitalization of destination communities to take center stage.

In recent decades, the cruising industry has experienced spectacular growth. With an eye to the future, the sustainability reports published by Carnival Corporation and Royal Caribbean Cruises, for example, are couched within the idiom of continuing growth and business expansion and they reflected a belief in continuing consumption. Under the banner "Enabling Responsible Growth," Royal Caribbean Cruises, for example, stressed that "as our company grows in revenue and geographical reach, we aim to achieve responsible growth" and that "as we visit each port we will be able to promote economic development through taxes, port fees, port development projects and most notably guest and crew spending at destinations" (Jones et al., 2016, p. 269). Royal Caribbean Cruises does not offer a definition of responsible growth per se, but its approach is rooted in the general belief that continuing economic growth will inevitably be accompanied by the more efficient use of resources. Only two of the leading ocean and river cruise companies have currently posted dedicated sustainability reports to detail how they managed the environmental, social, and economic impacts of their business operations. The majority of cruise operators provided limited information on their approach to sustainability, which is not a problem per se in that companies have no statutory obligation to report on sustainability and as such, may reflect the reality that collectively the world's leading cruise companies are at the beginning of what may well be a long and demanding journey toward sustainability. With that said, a number of issues merit discussion and reflection. If "developing a sustainable brand can help to manage reputational risks, enhance relationships with key stakeholders, and meet the requirements of a growing segment of consumers that place value on sustainability" (Jones et al., 2016, p. 280) within the industry, then the majority of cruise companies currently seem to be falling short of the mark in formally reporting their sustainability strategies and achievements. More specifically, reporting on sustainability may be important in helping to counter government, media, and pressure group criticism.

It is vital that tourism, as a "people-centered activity," delivers supreme customer service, raises public awareness, and creates a greater understanding of its strategic importance as well as the multitude of careers and entrepreneurial opportunities available. Tourism must also address relevant impacting issues, such as social inclusiveness and gender considerations as well as engender feelings of ownership and involvement. In fact, the human resource/people-centered requirements of the sector merit dedicated, focused, and systematic action at the national and regional level. The growth of the community-centered tourism is out of a recognition that it is a tactic used by tourism planners to organize communities to act to expand the reach of the industry's offerings (Dangi & Jamal, 2016). The goal is to promote socioeconomic opportunities and added value for local and foreign tourists. This process opens new niches for destinations, particularly natural, cultural, and adventurous destinations. The development of the community spirit enables individuals to be more informed of the value of their community assets—culture, heritage, food, and lifestyle. It mobilizes them to transform these into revenue-generating ventures while offering tourists a more dynamic and meaningful experience. Through community-centered business models, tourist destination residents learn to manage small businesses, improve the environment, produce goods, and deal with the market's vagaries. This type of tourism centered on people promotes a sense of ownership that is good for the sustainability of the industry, people's wellbeing, and the preservation of nature and natural resources (Korstanje & George, 2020). In inclusive and sustainable tourism, ecological, social, economic, and cultural sustainability are considered. The community is guided and governed to encourage visitors to learn about the culture and the local way of life without removing fringe elements. Essentially, the Caribbean region has enough policies that can address these issues but it only can be done with specific actions that deal with the following: (a) community involvement with tourism development; (b) research and communication with the general public and major stakeholders about the impacts of tourism; (c) training and awareness programs for the general public about the positive and negative impacts of tourism; (d) funding and management training to support small businesses; and (e) specific actions by the government and other major stakeholders to encourage linkages between tourism and the rest of the economy.

The tourism industry is growing at a record pace and there is little indication that this trend will subside. This chapter addresses some of the economic, sociocultural, and environmental impacts caused by tourism development. As the Caribbean region has been involved in mass tourism and an expansion of the cruise sector, it is clear that tourism and the cruise ship tourism industry have significant effects on destinations and local communities. There exists an interdependence between tourism industries, destination communities, and historic sites. For example, tourism is a business and competitive market for tourism industries and local communities rely on tourism revenue to generate taxes and economic development. The real challenge is how to balance preserving culture and authenticity while promoting a tourist economy. The literature points to the fact that the Caribbean region already has a good policy framework, now it is time for the region to put more emphasis on planning and policies for tourism development in a much more sustainable way.

This chapter also highlights the need for more dialogue between industry executives and community officials in the Caribbean region, forging a way forward for island governance and offering potential strategies involving public, private, and mixed partnerships in order to develop a tourism strategy that supports its development and sustainability. This suggestion is strong for the region's opportunities in favor of a beneficial integration between cruise tourism and land-based tourism. All stakeholders in the Caribbean region tourism industry have a responsibility to preserve and protect natural and cultural resources. The tourism industry has incredible power and responsibility to engage with communities ethically, particularly in locations dependent upon, and therefore, at the mercy of the industry. The public health threats of tourism on local communities will only increase post-COVID-19 pandemic. The economies of many tourist locations have been hit exceedingly hard, leaving locals even more exposed to health threats. Efforts must be made to quantify the harmful public health impacts of tourism, and a community-centered approach can facilitate this process (Okazaki, 2008; Tolkach & King, 2015). With locally specific public health impact assessments of tourist activity in hand, communities will be better poised to accept, adapt, or reject tourism activities (Robinson, 1999). Community consent is the cornerstone for achieving public health equity in tourism. To achieve sustainable tourism, a balance must be reached between economic development, social and cultural justice, and the natural environment. This effort will require holistic proactive planning solutions, facilitation, and dialogue among all stakeholders.

References

Abdool, A. (2002). *Residents' perceptions of tourism: A comparative study of two Caribbean communities* (Doctoral dissertation, Bournemouth University). ProQuest Dissertations and Theses Global. https://core.ac.uk/download/pdf/76947.pdf

Adrian, S. C. (2017). The impact of tourism on the global economic system. *Ovidius University Annals, Economic Sciences Series, 17*(1), 384–387.

Albattat, A. (2017). Current issue in tourism: Diseases transformation as a potential risk for travelers. *Global and Stochastic Analysis, 5*(7), 341–350.

Anderson-Fye, E. P. (2004). A "Coca-Cola" shape: Cultural change, body image, and eating disorders in San Andrés, Belize. *Culture, Medicine and Psychiatry, 28*(4), 561–595. https://doi.org/10.1007/s11013-004-1068-4

Aref, F., Gill, S. S., & Farshid, A. (2010). Tourism development in local communities: As a community development approach. *Journal of American Science, 6*, 155–161.

Bakar, N. A., & Rosbi, S. C. (2020). Effect of Coronavirus disease (COVID-19) to tourism industry. *International Journal of Advanced Engineering Research and Science, 7*(4), 189–193. https://doi.org/10.22161/ijaers.74.23

Baker, D. M. A. (2015). Tourism and the health effects of infectious diseases: Are there potential risks for tourists? *International Journal Safety and Security of Tourism and Hospitality, 1*(12), 18. https://www.palermo.edu/Archivos_content/2015/economicas/journal-tourism/edicion12/03_Tourism_and_Infectous_Disease.pdf

Baker, D., & Unni, R. (2018). Characteristic and intentions of cruise passengers to return to the Caribbean for land-based vacations. *Journal Tourism – Revista de Turism, 26*, 1–9.

Baker, D., & Unni, R. (2021). Understanding residents' opinions and support towards sustainable tourism development in the Caribbean: The case of Saint Kitts and Nevis. *Coastal Business Journal, 18*(1), 1–29.

Becken, S. (2014). Water equity-contrasting tourism water use with that of the local community. *Water Resources and Industry, 7*(8), 9–22. https://doi.org/10.1016/j.wri.2014.09.002

Becker, A. E. (2004). Television, disordered eating, and young women in Fiji: Negotiating body image and identity during rapid social change. *Culture, Medicine and Psychiatry, 28*(4), 533–559. https://doi.org/10.1007/s11013-004-1067-5

Becker, A. E., Fay, K., Agnew-Blais, J., Guarnaccia, P. M., Striegel-Moore, R. H., & Gilman, S. E. (2010). Development of a measure of "acculturation" for ethnic Fijians: Methodologic and conceptual considerations for application to eating disorders research. *Transcultural Psychiatry, 47*(5), 754–788. https://doi.org/10.1177/1363461510382153

Behsudi, A. (2020, December). Wish you were here. *Finance & Development*. https://www.imf.org/external/pubs/ft/fandd/2020/12/pdf/impact-of-the-pandemic-on-tourism-behsudi.pdf

Bellos, V., Ziakopoulos, A., & Yannis, G. (2020). Investigation of the effect of tourism on road crashes. *Journal of Transportation Safety & Security, 12*(6), 782–799. https://doi.org/10.1080/19439962.2018.1545715

Bohdanowicz, P., Simanic, B., & Martinac, I. (2004, October 27–29). Sustainable hotels—Eco-certification according to EU Flower, Nordic Swan and the Polish Hotel Association. In *Proceedings of the Regional Central and Eastern European Conference on Sustainable Building (SB04)*. Warszawa, Poland.

Brewster, R., Sundermann, A., & Boles, C. (2020). Lessons learned for COVID-19 in the cruise ship industry. *Toxicology and Industrial Health, 36*(9), 728–735.

Brida, J. G., & Zapata, S. (2010). Cruises tourism: Economic, socio-cultural and environmental impacts. *International Journal of Leisure and Tourism Marketing, 1*(3), 205–226.

Britton, S. (1989). Tourism, dependency, and development: A mode of analysis. *Europäische Hochschulschriften 10 (Fremdenverkehr), 11,* 93–116.

Bushell, R., & McCool, S. F. (2007). Tourism as a tool for conservation and support of protected areas: Setting the agenda. In R. Bushell & P. F. J. Eagles (Eds.), *Tourism and protected areas: Benefits beyond boundaries* (pp. 12–26). CABI International.

Butt, N. (2007). The impact of cruise ship generated waste on home ports and ports of call: A case study of Southampton. *Marine Policy, 31*(5), 591–598.

Cannonier, C., & Burke, M. G. (2019). The economic growth impact of tourism in small island developing states-evidence from the Caribbean. *Tourism Economics, 25*(1), 85–108.

Caribbean Hotel Association. (2014). *Advancing sustainable tourism, a regional sustainable tourism situation analysis: Caribbean*. https://caribbeanhotelandtourism.com/

Castillo-Manzano, J. I., Castro-Nuño, M., López-Valpuesta, L., & Vassallo, F. V. (2020). An assessment of road traffic accidents in Spain: The role of tourism. *Current Issues in Tourism, 23*(6), 654–658. https://doi.org/10.1080/13683500.2018.1548581

Castro, C. (2004). Sustainable development: Mainstream and critical perspective. *Organization and Environment, 17*(2), 195–225.

Chang, C., McAleer, M., & Ramos, V. (2020). A charter for sustainable tourism after COVID-19. *Sustainability, 12*(9), 3671. https://doi.org/10.3390/su12093671

Chappell, K., & Frank, M. (2020). *The most tourism-dependent region in the world braces for prolonged Coronavirus recovery*. Reuters. https://skift.com/

2020/04/20/the-most-tourism-dependent-region-in-the-world-braces-for-prolonged-coronavirus-recovery/

Charles, D. (2013). Sustainable tourism in the Caribbean: The role of the accommodations sector. *International Journal of Green Economics, 7*(2), 148–161.

Cheng, T. L., & Conca-Cheng, A. M. (2020). The pandemics of racism and COVID-19: Danger and opportunity. *Pediatrics, 146*(5), e2020024836. https://doi.org/10.1542/peds.2020-024836

Choi, H. C., & Sirakaya, E. (2006). Sustainability indicators for managing community tourism. *Tourism Management, 27*(6), 1274–1289.

Cole, S. (2014). Tourism and water: From stakeholders to rights holders, and what tourism businesses need to do. *Journal of Sustainable Tourism, 22*(1), 89–106. https://doi.org/10.1080/09669582.2013.776062

Cook, C. L., Li, Y. J., Newell, S. M., Cottrell, C. A., & Neel, R. (2018). The world is a scary place: Individual differences in belief in a dangerous world predict specific intergroup prejudices. *Group Processes & Intergroup Relations, 21*(4), 584–596. https://doi.org/10.1177/1368430216670024

Croes, R., & Vanegas, M., Sr. (2008). Cointegration and causality between tourism and poverty reduction. *Journal of Travel Research, 47*(1), 94–103.

Dangi, T. B., & Jamal, T. (2016). An integrated approach to "sustainable community-based tourism." *Sustainability, 8*, 475–507. https://doi.org/10.3390/su8050475

Darma, I. G. K. I. P., Dewi, M. I. K., & Kristina, N. M. R. (2020). Community movement of waste use to keep the image of tourism industry in GIANYAR. *Journal of Indonesian Tourism, Hospitality and Recreation, 3*(1), 49–57. https://doi.org/10.17509/jithor.v3i1.23439

Deloitte. (2012). *Sustainability for consumer business operations: A story of growth.* https://www2.deloitte.com/content/dam/Deloitte/global/Documents/Consumer-Business/dttl_cb_Sustainability_Global%20CB%20POV.pdf

Farmer, P. (2006). *AIDS and accusation: Haiti and the geography of blame.* University of California Press.

Findlater, A., & Bogoch, I. I. (2018). Human mobility and the global spread of infectious diseases: A focus on air travel. *Trends in Parasitology, 34*(9), 772–783. https://doi.org/10.1016/j.pt.2018.07.004

Ghadban, S., Shames, M., & Abou Mayaleh, H. (2017). Trash crisis and solid waste management in Lebanon-analyzing hotels' commitment and guests' preferences. *Journal of Tourism Research & Hospitality, 6*(3), 1000169. https://doi.org/10.4172/2324-8807.1000171

Gössling, S., Peeters, P., Hall, C. M., Ceron, J.-P., Dubois, G., Lehmann, L. V., & Scott, D. (2012). Tourism and water use: Supply, demand, and security.

An international review. *Tourism Management, 33*(1), 1–15. https://doi.org/10.1016/j.tourman.2011.03.015
Greening, A. (2014). *Understanding local perceptions and the role of historical context in ecotourism development: A case study of Saint Kitts* (Master's Thesis, Utah State University). ProQuest Dissertations and Theses Global.
Hanafiah, M. H., Harun, M. F., & Jamaluddin, M. R. (2010). Bilateral trade and tourism demand. *World Applied Sciences Journal, 10*, 110–114.
Harry-Hernández, S., Park, S. H., Mayer, K. H., Kreski, N., Goedel, W. C., Hambrick, H. R., Brooks, B., Guilamo-Ramos, V., & Duncan, D. T. (2019). Sex tourism, condomless anal intercourse, and HIV risk among men who have sex with men. *Journal of the Association of Nurses in AIDS Care, 30*(4), 405–414. https://doi.org/10.1097/JNC.0000000000000018
Haukeland, J. V. (2011). Tourism stakeholders' perceptions of national park management in Norway. *Journal of Sustainable Tourism, 19*(2), 133–153.
Haywood, M. K. (2020). A post COVID-19 future—Tourism re-imagined and re-enabled. *Tourism Geographies, 22*(3), 599–609. https://doi.org/10.1080/14616688.2020.1762120
Homans, C. G. (1958). Social behavior as exchange. *American Journal of Sociology, 63*(6), 597–606.
Hoppe, T. (2018). "Spanish Flu": When infectious disease names blur origins and stigmatize those infected. *American Journal of Public Health, 108*(11), 1462–1464. https://doi.org/10.2105/AJPH.2018.304645
Hung, C. H., & Wu, M. T. (2017). The influence of tourism dependency on tourism impact and development support attitude. *Asian Journal of Business and Management, 5*, 88–96. https://doi.org/10.24203/ajbm.v5i2.4594
International Ecotourism Society. (2004). *The triple bottom line of sustainable tourism*. https://www.coursehero.com/file/81910666/s1pdf/
Jamal, T., & Stronza, A. (2009). Collaboration theory and tourism practice in protected areas: Stakeholders, structuring and sustainability. *Journal of Sustainable Tourism, 17*(2), 169–189.
Johnson, D. (2002). Environmentally sustainable cruise tourism: A reality check. *Marine Policy, 26*(4), 261–270.
Jones, P., Hillier, D., & Comfort, D. (2016). The environmental, social and economic impacts of cruising and corporate sustainability strategies. *Athens Journal of Tourism, 3*(4), 273–285.
Jordan, E. J. (2014). *Host community resident stress and coping with tourism development* (Doctoral dissertation, Michigan State University, East Lansing, MI). ProQuest Dissertations and Theses Global.
Jordan, E. J., Lesar, L., & Spenser, D. M. (2021). Clarifying the interrelations of residents' perceived tourism-related stress, stressors, and impacts. *Journal of Travel Research, 60*(1), 208–219. https://doi.org/10.1177/0047287519888287

Jordan, E. J., & Vogt, C. A. (2017). Appraisal and coping responses to tourism development-related stress. *Tourism Analysis, 22*(1), 1–18. https://doi.org/10.3727/108354217X14828625279573

Kaseva, M. E., & Moirana, J. L. (2010). Problems of solid waste management on Mount Kilimanjaro: A challenge to tourism. *Waste Management & Research, 28*(8), 695–704. https://doi.org/10.1177/0734242X09337655

Klein, R. A. (2011). Responsible cruise tourism: Issues of cruise tourism and sustainability. *Journal of Hospitality and Tourism Management, 18*(1), 107–118.

Korstanje, M., & George, B. (2020). Demarketing overtourism, the role of educational interventions. In H. Séraphin & A. C. Yallop (Eds.), *Overtourism and tourism education* (pp. 81–95). Routledge.

Laville-Wilson, D. P. (2017). *The transformation of an agriculture-based economy to a tourism-based economy: Citizens' perceived impacts of sustainable tourism development* (Doctoral dissertation, South Dakota State University). South Dakota State University Open Prairie. https://openprairie.sdstate.edu/etd/2262/

Li, Y., & Galea, S. (2020). Racism and the COVID-19 epidemic: Recommendations for health care workers. *American Journal of Public Health, 110*(7), 956–957. https://doi.org/10.2105/AJPH.2020.305698

Lubin, D. A., & Esty, D. C. (2010). The sustainability imperative. *Harvard Business Review, 88*(5), 42–50.

Lyneham, S., & Facchini, L. (2019). Benevolent harm: Orphanages, voluntourism and child sexual exploitation in South-East Asia. *Trends & Issues in Crime and Criminal Justice, 574*. Australian Institute of Criminology. https://www.aic.gov.au/sites/default/files/2020-05/benevolent_harm_orphanages_voluntourism_and_child_sexual_exploitation_in_south-east_asia.pdf

Mackenzie, S., & Goodnow, J. (2020). Adventure in the age of COVID-19: Embracing micro-adventures and locavism in a post-pandemic world. *Leisure Sciences, 43*(10), 1–8. https://doi.org/10.1080/01490400.2020.1773984

MacNeill, T., & Wozniak, D. (2018). The economic, social, and environmental impacts of cruise tourism. *Tourism Management, 66*, 387–404.

Mansfield, B. (2009). Sustainability. In N. Castree, D. Demeriff, D. Liverman, & B. Rhoads (Eds.), *A companion to environmental geography* (pp. 37–49). Wiley. https://doi.org/10.1002/9781444305722.ch3

Mansfeld, Y., & Pizam, A. (2006). *Tourism, security and safety*. Routledge.

Manzoor, F., Wei, L., Asif, M., Zia ul Haq, M., & Rehman, H. (2019). The contribution of sustainable tourism to economic growth and employment in Pakistan. *International Journal of Environmental Research & Public Health, 16*(19), 37–85. https://doi.org/10.3390/ijerph16193785

Mawby, R. I. (2017). Crime and tourism: What the available statistics do or do not tell us. *International Journal of Tourism Policy, 7*(2), 81–92. https://doi.org/10.1504/IJTP.2017.085292

Miller-Perrin, C., & Wurtele, S. K. (2017). Sex trafficking and the commercial sexual exploitation of children. *Women & Therapy, 40*(1–2), 123–151. https://doi.org/10.1080/02703149.2016.1210963

Minooee, A., & Rickman, L. (1999). Infectious diseases on cruise ships. *Clinical Infectious Diseases, 29*(4), 737–743.

Murphy, P., & Murphy, A. E. (2004). *Strategic management for tourism communities.* Channel View Publications.

Nofriya, N. (2018, August 7). *Health and safety issues from tourism activities in Bukit Tinggi City, West Sumatra.* 13th IEA SEA Meeting and ICPH—SDev. http://conference.fkm.unand.ac.id/index.php/ieasea13/IEA/paper/view/622

Ohlan R., (2017). The relationship between tourism, financial development and economic growth in India. *Future Business Journal, 3*(1), 9–22.

Okazaki, E. (2008). A community-based tourism model: Its conception and use. *Journal of Sustainable Tourism, 16*(5), 511–529. https://doi.org/10.1080/09669580802159594

Osland, G. E., Mackoy, R., & McCormick, M. (2017). Perceptions of personal risk in tourists' destination choices: Nature tours in Mexico. *European Journal of Tourism, Hospitality and Recreation, 8*(1), 38–50. https://doi.org/10.1515/ejthr-2017-0002

Person, B., Sy, F., Holton, K., Govert, B., Liang, A., Garza, B., Gould, D., Hickson, M., McDonald, M., Meijer, C., Smith, J., Veto, L., Williams, W., & Zauderer, L. (2004). Fear and stigma: The epidemic within the SARS outbreak. *Emerging Infectious Diseases Journal CDC, 10*(2), 358–363. https://doi.org/10.3201/eid1002.030750

Peterson, R. R., Harrill, R., & Dipietro, R. B. (2017). Sustainability and resilience in Caribbean tourism economies: A critical inquiry. *Tourism Analysis, 22*(3), 407–419. https://doi.org/10.3727/108354217X14955605216131

Petkova, A. T., Koteski, C., Jakovlev, Z., & Mitreva, E. (2012). Sustainability and competitiveness of tourism. *Procedia - Social and Behavioral Sciences, 44,* 221–227. https://doi.org/10.1016/j.sbspro.2012.05.023

Qiu, R., Park, J., Li, S., & Song, H. (2020). Social costs of tourism during the COVID-19 pandemic. *Annals of Tourism Research, 84,* 102994. https://doi.org/10.1016/j.annals.2020.102994

Quevedo-Gómez, M. C., Krumeich, A., Abadía-Barrero, C. E., & Van den Borne, H. W. (2020). Social inequalities, sexual tourism and HIV in Cartagena, Colombia: An ethnographic study. *BMC Public Health, 20*(1208), 1–11. https://doi.org/10.1186/s12889-020-09179-2

Ram, Y. (2021). Me too and tourism: A systematic review. *Current Issues in Tourism, 24*(3), 321–339. https://doi.org/10.1080/13683500.2019.1664423

Ramesh, D. (2002). The economic contribution of tourism in Mauritius. *Annals of Tourism Research, 29*(3), 862–865.

Richter, L. K. (2003). International tourism and its global public health consequences. *Journal of Travel Research, 41*(4), 340–347. https://doi.org/10.1177/0047287503041004002

Rittichainuwat, B. N., & Chakraborty, G. (2009). Perceived travel risks regarding terrorism and disease: The case of Thailand. *Tourism Management, 30*(3), 410–418. https://doi.org/10.1016/j.tourman.2008.08.001

Robinson, M. (1999). Collaboration and cultural consent: Refocusing sustainable tourism. *Journal of Sustainable Tourism, 7*(3–4), 379–397. https://doi.org/10.1080/09669589908667345

Rosselló, J., Santana-Gallego, M., & Awan, W. (2017). Infectious disease risk and international tourism demand. *Health Policy and Planning, 32*(4), 538–548. https://doi.org/10.1093/heapol/czw177

Ryan, C., & Kinder, R. (1996). Sex, tourism and sex tourism: Fulfilling similar needs? *Tourism Management, 17*(7), 507–518. https://doi.org/10.1016/S0261-5177(96)00068-4

Schwartz, K. L., & Morris, S. K. (2018). Travel and the spread of drug-resistant bacteria. *Current Infectious Disease Reports, 20*(9), Article 29. https://doi.org/10.1007/s11908-018-0634-9

Sheller, M. (2004). Natural hedonism: The invention of Caribbean islands as tropical playgrounds. In S. Courtman (Ed.), *Beyond the blood, the beach, and the banana: New perspectives in Caribbean studies* (pp. 170–185). Ian Randle.

Sönmez, S., Wiitala, J., & Apostolopoulos, Y. (2019). How complex travel, tourism, and transportation networks influence infectious disease movement in a borderless world. In D. J. Timothy (Ed.), *Handbook of globalization and tourism* (pp. 76–88). Edward Elgar Publishing. https://doi.org/10.4337/9781786431295.00015

Sustainability Accounting Standards Board. (2014). *Cruise lines: Sustainability accounting standards*. http://www.sasb.org/wp-content/uploads/2014/12/SV0205_Cruise_ProvisionalStandard.pdf

Telfer, D. (2002). The evolution of tourism and development theory. In R. Sharpley & D. Telfer (Eds.), *Tourism and development: Concepts and issues* (pp. 35–78). Channel View.

The Caribbean Tourism Organization [CTO]. (2020). *Caribbean sustainable tourism policy and development framework*. https://caricom.org/documents/10910-cbbnsustainabletourismpolicyframework.pdf

Tolkach, D., & King, B. (2015). Strengthening community-based tourism in a new resource-based island nation: Why and how? *Tourism Management, 48*, 386–398. https://doi.org/10.1016/j.tourman.2014.12.013

Tosun, C. (2006). Expected nature of community participation in tourism development. *Tourism Management, 27*, 493–504.

UNCTAD. (2020). *Coronavirus will cost global tourism at least $1.2 trillion.* United Nations Conference on Trade and Development. Retrieved January 6, 2021, from https://unctad.org/news/coronavirus-will-cost-global-tourism-least-12-trillion

UNWTO. (2001). *Tourism highlights 2001.* World Tourism Organization. Madrid. https://doi.org/10.18111/9789284406845

UNWTO. (2019). *United Nations World Tourism Report 2019.* Available at: https://www.eunwto.org/doi/pdf/10.18111/9789284421152. Accessed 24 August 2020.

Walker, L., & Page, S. J. (2004). The contribution of tourists and visitors to road traffic accidents: A preliminary analysis of trends and issues for central Scotland. *Current Issues in Tourism, 7*(3), 217–241. https://doi.org/10.1080/13683500408667980

Wallen, B. (2020, November 30). Why some countries are opening back up to tourism during a pandemic. *National Geographic.* https://www.nationalgeographic.com/travel/article/are-economics-driving-countries-to-reopen-to-tourists-coronavirus

Waterman, T. (2009). *Assessing public attitudes and behavior toward tourism development in Barbados: Socio-economic and environmental implications.* Central Bank of Barbados.

Wilks, J., Stephen, J., & Moore, F. (2013). *Managing tourist health and safety in the new millennium.* Routledge.

World Conservation Union. (1996, October 13–23). *Resolutions and recommendations* [Meeting]. World Conservation Congress, Montreal, Canada. https://portals.iucn.org/library/sites/library/files/documents/WCC-1st-002.pdf

World Travel & Tourism Council (WTTC). (2019). *Economic impact reports.* https://wttc.org/Research/Economic-Impact

World Travel & Tourism Council (WTTC). (2020). *100 million jobs recovery plan: Final Proposal* (G20 2020 Saudi Arabia Summit). https://wttc.org/Portals/0/Documents/Reports/2020/100%20Million%20Jobs%20Recovery%20Plan.pdf?ver=2021-02-25-183014-057

Zheng, D., Luo, Q., & Ritchie, B. (2021). Afraid to travel after COVID-19? Self-protection, coping and resilience against pandemic 'travel fear.' *Tourism Management, 83*, 104261. https://doi.org/10.1016/j.tourman.2020.104261

CHAPTER 11

The Role of the Bahamas Government in Tourism

Madlyn Bonimy

Introduction

Government is public administration. According to Harmon and Mayer (1994), public administration is "the concern of all those who act on behalf of the public–on behalf of society in a legally mandated way—and whose actions have consequences for members of society" (p. 6). Further, the authors discussed how public administration is concerned with decisions that affect people's lives are "made in the name of the public, and use public resources" (p. 6). Denhardt and Denhardt (2000) asserted that "public administration is to serve citizens" (p. 555). In serving citizens, public administration makes decisions in the name of the public and it executes the public's business.

In general terms, governments exist for specific purposes and in fact, they intervene in every facet of life and their actions have consequences

M. Bonimy (✉)
University of Arizona Global Campus, San Diego, CA, USA
e-mail: mmbonimy@yahoo.com

C. Cannonier and M. Galloway Burke (eds.), *Contemporary Issues Within Caribbean Economies*, https://doi.org/10.1007/978-3-030-98865-4_11

for society. According to Mikesell, (2006 [1990]) "Governments exist to provide valuable services which business or individuals are unwilling to provide independently" (p. 2). Governments have economic functions as well:

> Stabilization, and growth, involves the combat against unemployment and inflation and provisions for increases in the standard of living for the citizenry […] distribution, the correction of perceived injustices in the distribution of wealth in society […] allocation, the provision of public or collective goods. These goods and services which are socially desirable but which ordinary business firms cannot be expected to provide in desirable amount […]. Public goods include services, such as natural defense, pollution control, disease control, police and fire protection, primary education and so on. (Mikesell, 2006 [1990], pp. 3–4)

In short, the government defends its territory, administers justice, protects its citizens, maintains order, collects taxes, and promotes growth of society. In the context of public administration, the government is occupied with trying to solve wicked problems in society (Gordon & Milakovich, 2012). Wicked problems have no easy solutions but have implications for society. In the end, the role that the Bahamas government plays in tourism has implications for society, the economy, and public finances.

Location of the Bahamas

The Bahamas is an archipelago of 700 islands and over 2,000 rocks or cays. Some 31 islands are inhabited (World Atlas, 2021). The country is situated in the Western Atlantic—50 miles east of the American state of Florida extending some 600 miles south eastward to within 50 miles of the island of Cuba. A former British Colony, the Bahamas gained independence on July 10, 1973. Dupuch (2000) pointed out how:

> At 12:01am, July 10, 1973, The Bahamas raised its own flag and ended more than 300 years of British colonial rule. Under Prime Minister Lynden Pindling, the country got to work putting in place an infrastructure that would declare to the world its independence. Key to this evolution was the opening of The Central Bank of The Bahamas on June 1, 1974….it was a fully Bahamian operation […]. The Bahamian economy […] shifted into a comfortable and confident cruise mode, triggered by steady gains in the tourism industry. (p.122)

The tourism industry is important to the Bahamas' economy.

Tourism Defined

As Sharpely (2018) suggested, tourism is all things to all people—it may be for relaxation, recreation, or escape for the stress of everyday life and work—as well as for those in the tourism business around the world. Simply, tourism by definition is a source of employment and income and simultaneously, governments may promote or encourage the development of tourism as it can be considered as an essential ingredient of broader social and economic development policies. To this definition should be added that tourism is also an industry that involves the caring of people (i.e., tourists). O' Reilly (1983) noted that no business is easy with tourism not being an exception as it deals with the most difficult element of all—people as there is moving, housing, feeding, and entertaining them as well as meeting their multitudinous needs, both as groups and individuals since tourists are paying to be pampered. Bonimy (2009) explained how "tourism involves providing recreational facilities and services, such as lodging, transportation, attractions, entertainment, and food for people traveling for rest, relaxation, sport, and access to culture and nature" (p. 16). Ardahey (2011) also pointed out that tourism involves a large array of retail and service businesses that includes the sectors most affected by tourism such as "hotels and other lodging facilities, eating and drinking establishments, and amusement and recreation facilities such as theme parks and ski resorts" (p. 214).

Thus, by its very nature, tourism is characterized by urbanization and commercialization and its obvious economic manifestations are job creation, foreign exchange earnings, and income tax revenues. Nunkoo and Gursoy (2019) argued that tourism contributes to economic development at the destination level as it generates income and foreign exchange, creates new employment opportunities for local people, and aids in diversifying the local economy. Similarly, Icoz and Icoz (2019) emphasized how "the tourism industry has a positive influence on the local economy by resulting in effects such as economic diversity, revenues, jobs, and tax revenue" (p. 97). Thus, the industry of tourism is built around the moving, the caring of people in a different setting and its most important characteristic seems to be that it provides for economic growth.

Tourism: Economic Engine of the Bahamas

Nature endowed the Bahamas with its potential for tourism: miles of gleaming white and pink sand beaches, clear translucent waters, a delightful climate, sporting activities, friendly inhabitants, and a slow pace of the Islands that make them ideal as a year-round haven for tourists. The Bahamas boasts three distinct tourist destinations.

1) Nassau, the capital city of the Bahamas that is located on the island of New Providence, is known for its historical charm, nightlife, casinos, and shopping facilities.
2) Freeport, located on the island of Grand Bahama, is renowned for championship golf courses, casinos, and shopping.
3) The "Family" Islands are the remaining islands grouped together. These "Out" islands, as the name suggests, are known for their beautifully untouched, uncrowded pink and white sand beaches plus their tranquil, relaxed, laid-back, and natural atmosphere.

The Bahamas has a population of approximately 402,953 (CountryMeters, 2022) and a gross domestic product of approximately $12.83 billion USD (Trading Economics, 2021). Tourist expenditures obtained through spending by visitors in 2019 were estimated to be $4.1 billion (Ministry of Tourism, 2019). Icoz and Icoz (2019) emphasized how the increase in the number of tourists has been parallel to the increase in gross domestic product (GDP), which leads to greater growth in employment and wealth when compared to other economies that do not specialize in tourism as well as employment rates higher than in those economies. With a total labor force of 214, 211 (Data World Bank, 2020), the economy depends heavily on the tourism sector to provide employment—some 110,490 people are employed as a direct result of tourism (Department of Statistics—Bahamas, 2019). Direct employment is necessary to serve the tourism industry and it is evident in the jobs created at hotels, restaurants, shops, and so forth, to directly serve the tourist. Indirect jobs are produced through the creation of the components of the infrastructure with skilled and unskilled jobs, such as mechanics maintaining rental cars, artisans creating items sold in shops, farmworkers, telecommunications employees, police, and all manner of other jobs created to serve the needs of the tourism industry in the Bahamas.

The Bahamas welcomed its first visitors as tourists in the eighteenth and the nineteenth centuries when invalids visited in order to benefit from an equable climate (Dupuch, 2000). However, with arable land and no mineral deposit, except salt, tourism as an export industry was first encouraged in the Bahamas in the 1950s (Dupuch, 2016). Tourism as an export sector, as described by Sharpley (2018), "...involves travel to and a stay of at least 24 hours or more in a country in which the tourist does not normally reside or work" (p. 2) and that it "differs from other exports inasmuch as it is consumed in the country where it is produced" (p. 2).

In 1950, tourist arrivals to the Bahamas numbered about 32,000 (Dupuch, 2016). This figure increased to over 100,000 visitors in 1954, to half a million visitors in 1963, followed by the 1 million visitor level in 1968, and then the 3 million visitor mark in 1986. The Bahamas hosted over 7.3 million visitors in 2019–2020 (pre-covid-19 coronavirus pandemic or the name of the illness caused by the coronavirus SARS-CoV-2 or severe acute respiratory syndrome coronavirus 2) (Tourism Today, 2019).

However, it is important to point out that in March 2020, the Bahamas shuttered due to the COVID-19 pandemic. From 2020–2021, COVID-19 forced the most significant restrictions on the movement of people. Globally, many countries introduced travel restrictions to contain the spread of the virus. Because of the COVID-19 pandemic, the Bahamas was also forced to close its borders to protect against this deadly virus, including its airports and hotels. Thus, understandably, with a largely tourism-driven economy, the Bahamas experienced a steep decrease in visitor arrivals; in fact, some 96.3% lower in July 2020 (the beginning of the fiscal year) than in the previous year (Bahamas Ministry of Finance, 2021). Unfortunately, this significant decline in visitor arrivals resulted in falling government revenue. For 2020, reduced government revenues translated into a substantial fiscal deficit of $1.3 Billion.

Nonetheless, in spite of the COVID-19 pandemic, the economic outlook of Bahamas rebounded in 2021. The country's resurgence was helped by the vaccine programs in the US and Canada, coupled with the US federal government's stimulus initiatives (Bahamas Government Bahamas Ministry of Finance, 2021). The Bahamas once again opened for international travel tourists (Bahamas Ministry of Tourism, n.d.). The Bahamas government has also implemented the Bahamas Travel Health Visa system (Travel Compliance Unit, n.d.) to support the country's implementation of its COVID-19 related guidelines for safely managing international travelers (both foreign and local), as well as inter-island travel.

It is important to point out that the Bahamas has faced other challenges and setbacks that have affected its tourism industry. In September 2019, Dorian, a category 5 hurricane, produced mass destruction to two of the Bahamas' major 16 islands: the northwest islands of Abaco and Grand Bahama (Mercy Corps, 2019). Both Abaco and Grand Bahama are two major tourist destinations of The Bahamas. Hurricane Dorian caused an estimated damage of $3.4 billion which is equal to one-quarter of the Bahamas' GDP (Mercy Corps, 2019). According to the Inter-American Development Bank (2019), the impact from hurricane Dorian was divided as 72% in damage and 21% in losses with the private sector absorbing almost 90% of total losses. Unfortunately, hundreds of people lost their lives too. Also, while it was the housing sector that suffered the highest damage, tourism suffered most of the losses (Inter-American Development Bank, 2019). Hurricane Dorian disrupted their tourist flows with damage to assets in each sector including buildings, machinery, equipment, means of transportation, furnishings, roads, ports, airports, telecommunications, and stocks of goods, among others (Economic Commission for Latin American & Caribbean, n.d).

Rightfully so, the Bahamas government has been present and in solidarity with Bahamians throughout these most difficult times. After Hurricane Dorian, the government immediately designated both Abaco and Grand Bahama as special economic recovery zones for an initial period of three years. Under this designation all Bahamian businesses and residents are to have access to duty-free purchase of all vehicles, materials, fixtures, furniture, and equipment for all businesses and residential construction rehabilitation efforts; waiver of business license fees; waiver of real property tax payable on all eligible properties that are reconstructed Restored or are otherwise inhabitable (McKenzie, 2019). In addition, the Bahamas government established a $10 million loan guarantee and equity financing program that allows Bahamian small- and medium-sized businesses an opportunity to secure up to $500,000 in financing to fund the restoration of businesses or the creation of new businesses (McKenzie, 2019).

The island of Abaco experienced much more damage than the Island of Grand Bahama. In fact, Abaco's Chamber of Commerce predicted the island's post-Dorian reconstruction would take an additional three to five years at minimum to complete (Hartnell, April 2021). The problem was exacerbated due to the public health measures related to the COVID-19 pandemic, such as lockdowns and travel restrictions, that both delayed and complicated rebuilding and reconstruction efforts in 2021. Abaco entrepreneurs have received over $3.7 million loans and grant applications through the Bahamas' Small Business Development Center to assist them in their rebuilding efforts. In spite of the deferments, the people in Abaco are voicing optimism and expressing hope for a long recovery.

While the island of Grand Bahama was less affected by Hurricane Dorian, recovery on this island is slow as well due to the COVID-19 pandemic restrictions and lockdowns. However, in 2020 the Bahamas government began to rebuild the business community in Grand Bahama. For example, again through the Bahamas' Small Business Development Center, over $3 million was disbursed to assist over 113 micro and small businesses affected by Hurricane Dorian in Grand Bahama and altogether, approximately $3.3 billion has been put directly into the hands of Bahamian companies and homes (Cooper, 2020).

Even though reconstruction efforts slowed after the COVID-19 pandemic, the islands of Abaco and Grand Bahama continue to be the focus of the Bahamas government which is committed over the long term to bringing back these two vibrant tourism economies. And as it should be, the Bahamas government is also committed to the rebuilding efforts and through completion for these two northern islands. Fortunately, the principal island of New Providence and the capital city of Nassau where 70% of the population of the Bahamas live, and which is also the hub of the Bahamas government, was largely spared and unscathed from hurricane Dorian except for some heavy rainfall.

In spite of the disasters and delays that have hampered tourism in the Bahamas, tourism still serves as an economic engine in the Bahamas and the government of the Bahamas has a central role to play in the development of tourism. Tourism used for economic development is a policy intervention endeavor with intentions of economic and social well-being of people (Choe & Roberts, 2011). Indeed, policymakers employ economic development to promote the standard and the economic health of areas (Gibbs, 2002). Consequently, the Bahamas government, preoccupied with improving the quality of life of Bahamians (the people of the Bahamas), has put in place appropriate legislation, policies, and programs focused on the economic growth and development of tourism. It is through the examination of these three components—(1) legislation,

(2) policies, and (3) programs—that the significant role the government of the Bahamas plays in tourism will be further evidenced.

Government Legislation in Tourism Development

There are several important pieces of government legislation essential for the development of tourism in the Bahamas. First, the central piece of legislation, key to fostering growth in the principal industry of the Bahamas, came through the passage of the Promotion of Tourism Act of 1964 (Bahamas Government Legislation, Promotion of Tourism Act, n.d.). The passage of this act empowered the government to appoint a Minister charged with the overall responsibility of the promoting of tourism. The idea behind this act was to create a Ministry that operated in a more flexible manner that was not subject to rigid procedures and bureaucratic controls and delays. Thus, The Bahamas Ministry of Tourism is the government's agency responsible for the promotion of tourism in the Bahamas. The vision of the Ministry of Tourism is "to be a global industry leader in destination marketing and management, contributing sustainably to a thriving national economy" (The Bahamas Ministry of Tourism, 2021, para. 1). The mission of The Ministry of Tourism is to "achieve its vision through a holistic approach that is research, data, and technology-driven" (The Bahamas Ministry of Tourism, 2021, para. 2). The Ministry of Tourism is funded by a direct subvention from parliament. In 2019–2020, the Ministry of Tourism operated with a budget of $130.4 million (Cartwright-Carroll, 2020).

The Ministry of Tourism & Aviation, as it is now known, functions today with a staff of several hundreds of people located both within the Bahamas and in offices overseas (the US, Canada, and Europe). The Ministry of Tourism is responsible for regulating the aviation industry. Aviation plays such an important role in the economic development of the Bahamas as it is responsible for moving passengers and goods for international and international commerce (Lexology Library, Aviation in the Bahamas, 2018). The duties of the Minister of Tourism & Aviation are related to organizing, carrying out, and encouraging measures such as (1) developing civil aviation; (2) promoting the safe and efficient use of civil aircraft; and (3) granting air transport licences (Lexology Library, Aviation in the Bahamas, 2018). It is important to note as well that the staff of the Ministry of Tourism & Aviation is not like civil servants. All authority concerning appointments, terminations, discipline, and other personnel matters rests with the Minister. The technical head of the Department of Tourism & Aviation is the Director General, who normally reports to the Minister and has direct access to him or her.

The primary concern of the Ministry of Tourism & Aviation is not in direct consumer sales, but to provide a positive environment for tour operators, travel agents, airlines, cruise ships, hotels, and promotion boards to successfully market the Bahamas to the consumer. The Ministry is also occupied with the quality and continued improvement of the tourism product to ensure that it lives up to the image created through promotion. To this end, the Bahamas Ministry of Tourism & Aviation develops and executes marketing campaigns to promote the Islands of the Bahamas; produces collateral material including brochures to promote the country as a whole; and works with various governmental and non-governmental agencies to improve the infrastructure and product of the Bahamas, thereby, ensuring adequate transportation systems, both air service and sea service.

The role of the government in the Bahamas in supplying modern infrastructure is vitally important to tourism. In fact, "without infrastructure of roads, bridges, transportation, waste disposal plants, water supply systems, airports, communication systems, power generating plants" (Axelrod, 1995, p. 100), the industry of tourism in the Bahamas would certainly deteriorate. While staying at a destination, Ardahey (2011) pointed out that such auxiliary entities and goods need to be created, further developed, or imported, depending on accessibility of how tourists need auxiliary goods and services while staying at a destination. To accommodate tourists and offer them needed services, Kocabulut, Yozukmaz, and Bertan (2019) noted that in addition to required infrastructure services (i.e., roads, streets, harbors, airports, electricity, water, and sewage systems), superstructure systems are needed, which refers to the components directly related to visitor needs such as reception centers, hotels, restaurants, car rental companies, tour operators, and retailers. In reality, the government of the Bahamas has spent tens of millions of dollars to improve roads, harbors, and water systems. In its 2019/2020 budget, the Bahamas government allocated $83.5 Million or 3.2% of recurrent expenditures to public enterprises and infrastructure (Bahamas Ministry of Finance, 2021), which include six international airports, extensive electrification, modern and extensive medical facilities, and modern telecommunications. These projects are the mainstays of economic stability in the Bahamas and essential to the existence and facilitation of tourism. Axelrod (1995) noted how only the national government can really cope with major economic problems. The role that the government of the Bahamas plays in tourism is politically essential and justified: the government of the Bahamas is preoccupied with the degree to which foreign exchange continues to grow as a result of a successful tourism economy; is concerned with the extent to which employment continues to increase at required rates as a result of a successful tourism economy; and is occupied with the degree to which the distribution of income continues to expand among all Bahamians.

A second piece of legislation indispensable to the development of the tourism industry in the Bahamas is the Hotels Encouragement Act that is administered through the Bahamas Investment Authority (BIA). The BIA, established in 1993, is a one-stop investment facilitator under the umbrella of the Office of the Prime Minister responsible for investment policy formulation, international and domestic promotion of investment opportunities in The Bahamas, as well as review and evaluation of investment proposals (Dupuch, 2000). The Hotels Encouragement Act became law in 1954 with subsequent amendments in 1965, 1966, 1974, and 1993 (Norville, n.d.). The act does a good job of encouraging the development of new hotels throughout the Bahamas and the expansion of operating ones by providing a number of concessions for hotel owners and investors. These concessions include: (1) customs duty refunds that refunds customs duty on the costs of materials purchased or imported for use in the construction and furnishing of a new hotel in order to allow the facility to open for business; (2) right to import construction plant, including heavy-duty machinery, free of duty on a customs bond, with the obligation to re-export it by a given date; and (3) tax exemptions that includes hotel investors having a 10-year exemption from real property tax with a minimum taxation per bedroom of $20.00 beginning in the eleventh year until a twenty-year period occurs from the date that the hotel opened (Office of the Attorney General & Ministry of Legal Affairs, 2010). These concessions apply to all amenities offered in conjunction with the hotel such as golf courses, marinas, harbors, roads, airfields, and landscaping. The only qualification demanded by the Bahamas government is that under the Hotels Encouragement Act, premises established as a new hotel or residential club "in New Providence or Paradise Island must have at least 20 bedrooms and suitable public rooms for the accommodation and entertainment of guests. A new hotel in the Family Islands must have at least five bedrooms" (Dupuch, 2000, p. 485) for the accommodation of guests.

Following the Hotels Encouragement Act came the passage of the Hotels Act of 1970. This legislation provided for the establishment of a Hotel Licensing Board, charged with the responsibility for licensing hotels throughout the Bahamas (Norville, n.d.). It was through the passage of this act that the Bahamas government introduced standards in hotel accommodations. For example, every interior part of the structure (e.g., fittings, fixtures, mattresses, draperies, upholstery, and flooring) of every hotel should be kept clean and in good condition and repaired; every exterior part of the structure of every hotel should be kept clean and in good condition; every room should be adequately lighted and ventilated with a form regarding accommodations posted on the back of every hotel room entrance; and all reasonable precautions should be taken to prevent fire in the hotel and to maintain all fire equipment therein in good working order and publish fire procedures within the hotel fires (Office of the Attorney General &Ministry of Legal Affairs, 1971). Furthermore, as Norville (n.d) noted, "a 4% room toll was introduced, payable to the central government (since amended to 6%)" (para. 4).

These aforementioned standards are of vital importance to the survival and growth of the tourism industry. Also, overall, the Bahamas' Government legislation has an impact on tourism development as it offers incentives for foreign direct investment in the hotel sector. Having international standard hotel accommodations in the Bahamas attracts tourists and having a variety of hotel accommodations offers a wider appeal for tourists. The problem is that many of the hotels in the Bahamas are foreign-owned by hotel operators such as Hilton, Hyatt, Margaritaville, Wyndham, and Atlantis Resorts. These foreign-owned companies transfer some of their earnings, such as profits, wages/salaries, to their home country. This transfer of profits from outside of the local area is known as export leakage and is a negative economic cost of tourism. As Icoz and Icoz (2019) reported, such leakage results in financial processes through which less money gets back into the economy.

In addition, all-inclusive accommodations, such as Breezes, Club Med, Riu, and Sandal Resorts, impact the local economy in the Bahamas. Guests staying at these hotels undergo a process in tourism known as "eclavisation," which is an economic cost of tourism. The problem with enclave tourism is that tourists pay for their entire stay in their home country and are then dissuaded from spending any money outside of their hotel at their vacation destination. In addition, they often spend their entire vacation at the same resort confined to their environmental bubble throughout their trip; thus, not contributing to the local economy. Icoz and Icoz (2019) pointed out that while all-inclusive hotels generate the largest amount of revenue, their impact on the local economy is smaller per dollar of revenue when compared to other hotels.

Certainly, foreign direct investment in the hotel sector adds jobs to the Bahamas' workforce. Smaller family operated hotels and inns augmented with apartments, cottages, and villas could translate into more linkage with the local economy as more local materials and techniques would reflect the indigenous character of the surroundings.

In addition, a major economic cost is that a substantial amount of what the Bahamas earns in foreign exchange is expended out due to imports, especially buying foreign supplies, including food to satisfy the tourists' needs. Supradist (2004) argued that the most significant leakage caused by tourism is import leakage where tourists demand goods that the host country cannot produce or supply. The Bahamas must do a better job to create more linkages from the tourism industry to other industries within the economy, such as with an indigenous agricultural industry thus reducing imports and producing and supplying food to help feed tourists.

Government Policy in Tourism Development

In addition to the legislation focused on the economic growth and development of tourism, the government of the Bahamas has put in place several specific policies as well. The term policy refers in general to a purposive course of action that an individual or group consistently follows in dealing with a problem (Anderson, 2015). Public policy is what the government chooses to do and not to do (Dye, 1987) and is also the battle of ideas (Ripley & Franklin, 1991). In fact, Lowi (1964) discussed how all government functions can be classified into three types of policies: (1) distributive, (2) redistributive, and (3) regulatory. In this section, two types of policies in particular are examined that the Bahamas government practices in helping to advance the tourism industry—distributive and regulatory.

First, unlike redistributive policies which "provide benefits to one category of individuals at the expense of another, [...] and often reflect ideological or class conflict, [such as with] Welfare and Social Security

[…]" (Kraft & Furlong, 2018, p. 112), distributive policies are "individual programs or grants that a government provides without regard to limited resources […]" (Kraft & Furlong, 2018, p. 111). Gordon and Milakovich (2012) further detailed how "distributive policies deliver large-scale services or benefits to certain individuals or groups in the population. Examples are loans and loan guarantees provided by the national government" (p. 346). Essentially, the Bahamas government offers a soft window of loans and loan guarantees through the Bahamas Development Bank (BDB). The bank, established by an Act of Parliament on October 8, 1974, opened its doors to the public on July 21, 1978 (Dupuch, 2000) and was created specifically to assist Bahamian entrepreneurs in establishing new businesses or expanding through the provision of concessionary funding and technical assistance. There is a focus on projects that generate jobs and contribute to the economic growth and development of the Bahamas with major sectors financed by the BDB that include tourism and ancillary services; industrial enterprises; agro-based industrial enterprises; farming; fishing; marine and land transportation; and small businesses. There are also loan guarantee provisions for touristic resorts in the Family Islands.

Through its 2021 budget communication, the Bahamas Government allocated the Bahamas Development Bank an additional $4.0 million to assist Bahamian entrepreneurs (Bahamas Ministry of Finance, 2021). The Bahamas Ministry of Finance has also committed $20 million in financing for the 2021–2022 fiscal year to the Bahamas Development Bank to recapitalize the BDB so that it may fund opportunities for small businesses in The Bahamas (Hartnell, March 2021). The Recapitalizing of the BDB by the Ministry of Finance is a contributory government policy as it serves as a financing source for the self-employed, cooperatives, and small Bahamian businesses which contribute to enhancing the economic growth and development of the Bahamas. They not only create new job opportunities, but they also use local materials, reduce imports, and contribute to placing capital and wealth in the hands of Bahamians.

The second kind of policy pursued by the government of the Bahamas in fostering the growth of the tourism industry is regulatory by nature. Meier (1993) argued that "regulatory policy is government restriction of individual choice to keep conduct from transcending acceptable bounds" (p. 82). Gordon and Milakovich (2012) emphasized that regulatory policies really promote restrictions on the freedom to act of those subject to the regulations. Furthermore, Redford (1965) explained that licensing is a major type of regulation. In essence, with licensing, government consent must be obtained before action is taken. To foster growth and development, the government of the Bahamas established the Hotels Regulations of 1971 (Office of the Attorney General & Ministry of Legal Affairs, 1971) that regulates hotels through hotel inspections. The Hotels Regulations of 1971's power lies in its ability to grant a license, refuse a license, grant a temporary license, or cancel a license. Hotel operators can even be prosecuted for contravening hotel regulations, such as for non-payment of hotel guest tax and for failure to maintain the hotel's physical facilities at an acceptable standard. In fact, every hotel operator must make a check payable to the Public Treasury each month for the amount of the hotel guest tax that must reach the office of the Chief Licensing Inspector no later than the fifteenth day of the month following the month in which the check is due.

Other important regulatory policies concern environmental issues. The environment and its resources contribute to sustainable tourism development. Brundtland (1987) defined sustainable development as "development which meets the needs of the present generation without compromising the ability of future generations to meet their own needs" (p. 42). The government of the Bahamas has regulatory policies in place to protect against littering, pollution of coastal waters, cruise ships dumping at sea, the depletion of non-renewable and extremely fragile marine life. The violation of the environmental policy is illegal and punishable through the levying and payment of a heavy fine.

The sea and lakes in the Bahamas not only add to the visual beauty of the islands, forming an attractive landscape, but also offer the possibilities of swimming, sailing, canoeing, and fishing. As the Bahamas is overwhelmingly a marine country, it is highly vulnerable to environmental threats to its marine resources (Government of the Bahamas, 2018). In protecting the marine environment, the Department of Marine Resources identified land-based impacts and coastal development as significant threats to coastal and marine environments. Threats to the marine environment are also seen through the direct impacts of dredging, removal of mangroves, landfilling, altering of beaches for human activities, construction of unregulated buildings on coastlines, and indirect impacts from pesticides, sewage discharge, and runoff (Government of the Bahamas, 2018). Even the building of marinas can alter water levels and disturb fauna and flora. In the Bahamas, marine ecosystems include, for example, seagrass beds, coral reefs, blue holes and open oceans that provide refuge and feeding grounds for fish and other marine life and support habitats and vast oceanic food webs. Unfortunately, like many other Caribbean islands, the Bahamas ranks among the most water scarce small island developing states in the world (Government of the Bahamas, 2018). In addition, since the 1990s, environmental degradation and ecological vulnerability have drastically increased with many Bahamian ecosystems already depleted or under threat of further degradation due to overextraction and fragmentation of natural habitats (Government of the Bahamas, 2018).

Since environmental quality in the form of physical location, air, land, space, climate, flora, and fauna, attracts tourism (Bonimy, 2011), changes in the state and condition of tourism resources result in impacts on the bio-physical environment. The Bahamas National Trust (BNT) is responsible for conserving the natural resources of the Bahamas. To protect natural resources, the goal of the BNT is.

> To make the BNT and the environmental field, in general, more accessible for younger generations who are the future of The Bahamas; while remaining true to what has always been at the core of our identity: passion, dedication, commitment, protection, stewardship, conservation, and transparency. The BNT is responsible for 32 national parks over 2 million acres of land and sea throughout The Bahamas. (The Bahamas National Trust, 2021, paras. 3–4).

In fact, the BNT works with the Government of The Bahamas (GOB) and other partners to establish more protected areas; research and monitor the areas using species identified as sensitive to climate change; develop climate-smart management plans; enforce the management strategies; restore areas as needed; and adapt the plan as circumstances change (Government of the Bahamas, 2018). One government ministry with which the BNT works to conserve the natural resources of the Bahamas is the Bahamas Ministry of Environmental Planning and Protection. Created in 2019, this ministry provides for the prevention or control of pollution, the regulation of activities, and the administration, conservation, and sustainable use of the environment (Bahamas Department of Environmental Planning & Protection, 2021).

The Bahamas also has in place a National Maritime Policy to regulate maritime activities. The National Maritime Policy, implemented in 2017, addresses several key thematic areas including: (1) Ocean governance to support future economic investments; (2) Regulation and enforcement of maritime space and activities; (3) Healthy and productive marine environment; (4) Climate change and resilience; and (5) Education, awareness and participation for coastal inhabitants and visitors to the islands (Government of the Bahamas, 2018).

Tourism can be viewed in conflict with sustaining the environment. On one hand, it is environmental quality that attracts visitors. On the other hand, the problem is that tourism can be responsible for effects on the environment with, for example, congestion, air pollution caused by increased automobiles, loss and disappearance of beaches to hotel development, oil spills from cruise ships, discharging of raw sewage into onshore waters by cruise ships, and littering of glass and tin cans from beachgoers. Obviously, the Bahamas government's regulatory policies are in place to protect the tourism environment. It is now imperative that these policies work to help preserve the natural environment and resources in the Bahamas. Islands like the Bahamas are especially vulnerable as the sea comprises about 95% of the Bahamas' geographical area and little land is available. As a signatory to the United Nations Paris Climate Agreement in April 2016 (Scavella, 2016), and although a low emitter of greenhouse gas emissions on sa global scale, the Bahamas' participation in this global policy accord serves as clear evidence of its commitment to the environment and to the global conversation about climate change, its effects, and the course of action needed to address it.

Government Programs in Tourism Development

The government of the Bahamas, focused on national prosperity throughout the economy and society, has implemented a plethora of programs designed to position the Bahamas as an attractive, viable tourist, and investment destination. Three such areas of focus deal with investment, education and job training, and national security.

First, to lure foreign investors, the government offers attractive incentive programs, not the least of which is complete exemption from taxes on all earnings. This translates into no corporate taxes, no sales taxes, no personal income tax, no capital gains tax, no profit tax, no real estate tax, and no inheritance tax. Regarding the investment environment, Dupuch (2000) asserted that "To undergird the National Investment policy, the government will provide [...] an environment in which freedom from capital gains, inheritance, withholding, profit remittance, corporate, royalty, sales, personal income, dividends, payroll and interest taxes is ensured" (p. 502). This tax freedom is available to all resident corporations, partnerships, individuals, and trusts. It must be noted that the investment environment of the Bahamas is particularly strong because the Bahamas is one of the most politically stable countries in the Western Hemisphere. In fact, Parliamentary democracy was introduced there in 1729 and has been uninterrupted for over 292 years. The investment plan to lure foreign investors to the Bahamas benefits Bahamians who work in the tourism industry. Foreign investment also helps to grow the Bahamas' tourism product and, as a result, both direct and indirect jobs are created to serve the needs of the tourism industry in the Bahamas.

In addition to attractive investment incentive programs, educational and job training programs of the Bahamas government are vital to the advancement of tourism and improvements in education can create a positive socioeconomic impact on tourism. The Bahamas society has an adult literacy rate of 85% due largely to the free and compulsory education up to high school. Education in the Bahamas falls under the jurisdiction of the Ministry of Education that oversees free education in Ministry schools throughout The Bahamas (Dupuch, 2000).

It is a good idea to develop tourism education to balance the tourism development demand for fulfilling the broader perspective of managing tourism (Malihah & Setiyorini, 2014). Through education, Bahamians become experienced and more highly trained. Of particular relevance to the tourism industry are government-operated institutions of higher learning. Inui et al. (2006) suggested that there are two reasons for educating future professionals—employability and providing students with a wider foundation for decision-making strategies as well as for professional preparation.

The Bahamas Hotel Training College has played an important role in the preparation of young persons for employment in the hotel and entrepreneurial sectors. The school was established to meet demands of the developing tourism industry in the Bahamas, the Caribbean, and other Commonwealth countries through the development of human resources for national and international tourism, hospitality, and allied industries (Dupuch, 2000). In August 2000, The Bahamas Hotel Training College "was amalgamated with the University of the Bahamas, producing the School of Hospitality and Tourism Studies, later known as the Culinary and Hospitality Management Institute" (University of the Bahamas, n.d., para. 7).

The University of the Bahamas plays an important role in educating Bahamians for employment in the tourism industry. While the Bahamas government is committed to education, unfortunately, the reduction in budget in 2020–2021, by approximately $16.1 million to the University of the Bahamas, came about because of reduced tourism revenues due to hurricane Dorian and to the COVID-19 pandemic. Hence, education impacts tourism and tourism impacts education.

A third program focuses on the government of the Bahama's role in national security and law enforcement, which it is paramount for the leadership of the government because security of life and of personal property is vitally important to the tourism industry. The government entity charged with ensuring public security of the Bahamas is the Ministry of National Security that oversees the major agencies in the country responsible for ensuring law and order, defense, and correction such as the Royal Bahamas Police Force, the Royal Bahamas Defence Force, and the Bahamas Department of Corrections (Bahamas Ministry of National Security, n.d.). The Royal Bahamas Police force is a law enforcement agency with over 4,000 officers, reserves, and police civilians that provides policing services to all residents and visitors of The Bahamas (Royal Bahamas Police Force, n.d.). The Royal Bahamas Defence Force, the second arm of law enforcement in the Bahamas, has the mandate for protecting border security (Royal Bahamas Defence Force Maritime Security Plan, 2021). The Bahamas Department of Corrections "contributes to the protection of society by optimizing staff development, while maintaining inmates in a controlled, safe, secure and humane environment that encourages rehabilitation and successful reintegration into society" (Bahamas Department of Correctional Services, Mission Statement, n.d., para. 1). An example of the commitment of the government of the Bahamas to law enforcement is demonstrated by the fact that law enforcement and national security matters received the second highest budget allocation, just behind education in the most recent recurrent budget. Axelrod (1995) mentioned how the budget reflects the aspirations, values, social and economic policies, and services of government.

On one hand, some studies (e.g., Andereck et al., 2005; Rothman, 1978) advanced how tourism has been found to lead to increased crime rates. On the other hand, scholars, such as Loureiro et al. (2019), argued that "Tourists tend to enjoy the night and consume more alcohol, leading to increases in levels of noise, prostitution, and crime due to bad behavior and drug and alcohol abuse" (p. 52). Nonetheless, with more than seven million visitors visiting the Bahamas every year, crime against tourists would definitely be an attack on tourism. In fact, the Bahamas government has reported that out of the millions of visitors that visit the Bahamas every year "less than half per cent are impacted by crime" (*Eyewitness News*, 2018, para. 6). Obviously, just one instance of crime can ruin a visitor's vacation; therefore, safety and security continue to be a very important issue for the Bahamas government. Through its national security budget allocation, the Bahamas government is dedicated to keeping both its citizens and tourists safe.

The three examples of governmental programs—investment incentive programs, education, and national security—confirm and further attest to the commitment and the significant role that the government of the Bahamas plays in the development of tourism. While all three of these programs are important in the development of the tourism industry, the education of Bahamians and keeping visitors and citizens safe are among the highest budget allocations. These budgets not only communicate national priorities but also the economic goals of the Bahamas government.

Conclusion

The purpose of this chapter was to examine the role that the Bahama government plays in tourism. The Bahamas government influences its economy directly for the continued development of tourism and is a source of investment (Levine et al., 1990) for the continued development of tourism. By raising or lowering taxes and expenditures, the Bahamas government attempts to promote economic growth, and maintain high levels of employment (Axelrod, 1995). The Bahamas government also regulates entities of tourism as "licensing is one of the most persistent forms of government control" (Redford, 1965, p. 36).

Evidently, tourism is big business in the Bahamas. As the largest sector in the Bahamian economy, tourism is the principal generator of employment. In fostering the growth of tourism, the government of the Bahamas combats against unemployment and provides for increases in the standard of living for all Bahamians. In a country where 60% of the workforce is directly employed because of the tourism industry and where 60% of government revenue is derived from the tourism industry, the role of the government in this industry has to be extensive and significant.

The government of the Bahamas has to be committed to the continued development of the country's tourism product, which is the dominant economic force for creating jobs and entrepreneurial opportunities.

Nonetheless, the tourism industry is a fickle industry open to the environment and worldwide prosperity, but the industry is open as well to economic recessions, employment fluctuation, changing fashions, impacts of natural disasters such as hurricanes, global pandemics, and changing tourist preferences. To enhance the economy, the government of the Bahamas must make more efforts to diversify its economy. Already, banking is the second industry; however, more focus should be placed on creating greater linkages with the agricultural sector to emphasize more local materials and techniques that reflect the indigenous character of the surroundings. The Bahamas must also continually try to indigenize its tourism product. The indigenization of the tourism product translates into, for example, continued involvement and education of locals to a higher degree as well as fostering a strong commitment to the development of tourism industries, especially an indigenous agricultural industry thus reducing imports.

As for enclave tourism, to combat against the environmental bubble that comes with all-inclusive resorts that do not provide contacts with local people or discovery of local culture, the Bahamas government should continue its efforts to improve upon massive educational programs such as the People-to-People program. This program puts visitors in contact with Bahamians who share their profession, interests, or social clubs. In promoting this form of authentic experience, tourism serves both local residents and visitors. On one hand, the program provides visitors with an understanding and appreciation of the customs of Bahamians. On the other hand, the program serves to strengthen the locals' awareness and pride in their own culture and traditions.

Tourism is the lifeblood of the Bahamian economy; however, the Bahamas tourism industry has experienced other challenges and setbacks (e.g., hurricane Dorian and the COVID-19 pandemic). Nonetheless, in spite of these challenges that have affected its tourism industry, total Bahamas government revenues are projected at $2.247 billion dollars (Bahamas Ministry of Finance, 2021). This revenue represents an increase of approximately $588.3 million or 35.5% over the projected 2020–2021 fiscal year (FY2020/21) total revenue. These additional monies will go a long way in helping the Bahamas government to promote economic growth and tourism throughout the country.

One new initiative that the Bahamas government has invested in is the home porting of cruise ships. Following on the heels of a very successful and record-breaking cruise industry in 2019, when 5.4 million cruise passengers came to the Bahamas pumping some $400 million directly into the hands of Bahamians and Bahamian businesses and providing another $100 million in entry taxes, the Bahamas government began investing in home porting. Royal Caribbean began operating weeklong cruises from its home port in Nassau, Bahamas and sailing to destinations within the Bahamas. Estimations were that home porting would bring approximately 30,000 to 35,000 cruise visitors to the Bahamas in 2021, expecting them to spend approximately $50 million during their stay in the Bahamas. Home porting is expected to positively impact the Bahamian economy as taxi drivers and tour drivers, custom agents, port workers, shop and store employees, and hotel and restaurant workers will all benefit (Bahamas Ministry of Finance, 2021).

The government in the Bahamas assumes its proper role as regulator and facilitator of economic development. Without the protection and enforcement of a government legal structure, such as the Promotion of Tourism Act and the Hotels Encouragement Act; without specific tourism-related policies such as loans and loan guarantees to assist Bahamian entrepreneurs in establishing businesses in the tourism industry; without special governmental programs targeted to educating Bahamians for employment in the tourism industry through government-operated institutions of higher learning; without governmental programs in national security to keep citizens and visitors safe; without attractive investment incentives to lure foreign investors; and without government regulations in hotel standards and hotel licensing, the tourism industry in the Bahamas could not exist in its current form.

References

Ardahey, F. T. (2011). Economic impacts of tourism industry. *International Journal of Business & Management, 6*(8), 206–215. https://doi.org/10.5539/ijbm.v6n8p206

Andereck, K. L., Valentine, K. M., Knopf, R. C., & Vogt, C. A. (2005). Residents' perceptions of community tourism impacts. *Annals of Tourism Research, 32*(4), 1056–1076. https://doi.org/10.1016/j.annals.2005.03.001

Anderson, J. E. (2015). *Public policymaking* (8th ed.). Cengage Learning.

Axelrod, D. (1995). *Budgeting for modern government*. Martin's Press, Inc.

Bahamas Department of Correctional Services. (n.d.). *Mission statement.* Retrieved June 15, 2021, from https://www.corrections.direct/the-bahamas/nassau/corrections/bahamas-department-of-correctional-services-3652
Bahamas Department of Environmental Planning and Protection. (2021, June). *About us.* https://www.depp.gov.bs/
Bahamas Ministry of Finance. (2020, December). *Mid-Year budget statement on the six months ending December 31, 2020.* https://bahamasbudget.gov.bs/2020/news-centre/latest-news/2021/02/24/mid-year-budget-statement-on-the-six-months-ending-december-31-2020/
Bahamas Ministry of Finance. (2021, February 24). *Mid-year budget statement on the six months ending December 31, 2020* [Speech transcript]. Retrieved June 14, 2021, from https://www.bahamas.gov.bs/wps/wcm/connect/024d5d6d-b046-41a1-9224-32475b18cd4e/2021_22_BudgetCommunication_FINAL.pdf?MOD=AJPERES
Bahamas Ministry of National Security. (n.d.) *Overview.* Retrieved June 15, 2021, from https://www.devex.com/organizations/ministry-of-national-securitybahamas-127403
Bahamas Ministry of Tourism. (n.d.). Retrieved May 30, 2021, from https://www.tourismtoday.com/bahamas-ministry-tourism
Bahamas Ministry of Tourism. (n.d.) *We're ready to welcome you.* Retrieved August 1, 2021, from https://www.bahamas.com/travelupdates
Bonimy, M. (2009). *Environmental impacts: Citizens' views and participation in Pigeon Forge.* Tennessee. VDM Verlag Dr.
Bonimy, M. (2011). Urban residents' perceptions of environmental impacts. *International Journal of Hospitality and Tourism Administration, 12*(4), 330–354. https://doi.org/10.1080/15256480.2011.614554
Brundtland, G. H. (1987). *Report of the world commission on environment and development: Our common future.* Oxford University Press.
Cartwright-Carroll, T. (2020, May 28). *Bahamas reduces budget.* The Nassau Guardian. https://thenassauguardian.com/govt-reduces-budget-of-42-ministries-and-departments/
Choe, K. A., & Roberts, B. H. (2011). *Competitive cities in the 21st century: Cluster-Based local economic development.* Asian Development Bank.
Cooper, A. (2020, October). *GB economic progress post hurricane Dorian.* Compass Bahamas. https://www.thecompassbahamas.com/gb-economic-progress-post-hurricane-dorian/
Countrymeters. (2022). *Bahamas population.* https://countrymeters.info/en/Bahamas#population_2021
Data World Bank. (2020). *Labor force, total: The Bahamas* [Databank]. Retrieved May 15, 2021, from https://data.worldbank.org/indicator/SL.TLF.TOTL.IN?locations=BS.

Denhardt, R. B., & Denhardt, J. V. (2000). The new public service: Serving rather than steering. *Public Administration Review, 60*(6), 549–559. https://doi.org/10.1111/0033-3352.00117

Department of Statistics—The Bahamas. (2019, May). *Bahamas government labour force report*. Retrieved May 15, 2021, from https://www.bahamas.gov.bs/wps/wcm/connect/819a4a40-602b-47a3-9da7-c90eeae0f679/Labour+Force+Report+May_2019.pdf?MOD=AJPERES

Dupuch, E. (2000). *The Bahamas handbook*. Publications Ltd.

Dupuch, E. (2016). *The Bahamas handbook*. Publications Ltd.

Dye, T. (1987). *Understanding public policy* (6th ed.). Prentice Hall, Inc.

Economic Commission for Latin American & Caribbean. (n.d.). *Assessment of the effects and impacts of hurricane Dorian in the Bahamas.*. Retrieved September 12, 2021, from https://reliefweb.int/sites/reliefweb.int/files/resources/EZSHARE-1256154360-486.pdf

Eyewitness News. (2018, October). Crime affecting tourism. https://ewnews.com/crime-affecting-tourism

Gibbs, D. (2002). *Local economic development and the environment*. Routledge, Taylor & Francis Group.

Gordon, G.J. & Milakovich, M. (2012). *Public administration in America*. Wadsworth Cengage Learning.

Government of the Bahamas. (2018, July). *The Bahamas: Voluntary national review on the sustainable development goals to the high level political forum of the United Nations Economic and Social Council*. https://sustainabledevelopment.un.org/content/documents/19874VNR_document_03.07.18_master_document.pdf

Harmon, M., & Mayer, R. T. (1994). *Organization theory for public administration*. Chatelaine Press.

Hartnell, N. (2021, March 18). Govt to recapitalise Bdb in $20m outlay. *The Tribune*. http://www.tribune242.com/news/2021b/mar/18/govt-recapitalise-bdb-20m-outlay/

Hartnell, N. (2021, April 14). Abaco hurricane Dorian recovery. *The Tribune*. http://www.tribune242.com/news/2021a/apr/14/further-3-5-years-minimum-abacos-dorian-recovery/

Icoz, O. & Icoz, O. (2019). Economic impacts of tourism. In D. Gursoy & R. Nunkoo (Eds.). *The Routledge handbook of tourism impacts, theoretical and applied perspectives* (pp. 95–108). Routledge. https://doi.org/10.4324/9781351025102-8

Inter-American Development Bank. (2019, November 15). Damages and other impacts on Bahamas by Hurricane Dorian estimated at $3.4 billion: Report [News Release]. https://www.iadb.org/en/news/damages-and-other-impacts-bahamas-hurricane-dorian-estimated-34-billion-report

Inui, Y., Wheeler, D., & Lankford, S. (2006). Rethinking tourism education: What should schools teach? *Journal of Hospitality, Leisure, Sport and Tourism Education, 5*(2), 25–35. https://doi.org/10.3794/johlste.52.122

Kocabulut, O., Yozukmaz, N., & Bertan, S. (2019). Environmental impacts of tourism. In D. Gursoy & R. Nunkoo (Eds.). *The Routledge handbook of tourism impacts, theoretical and applied perspectives* (pp. 281–297). Routledge. https://doi.org/10.4324/9781351025102-22

Kraft, M. E., & Furlong, S. R. (2018). *Public policy, politics, analysis, and Alternatives* (6th ed.). SAGE.

Levine, C. H., Peters, B. G., & Thompson, F. J. (1990). *Public administration, challenges, choices, consequences*. Scott.

Lexology Library. (2018, October). *Aviation in the Bahamas*. https://www.lexology.com/library/detail.aspx?g=721ac683-3807-4dbb-9762-abc363024c77

Loureiro, S. M. C., Sarmento, E. M., & Ferreira do Rosario, J. (2019). Overview of underpinnings of tourism impacts, The case of Lisbon destination. In D. Gursoy & R. Nunkoo (Eds.) *The Routledge handbook of tourism impacts, theoretical and applied perspectives* (pp.49–61). Routledge. https://doi.org/10.4324/9781351025102-4

Lowi, T. (1964). American business, public policy, case studies, and political theory. *World Politics, 16*(July), 667–715. https://doi.org/10.2307/2009452

McKenzie, N. (2019, September 25). *DPM: Order on economic recovery zone incentives to be released in 'full detail' by Thursday*. https://ewnews.com/dpm-order-on-economic-recovery-zone-incentives-to-be-released-in-full-detail-by-thursday

Malihah, E. & Setiyorin, H. P. D. (2014, October) *Tourism education and edu-tourism development: Sustainable tourism development perspective in education*. The 1st International Seminar on Tourism (ISOT), Bandung—Eco-Resort and Destination Sustainability: Planning, Impact, and Development. https://www.researchgate.net/publication/317168362_Tourism_Education_and_Edu-Tourism_Development_Sustainable_Tourism_Development_Perspective_in_Education_1

Meier, K. J. (1993). *Politics and the bureaucracy: Policymaking in the fourth branch of government*. Brooks/Cole.

Mercy Corps. (2019, September). *The facts: Hurricane Dorian's devastating effect on The Bahamas*. https://www.mercycorps.org/blog/quick-facts-hurricane-dorian-bahamas

Mikesell, J. L. (2006 [1990]). *Fiscal administration: Analysis and application for the public sector* (7th ed.). Thomson Wadsworth Publishing.

Ministry of Tourism. (2019). *Bahamas tourist expenditures: 2019/2018 expenditure comparisons preliminary* [Research and Statistics Department]. https://www.tourismtoday.com/sites/default/files/expenditure_by_quarter_2019_and_2018.pdf

Norville, L. (n.d.). *Tourism today—Sstructure and functions*. Ministry of Tourism. Retrieved September 7, 2021, from https://www.tourismtoday.com/about-us/structure-functions

Nunkoo, R., & Gursoy, D. (2019). Introduction to tourism impacts. In D.Gursoy & R. Nunkoo (Eds.) *The routledge handbook of tourism impacts, theoretical and applied perspectives* (pp.1–20). Routledge. https://doi.org/10.4324/9781351025102-1

Office of the Attorney General & Ministry of Legal Affairs. (1971). *Chapter 288: Hotels—Hotel regulations* [Statute Law]. http://laws.bahamas.gov.bs/cms/images/LEGISLATION/SUBORDINATE/1971/1971-0008/HotelsRegulations_1.pdf

Office of the Attorney General & Ministry of Legal Affairs. (2010, January). *Chapter 289: Hotel encouragement* [Statute Law]. http://laws.bahamas.gov.bs/cms/images/LEGISLATION/PRINCIPAL/1954/1954-0030/HotelsEncouragementAct_1.pdf

O'Reilly, A. M. (1983). Tourism in the eighties from the commonwealth Caribbean perspective: Change, challenge and renewal. In *The changes of tourism in the eighties and their consequences*. Editions AIEST.

Redford, E. (1965). *American government and the economy*. Macmillan Company.

Ripley, R. B., & Franklin, G. A. (1991). *Congress, the bureaucracy, and public policy* (5th ed.). Brooks/Cole Publishing Company.

Rothman, R. A. (1978). Residents and transients: Community reaction to seasonal visitors. *Journal of Travel Research, 16*(3), 8–13. https://doi.org/10.1177/004728757801600303

Royal Bahamas Defence Force. (2021, June). *Maritime security plan 2021*. http://rbdf.gov.bs/wp-content/uploads/2021/02/Maritime-Security-Plan-2021.pdf

Royal Bahamas Police Force. (n.d.). *About the royal Bahamas police force*. Retrieved May 15, 2021, from http://www.royalbahamaspolice.org/aboutus/?aboutus_id=1

Scavella, N. (2016, November 4). *Bahamas has 'great stake' in climate change conversation. The Tribune*. http://www.tribune242.com/news/2016/nov/04/bahamas-has-great-stake-climate-change-conversatio/

Sharpley, R. (2018). *Tourism, tourists and society* (5th ed.). Routledge. https://doi.org/10.4324/9781315210407

Supradist, N. (2004). *Economic leakage in tourism.* Master's thesis, Lund University. https://lup.lub.lu.se/luur/download?func=downloadFile&recordOId=1329250&fileOId=1329251
The Bahamas Ministry of Tourism. (2021, May). *About us.* https://www.tourismtoday.com/about-us/vision-mission
The Bahamas National Trust. (2021, April). *Bahamas National Trust rebrands after 60 years.* https://bnt.bs/latest-news/bahamas-national-trust-rebrands-after-60-years/
Tourism Today. (2019). *The Bahamas Ministry of Tourism visitor statistics: Total foreign arrivals to the Bahamas by air and sea–1971–2019.* https://www.tourismtoday.com/sites/default/files/air_sea_arrivals_71_thru_2019.pdf
Trading Economics. (2021, September). *Bahamas GDP.* https://tradingeconomics.com/bahamas/gdp
Travel Compliance Unit, Government of Bahamas. (n.d.) *Bahamas travel health site.* (n.d.). Retrieved June 15, 2021, from https://travel.gov.bs/
University of the Bahamas. (n.d.). *History.* Retrieved May 15, 2021, from https://www.ub.edu.bs/about-us/history/
World Atlas. (2021, September). *How many islands are in the Bahamas?* https://www.worldatlas.com/articles/how-many-islands-are-in-the-bahamas.html

Index

C. Cannonier and M. Galloway Burke (eds.), *Contemporary Issues Within Caribbean Economies*, https://doi.org/10.1007/978-3-030-98865-4

E

F

G

H

W

Kolibri 360 GmbH
Ferdinand-Jühlke-Straße 7
99095 Erfurt, Deutschland
produktsicherheit@kolibri360.de